AMONGST THE SHANS.

AMONGST THE SHANS

AMONGST THE SHANS

BY

ARCHIBALD ROSS COLQUHOUN

GYAN

Published by

GYAN

Gyan Publishing House
5, Ansari Road
Daryaganj, New Delhi-110002
Phone: 011-47034999, 9811692060
E-mail: books@gyanbooks.com

Distribution Network
gyanbooks.com
India, USA, Canada, UK, Australia

ISBN: 978-93-6208-353-1 (PB)
First Published, 1885

2nd Impression 2024

Printed at: Gyan Press, Delhi.

AMONGST THE SHANS
Author: ARCHIBALD ROSS COLQUHOUN

RAPIDS AT KENG-LUONG, ON THE MEKONG RIVER.

AMONGST THE SHANS

BY

ARCHIBALD ROSS COLQUHOUN

A.M.I.C.E., F.R.G.S.

Author of "Across Chrysê," etc.

With upwards of Fifty whole-page Illustrations

AND AN HISTORICAL SKETCH OF THE SHANS

BY

HOLT S. HALLETT, M.T.C.E., F.R.G.S.

PRECEDED BY AN INTRODUCTION ON

THE CRADLE OF THE SHAN RACE

BY

TERRIEN DE LACOUPERIE

Professor of Indo-Chinese Philology, University Coll. Lond., Author of "The Oldest Book of the Chinese," etc., etc.

NEW YORK:

SCRIBNER & WELFORD.

1885.

CONTENTS.

INTRODUCTION

BY

PROFESSOR T. DE LACOUPERIE.

THE CRADLE OF THE SHAN RACE.

AMONGST THE SHANS.

CHAPTER I.

b

PAGE

CHAPTER VI.

CHAPTER VII.

CHAPTER VIII.

PAGE

CHAPTER XIV.

CHAPTER XV.

CHAPTER XVI.

SUPPLEMENTARY CHAPTERS.

BY HOLT S. HALLETT.

PART I.

HISTORY OF UPPER SHAN.

PART II.

HISTORY OF LOWER SHAN.

LIST OF ILLUSTRATIONS.

N.B.—The titles of the illustrations,—from F. Garnier's "Voyage d'Exploration dans l'Indo-Chine,"—should be read according to the preceding list, where several errors of the context have been amended.

INTRODUCTION.

THE CRADLE OF THE SHAN RACE.

SUMMARY.

Ancient Indo-Chinese inseparable from the formation of the Chinese nation. Their Chinese affinities originated before they settled in their present seats.

Misunderstandings still current on China, and recent researches —How to explain the affinities of civilization—Reasons of the similitudes—How they are illustrated in China and Indo-China.

Causes of the misunderstandings—Special arrangement of the Chinese Annals—Geographical and administrative divisions of the Chinese Dominion.

Avowed existence of non-Chinese populations—Slow extension of the dominion of the Chinese—Distinction between their dominion and their influence.

Ancient intrusive races—TEK and TOK race—*Jung* or NUNG race —Woman-ruled tribes—*Lolos*, etc.

Non-intrusive races—Tattooed, dwarf, long-legged, tribes.

MÂN or MÔN race—*Ngu*—*San Miao*—*Pang*—*Kuei* divisions.

KING race—Karen tribes and the Non-Chinese state of Tsu or *Teru*.

TAÏ-SHAN race—*Mung*—*Pa-y*—*Lao*—*Leao*—*Tchao* divisions.

Conclusion.

THE valuable description of a branch of the great Taï race, which is the subject of Mr. Archibald R. Colquhoun's new book *Amongst the Shans*, as well as his former account of his journey *Across Chrysê*,[1] is not an unimportant contribution to ethnology. The two works contain a good deal of information taken *in situ*, which increases the knowledge, hitherto so unsatisfactory, of a large number of the independent and semi-independent non-Chinese tribes still existing within and without the southern boundaries of the Chinese Empire. Remnants of the non-absorbed and non-Sinicised parts of larger stocks of several races, gradually driven south-westwards, these tribes are now scattered, on a large area, into an undefined number of fragments, intermingled to a great extent, and often difficult to trace individually up to their original stems. With the exception of the northern region, which was supplied with a constant renewal of Altaic and Ugro-Finnish blood pouring into the Chinese agglomeration, they formerly composed the native population of China Proper. Their modern descendants are the representatives (much altered and modified by multiplied crossings and re-crossings) of those ethnic stocks, of which the southern off-shoots have gradually and successively migrated to Indo-China, and developed there into several nations of importance.

Therefore the ancient history of the Indo-Chinese populations is so completely interwoven with that of

[1] *Across Chrysê, being the narrative of a Journey of Exploration through the South China border lands from Canton to Mandalay, by Archibald R. Colquhoun*, 1883. The gold medal of the Royal Geographical Society has been awarded to the intrepid explorer. *Across Chrysê* has already been translated into French (Paris, Oudin) and German (Leipzig, Brockhaus).

the formation of the Chinese themselves, that, unless we dwell upon the peculiarities of this formation, the study of the former is incomplete and partly misunderstood. In the surviving aboriginal tribes and the valuable archives of the huge country, we have documentary evidence of the early movements of those races, and we shall see further that the cradle of the Taï-Shan race was in China Proper. The truthfulness of this history unwritten and written is simply wonderful, and the only task of the modern critic is to disintegrate the genuine information from the tribal interminglings and the marvellous details added to the ancient records in later ages under non-Chinese influence.

Since we have known anything of the Indo-Chinese, the considerable proportion contributed by China to their languages, culture, and blood, has been a matter of bewilderment. And the more extensive grew the knowledge, the more irrefutable were the affinities detected on the two sides. No satisfactory explanation has been forthcoming, because too little was known of the ethnological history of the Flowery Land. The hypothesis of a common descent goes beyond the mark, inasmuch as the ground of the Chinese languages, shown by their evolution, grammar, and vocabulary, is not Indo-Chinese. The same must be said of the races and of the civilizations. A few glimpses obtained by the learned explorer, Francis Garnier, had led him to guess the truth, so far as concerns the presence in ancient times of the Shan race in Southern China. The whole problem, however, was grasped by the late Capt. C. J. Forbes, of Burmah, when he wrote that "the close affinity of words and root forms which exists between the Chinese and the languages of Ultra-India . . . must have originated before the different races speaking these languages came into their present seats." The next step towards the solution is that this affinity is not identical throughout, and differs in the various groups.

***

The stock-in-trade of misunderstanding, bias, and untrue statements with regard to China, its languages and races, which is commonly used and credited in proof of speculations, or in illustration of a peculiar development, is simply appalling and ought to be thoroughly revised. It might be suggested, with sufficient reason, that the best plan would be to make a *tabula rasa* and begin the matter afresh, trusting no other sources than the ancient Chinese works and a few important books published in late years by eminent Sinologists.

The ancient Sinologists accountable for this deplorable state of things, however, must not be criticised with too much severity. They have done their best with the materials they had at hand, but were not able, either by training or position, to use an effective criticism. They could only accept *grosso modo* the various statements derived from the books they could read for themselves, or which were explained to them. They had not at their disposal the means of verifying these statements; so that, without supporting in its full bearing the appellation of "gobe-mouches," which has been lately applied to the ancient Jesuit missionaries by an eminent Russian scholar, we cannot help saying that, severe as it is in respect of their position and time, this judgment from our present standpoint is not altogether undeserved.

The researches and disclosures of late years on ancient China have revealed, in the evolution of that country, a state of things very dissimilar from that which was supposed to have existed. The history of China was considered to be that of the self-growth, during the protracted period required for such an evolution, of an homogeneous race occupying nearly the whole territory of China Proper, from savage life to a state of culture unparalleled by any western nation five hundred years ago. Now it turns out that neither one nor the other of these assumptions have been confirmed by the progress of knowledge.

Important deductions for the philosophy of history and science of politics, have been drawn from the existence of this supposed self-rise and development of an important focus of civilization. Obvious similarities with our own culture, which could not be traced to a recent importation, have been explained away, as the outcome of the identity of human mind everywhere. Chinese of high education and rank, acquainted with European culture, and struck with the

c

many similitudes between our institutions and their own as they are framed in the Code of Rites of the Tchou dynasty (B.C. 1050-778),[1] have ventured to explain the difficulty in their own way. They held that Lao-tze, their great philosopher of the sixth century, who was the librarian and keeper of the Museum at Loh, the capital of the Tchou dynasty, had taken away with him a copy of the said code, the *Tchou-Li*, when he left China to disappear in the West. Leaving aside this childish speculation, which is contradicted by all that we know respecting the book and the man, and without mentioning the other impossibilities of the case, let us consider the question from a higher point of view.

In researches of this kind, it should be borne in mind that communication of culture from one people to another may be either (*a*) complete, more or less,—by common descent, migration, intermingling, protracted intercourse, religious conversion, vicinity, or conquest; or (*b*) incomplete and more or less fragmentary,—by trade, fortuitous communications, and occasional intercourse in one or more cases.

On the other hand, it must now be admitted, apart from any system and theory, that, without outside pressure from a focus of culture of a higher standard, progress, in the common sense of the word, does not seem to be the natural course of the ever-growing evolution of men and things, except in the case of the

[1] The chronology followed here is that of the Annals of the Bamboo Books, the only one which has a semblance of veracity.

idealistic and speculative race to which we belong. The pressure may be the result of a regular intercourse or only of occasional communications, the character and frequency of which produce the amount of similarity.

Beyond a rather low level of civilization, within which the natural evolution takes place, there is no hope, for a secluded race of wild men, of real advance from their point of departure. And a civilized community will return after protracted seclusion to the low level of civilization we are speaking of. Otherwise no savages would be met anywhere after so many centuries of known habitation of man on the earth. That there is, as a rule, a common capacity of the human brain to produce in independent societies a low standard of somewhat similar culture, in any country whatever, nobody will deny; with this reserve, however, that the superior laws of surrounding circumstances of nature, such as climate, food, and race, introduce peculiarities of a different order and cause discrepancies.

Incomplete similarities, half-resemblances, diversification from a groundwork obviously identical, are often the result of occasional communications. Informal teaching, through persons unprepared for their unexpected task of civilizers, cannot produce any other results. And when the inquirer has to face difficulties such as those which would happen in events of this sort, surely it is there that he will find the explanation. The occasional communications between two seats of different culture are the most deceitful agents in the study of the history of civilization, and it is undeniable that such communications have been much more frequent than is generally supposed. Bold travellers, lost families, drift-away boats, are not uncommon facts; their repetition, of course, is of rarer occurrence, though not without many instances. Every day, new discoveries show that man is much older and has always travelled much more than was formerly believed.[1] The world is indeed small for the activity of man if unlimited by time. These considerations should always be remembered when studying civilizations. The similarities and affinities of so many sorts which are met with amongst the most distant nations, are better explained as the outcome of a series of interchanges, by direct or indirect channels, than as the common products of the human mind. Large allowance must be made for concidences, and for the operation of this human mind within a limited area, and bounded by circumstances.

The value of the loan of culture differs according to its causes and intermediaries. The latter, in case of occasional communications, are seldom the best channels which could be selected for the transmission

[1] "Chaque jour, en effet, quelque découverte nouvelle nous montre que l'homme est bien plus vieux et a été de tout temps beaucoup plus voyageur qu'on ne le croyait naguère."—A. de Quatrefages, *Hommes fossiles et Hommes sauvages* (Paris, 1884, 8vo), p. 162.

of knowledge. If they are men of the million, they do not know much, and cannot teach more unless they invent. A European sailor is a scholar among savages. If it is the reverse, and should the lost party belong to, or possess among them, men of highly cultivated minds, so much the better for the receivers; the fragmentary loan will be of a higher standard, and the affinities or similarities will be more genuine and more striking; and the impression produced on the minds of the people will be deep enough not to disappear in after ages.

The beginnings of Chinese civilization, as well as the Chinese affinities of the intrusive and aboriginal tribes enumerated below, plainly illustrate these facts.

China has received its language (since altered), and the elements of arts, sciences, and institutions, from the colonies of the Ugro-Altaic *Bak* families who came from Western Asia some twenty-three centuries B.C., under the conduct of men of high culture, acquainted, through their neighbours the Susians, with the civilization which emanated from Babylonia and was modified in its second focus. This general statement is now beyond any possibility of doubt, for the evidence in its favour is overwhelming. But this channel was not the only one through which ancient China was enabled to acquire so many notions similar to, and borrowed from one common source with, our own.

The non-Chinese races of the Flowery Land with

their younger cognates of Indo-China, show, in the unequal amount of affinities and parallelisms they possess with the Chinese, that some received them during a temporary vicinity, while the others had them from intermingling.

***

The reason of the misunderstanding, so far as regards the political and ethnological state of ancient China, is rather curious; it lies in the special divisions of the Chinese Annals, and the peculiarities of the geographical division of the Empire for the administrative management.

The three thousand volumes of which the Historical Annals of China are composed, do not constitute a cleverly interwoven narrative of all the political, social, artistic, scientific, and economic events, such as would make an acceptable history answering our western requirements. In relation to their distribution, their characteristic is much more analytic and encyclopædic. Everything is treated separately.

First come the Imperial Records, which contain the purely political events of each reign (giving special prominence to the deeds of the Emperor). Then follow sections on Chronology, Rites, Music, Jurisprudence, Political Economy (lit. food and commerce), State sacrifices, Astronomy, Elemental influences, Geography, Literature, Biographies, and Records of foreign nations and countries. As the unsubdued aborigines—

Miao, Man, Lao, Pang, Ngu, etc., etc.,—albeit within the Chinese boundaries, were non-Chinese, they were classified as foreigners in the last division of each part of the Annals, where all the facts and events concerning them were enumerated.

And as the histories of China hitherto written by Europeans have been constructed mainly from the chronological parts of these annals, the result is that the Chinese seem to have always been in full possession of their domain, and that their history is so dry that scarcely anybody can be interested in it.

The other features which have misled former orientalists, and notably Klaproth in the compilation of his *Tableaux historiques de l'Asie*, are the administrative divisions which, as said above, are indicated for the whole country as though it were equally occupied by the Chinese proper.

Enclosed partly or *in toto* within the subdued territory, the dominions of the aborigines were included within the great administrative divisions of the Empire, and considered as ruled by the principal officer of the division. The ruling of the independent aboriginal regions by their own chiefs, upon whom the Chinese government bestowed Chinese titles, was the oldest system followed, because it would have been impossible to embrace them otherwise. A simple recognition of the suzerainty of the Chinese Emperors, with the payment of a small tribute, and the grant of a new geographical name, was all that was required before the time of the second Han dynasty (A.D. 25), to include the region among those composing the Empire. With the appointment of officers residing somewhere on the borders of the districts newly defined, the exigencies of the government were satisfied.

The supposed homogeneous dominion of Shi-Huang-ti, the founder of the Chinese Empire, 221 B.C., included, from the Yang-tze-Kiang southwards, large tracts which he made Chinese only in name. And when the Han dynasty carried its authority into Yunnan and Kwang-si it was the repetition over and over again of the same impotent domination. But if the central government was satisfied, the Chinese officials appointed to preside over the non-Chinese districts were not; they could not suffer the gradually decreasing payment of the tribute and border duties, which were their only means of living. The progress of organization in the Empire was apparent, and the homogeneity was gaining ground. Feeling themselves backed by a firmer government, these officials grew gradually more oppressive in their exactions, and the result was that the yoke became unbearable. Rebellion after rebellion, risings on all sides, were of daily occurrence, and during several centuries it was an incessant fight to quash these movements. The success was not always on the side of the Imperial armies; and the boldness of the indigenous tribes, enhanced by the weakness of the Empire divided among several contemporaneous dynasties, compelled the Chinese government, under the Wei dynasty (fifth century), to reverse its policy towards them. The appointment of Chinese official governors and others was suppressed in the non-Chinese districts, and the indigenous chiefs themselves were recognised as Chinese officials, by the addition of Chinese titles of office to their own native dignity. An instance will show better than longer explanations what was the situation. In the latter part of the fifth century of cur era, the chief of the Pan-hu race was recognised by the Chinese Emperor as King of Siang-yang (Hupeh), and Governor of Kingtchou. His realm, containing 80,000 villages, covered the provinces of the centre and extended northwards near the Yellow River. In the twelfth century they were still occupying the eastern part of Setchuen, and Kweitchou, Hupeh and Hunan provinces. Under Chinese pressure they gradually disappeared, but have still many independent representative tribes in the southern provinces.

So that, under the cover of Chinese titles and geographical names, large regions occupied by populations entirely non-Chinese were included as homogeneous parts of the nation, with the effect of concealing the real weakness of the Chinese Empire previous to the last few centuries.

***

That the Chinese are not the earliest occupiers of

any part of their country is a statement which is readily acceptable. That they say so is more astonishing. Such is, however, the result of a comparative study of what is hidden in their traditions.

The existence of non-Chinese tribes more or less uncivilized in Kweitchou and Kwang-si provinces, —remnants of the ancient Miao-tze mentioned in the first parts of the Shu-King,—was a fact known from the writings of the Jesuit missionaries in the last three centuries; that the present Mandchu dynasty ruling in China had to repress occasional risings of these tribes, was also known. But how far they extended their power during the whole course of the Chinese history, what were their independence and strength, which in several occasions nearly jeopardised the Chinese dominion, is known only to a few scholars. The latest histories of China do not mention this state of things, and consequently the formation and evolution of the Chinese nation have been hitherto misunderstood. If China did not extend in former times further than it did previous to the now ruling dynasty, it was because of its internal weakness. Immense regions inside China proper were non-Chinese, and the Sons of Heaven had no more power than was necessary to keep a check upon these internal and inveterate foes, always ready to break the net which from time to time was spread over them.

Without any incitement from a higher focus of culture, the Chinese slept sheltered under the greatness of their founders, and no progress was made by them from the time of their settlement in the Flowery Land up to the establishment of the Tchou (B.C. 1050). Far from that, a serious decay took place, as is proved by manifest indications of their progressive neglect and oblivion of practical arts and scientific notions which had been possessed by their earlier rulers. The history of their writing, besides the statements with regard to astronomical instruments afterwards forgotten, which are mentioned in the first parts of the Shu-King, are cases in point.

One, if not the most striking, discovery of modern researches is the comparative youth of the Chinese as a great homogeneous and powerful people. Under the Shang-Yn and Tchou dynasties their dominion, though not extending more than midway between the Huang-ho and the Yang-tze-Kiang, was an area much too large for their own race; it was in fact interspersed with the aborigines, who were kept in check by the higher culture which the new comers endeavoured to impart to them. The Bak tribes, or *Peh Sing* (name of the Chinese immigrants), were overpowered by the numerous populations which had preceded them in the occupation of the country. The Flowery Land, long before their immigration, had gained fame, for its milder climate and the fertility of its soil, among the nomadic races of the barren and cold regions of Central Asia.

And it was not before the first quarter of the third century B.C. that the Chinese political power, then in the hands of the Prince of Ts'in, permitted them to cross the Yang-tze-Kiang which nearly separates the country in two parts north and south. However, the sway of the Chinese authority was in fact so ineffective that at the end of the sixth century, about 566 A.D., under the N. Tchou dynasty, the Emperor Wu-ti was obliged to protect the passages of the Yang-tze west of Y-tchang with ramparts in order to prevent the raids of the barbarians.

There is a broad distinction to be drawn between the extension of the Chinese dominion politically so called, and that of their influence. The latter, with the benefits of their higher culture, was carried throughout by the system of slow and continuous infiltration peculiar to the tenacious character of their race, a system pervading in all directions. Small colonies or private individuals, for trade purposes or to escape the regular authority, intermingling with the indigenous tribes, gradually paved the way to the acceptation by the latter of the Chinese yoke in the bordering regions. And this yoke in the newly-attached districts was not heavy; except after rebellions, it did not imply the sweeping and drastic measures with which we are familiar in the history of other countries. Military posts were however established to check the native authorities; but the latter, as we have seen, were almost always maintained in possession with a modified appellation and an additional Chinese title accompanied by the seal and ribbon of office. And when the yoke happened to be heavier under the pressure of the extraordinary growth of the suzerain people, who required a more positive territorial extension, the feudal states had to yield, and their population was mixed with and absorbed by the Chinese, or else they objected to the complete assimilation. In the latter case, they either migrated, or, if strong enough, resisted bodily. Such native states entirely enclosed in Chinese territory did last for many centuries, and the broken tribes still in existence in the southern provinces of China are fragments of their population. Segmentation, intermingling, and transfer from one place to another, have happened on so extensive a scale that hybridity is much more to be met with than purity in any degree, yet of those who migrated southwards and were progressively driven outside the modern Chinese frontiers, there are in Indo-China not a few remnant tribes or reconstituted nations, representative, in a decayed or in an improved state of culture, of former communities or important races and states which once were located in Central and Southern China.

***

We are now enabled by the perusal of a few works of recent years, by the examination of the remaining tribes of aborigines and non-Chinese races of China, and by the study of their traditions, to draw the general outlines of an ethnological history of the region known as China Proper, which, among other notable facts, will show the beginnings of the Shan race.

In order to clear the ground, we have to proceed with the pre-modern intrusive races, before considering the main aboriginal stocks, inasmuch as they exhibit this sort of fragmentary similarities in their Chinese affinities which are the outcome of temporary vicinity of a higher focus of culture, as mentioned above.

Towards the end of the Shang-Yn dynasty, in the S.E. of Shensi province, we hear of the TEK and TOK; the latter, apparently a division of the Tek, branched off about 1276 B.C., and were the first to begin intercourse with the Chinese; after some 200 years they overthrew the Shang-Yn dynasty, and established, in 1050 B.C., their own, which is commonly known as that of *Tchou*, the modern pronunciation of their ancient name Tok. They were, to a certain extent, the channel through which Iranian views, notions, and more or less corrupted words, entered into the Flowery Land. The Tek, commonly called Tih (after the same reason that Tok is Tchou), of whom we have no other ethnological information than their tribal names, seem to have some connection with Turkish tribes, and are the indirect ancestors of the Karens; some of them shared in the formation of the Karen (?) primitive nucleus of the Teru or Tsv, which became the great state of Southern China during the Tchou dynasty, and on which we shall have further to dwell. These Tek and their subdivisions, the Kiptchak and others, had apparently picked up during their wanderings, before their advance towards the East, some notions received from the Iranian formation.

A larger stock of notions derived from the latter formation seems however to have been in the possession of another race which had appeared in the West outside China, in the beginning of the sixteenth century B.C. They were a mixed offshoot of the white race to which we belong, and are known by the generic name of *Nung*, or JUNG, which is the modern pronunciation of the former. Much more numerous than the Tek, their warlike dispositions made their name equivalent to that of warriors, and later on it was at last chiefly used in that general sense. Twenty and more tribes of them are mentioned in history; but the larger number of their names are mere geographical indications, and only a few are interesting for ethnology, such as the Ion or Joan, the Yam, the Mao, the Lu-tzi, the Lokku, the Lok-lai, etc. While some of their hordes penetrated eastwards amidst the interspersed Chinese dominion, stepping after eleven hundred years on the very trails of the pre-Chinese Bak tribes in their immigration into the Flowery Land, others remained in the vicinity of the Tchou or Tok, with whom they were on good terms and intermingled. They had their share of the plunder on the overthrow of the Shang-Yn dynasty, but as they objected to submit to the laws of the settled populations, they proved a thorn in the side of the Chinese agglomeration. In B.C. 770, some hordes of the same race which had not become fused with the Chinese population, the Lu-tzi, were strong enough to overthrow the Tchou dynasty from its seat in Shensi, and to kill the king. By the joint action of the Chinese rulers of several principalities, the Tchou dynasty was revived in Honan, but its authority was henceforth a mere shadow, and never recovered from this dreadful blow.

The Jung, who were not swallowed up at the time of the encroachments of the state of Ts'in and its final extension into the Chinese Empire, disappeared south-west of Kansuh province towards Tibet. They were cognate to those woman-ruled states in this region, of which we have heard so much in the embellished records of the travels of King Muh to the states of the Western Queen, in the romantic geography of the Shan haï King, and in the more modern records mentioning states ruled by a queen. The *Si Wang Muh*, *Niu tsi*, *Niu tze*, and *Tung Niu*, are the several names under which they appear successively in Chinese books; female sovereignty was given up by the latter state in 742 A.D.

The descendants or modern representatives of the Jung, unequally diversified by incessant crossings with Altaïc races of Tibet, outside the borders of China, are: the Lu-tze or Anung, the Lissu or Leisu, the Mosso or Na-shi, and several smaller tribes, all on the south-west frontiers; more westwards, an important ethnologic part of the Muni-pur-Chittagong, and of the Kiranti groups; and within the borders of the Chinese dominion, the Lo-kwei or Laka, Luh-lu or

Lolo, of whom we have heard a good deal from that scholarly traveller and charming writer, Mr. E. Colborne Baber. The important position formerly occupied by women in their social organization has not altogether disappeared, but has left many traces in their habits and customs; while their curious head-dress, shaped like a horn, may be traced to Western Tibet and Northern India. They possessed for a while in the third century A.D. a prominent political dominion in the Eastern Setchuen and Kweitchou provinces; and when they were obliged to retrace their steps to their former seats in Western and North-Western Setchuen, they left behind them a not inconsiderable number of broken tribes, which, intermingling with other races, have produced an inextricable imbroglio of hybrid communities.[1]

***

We come now to the survey of the non-intrusive or aboriginal races which will lead us to the beginnings of the Shan race, and which display, in opposition to the intrusive races, a large number of special

[1] As a rule, the northern races, that is to say, those which reached China from the north, unless disturbed by a subsequent intermingling strong enough to disintegrate their grammar, have an indirect ideology (where, for instance, adjective and bare genitive precede the noun). Those originally from the south show the reverse phenomena. Moreover, several of the modern dialects of aboriginal tribes, such as those of the White Miao, Hua Miao, Yao Miao, etc., present the interesting feature of a mixed ideology, thus testifying to the interminglings which have taken place.

d

resemblances and parallelisms which can only result from a manifold and protracted intermingling.

At the outset of their relations with the natives, the Chinese became acquainted in their new country with tattooing populations, and with two races the characteristics of which are peculiar enough to be still wondered at by modern travellers. One was a race of pigmies, the Tiao, who are still represented by (*a*) the Trao, now located east of Bienhoa, in Cochin-China, almost the shortest of men; (*b*) the Hotha Shan, in south-west Yunnan; (*c*) the Mincopies of the Andaman Islands; (*d*) the Simangs of the Malay Peninsula and (*e*) one of the native races of Formosa, all diversified representatives of the once widespread Negrito race. The other race of men, established not far from the early Chinese settlements, *i.e.* around the great bend of the Huang-ho, was that of the *Tchang Kioh*, or "Long-legged" people. Now it happens that the French explorers of the "Expedition du Mekong" noticed that long legs were a remarkable characteristic of the Moïs, Phnongs, and Khas of the Southern Indo-Chinese Peninsula.

The fact that modern representatives of these peculiar men are in proximity one to the other, seems to confirm the early Chinese acquaintance with both of them, and to imply that their settlements were near Northern China, whence they must have been driven southwards, since the Chinese had then no knowledge whatever of the regions and races south of the Yang-tze-Kiang.

A careful comparison of traditions in history and geography discloses the unexpected fact that when the Chinese immigrants reached their new country, all the region around the great bend of the Yellow River, eastwards to the sea, and southwards to an undefined distance, was occupied by one race divided into several small groups. They were called by the new-comers "Great Bowmen" or Y, from the remarkable size of their bows. Their main characteristics were that they tattooed their bodies, cropped their hair, were good potters, spoke a language of the Mon-Annam class, and possessed traditions concerning the origin of their race, in which the egg has an important share. Their most ordinary name was NGU, which may be used as the denomination of their populations. These were nothing else than a branch of the Mōn race. The name of *Man* was also used in China as a general denomination of all the southern barbarians, but it was at first applied distinctly to these populations, and more especially to those occupying the modern provinces of Ngan-huy and Kiang-si. The ethnological name *Ngu* is represented by several regional forms, such as Nguei (modern Wei), Ngu (modern Wu), Ngou, Ngoh, Ngo-loh, etc., etc. Ngo or Ngu must not be mistaken with those of *ngai*, *ngioh* and *ngiu*, which are mere qualifications of divisions of the Taï race. During the reign of the first emperor Ts'in Shi Huang-ti, in 215 B.C., the Chinese general, Jen Hiao, sent to succeed general T'u Sui, who had been defeated and slain by the natives, repelled and drove out the population of Kuangtung, Kuang-si, and Tung

King, and settled in their place 500,000 colonists from the west of Tcheh-Kiang province and elsewhere. The new-comers, intermingled with the remnant of the natives, are now represented by the Annamites. We neglect several offshoots of the primitive race which had found their way westwards into Central China, and are still represented in the mixed tribes called Miao.

West of the preceding were the SAN MIAO, or Three Miao, apparently so called from such a number of natives states around and westwards of the Poh-yang Lake. The Chinese, according to their usual practice, by a punning approximation of one of their native names (Mao), have called them *Miao*, comparing their barbarian tongue to the mewing of cats, an animal the head of which was ideographed by the character used to write the word. It was against these Miao that the Great Yü was unsuccessful, and it was in the Ngu country (Kwei Ki), near the mouth of the Yang-tze, that he died under circumstances rather ominous for the successes of the Chinese arms.

In the centre were the PANG, of whom we hear at a very early date under more or less fabulous appearances. Historically they are mentioned as being very friendly with the Chinese since the beginning of the Hia dynasty, *i.e.* the 20th century B.C., helping them against their own internal divisions. They were settled in the north of Setchuen and Hupeh provinces, and the political existence of the Great Pang state was said to have been destroyed by SHANG Wu-ting, in 1231 B.C., after a lapse of 767 years, which were afterwards fabulously considered as the lifetime of their first chief, "the Patriarch Pang." Confucius (*Lun-yu*, vii. 1,) speaks of "Our old Pang." Undoubtedly moved by a spirit of revenge, they rallied the Tchou, then beginning to gain power, and helped them to overthrow the decaying Shang-Yn dynasty.

Their secondary seat was between the Yuen and the Wu Rivers, west and south-west of the Tung-ting lake, a mountainous region, which was highly favourable to gratify their hatred of Chinese yoke.

While *Pang* is the form of his name in the ancient Chinese records, *Pan-hu* is that by which the later Chinese have heard of him among his descendants, in Hunan province, where they have more or less diverged from their original type. He is the object of a curious legend which has grown out of a mythological misuse of words, coupled with a faint echo of Central Asiatic folk-lore. He was reputed to be a dog that married a daughter of Yao, or, as others say, of Ti Ku, as a reward for his help to the Chinese. The tradition was still common among their cognates the Peguans at the time of Camoens.

The central group of the Panhu race was included in the political agglomeration of Teru or Tsu, and regained, after a good deal of transformation, their independence after the collapse of the Ts'in Empire, 209 B.C. They did not acknowledge the Chinese supremacy before the end of the 11th century, under the Sung dynasty, and this acknowledgment was the cause of many of their small communities migrating southwards. Previous to that time, their temporary submissions to the Chinese government were of the desultory fashion we had occasion to explain in the first part of this account. Again and again they revolted against the Chinese yoke, and their vitality and strength were sufficient to permit them to assume the offensive, and once even to repulse the Chinese northwards out of Honan province.

Another important branch was that of the KUEI tribes.

There are reasons to believe, from linguistic and other similarities, that the Kuoi, Por, Samré, Phnong, Stieng and Pru, and their cognate tribes in Cambodia, who all speak tonic languages, are the modern representatives, diversified by subsequent interminglings, of two successive migrations of tribes formerly settled on Chinese soil. They were driven out of the Kuangtung and Kuangsi provinces in 215 B.C., of which they then formed the population, but their location was formerly much further north, viz. on the north banks of the Yang-tze, on the borders of Setchuen and Hunan, whence they had been driven away by the growth of the Shan race. We hear of them as early as the time of the Emperor Shun (2049-1990 B.C.), and notably of the *Kuei*, the chief of whom was musician to the court of the Chinese Ruler, whom he taught the five tone music of Scotch and Cochinchinese notoriety. They had frequent intercourse while in Chinese territory with the Lokuei, Tai-shan, and Môn races; and these, coupled with the Chinese infiltration, formed their ethnologic types, exclusively of the other influences which impressed them after their settlement in the extreme south.

***

West of the eastern divisions of the Mōn race, from which they were separated by an important branch of the Taï-shan mentioned below; and around the Tungting lake, between the Yang-tze, the Han rivers and southwards, were several native agglomerations, the oldest of which was apparently the *King* tribes that, latterly driven to the south, are represented by the modern Khyens (Hiŭ or Shu) of Burmah. They were urged southwards by the growth of the Teru (modern Tsu, Tch'u) state, which developed itself from the eleventh century B.C., under the influence of a branch of an intrusive race, the Karen, as we have mentioned above. In the ancient form of the very name of that state, *Tero*, as well as in that of *Kilien*, the immediate ancestor of the Me, its ruling clan, and also in that of the *Pok* tribes, which formed an important part of the same agglomeration, we have no doubt the antecedents of the Taru, Karoon, and Pgau, names of Karen tribes. They were expelled from China *viâ* Yungtchang (E. Yunnan), numbering some 200,000 families, in 778 A.D., by the powerful king of Nantchao, when he destroyed the western part of the Tsuan state (in N. Kuangsi). They are still represented in China (Kweitchou province) by the

Kihlao or Kihtou tribes, whose grammar and vocabulary (the latter with a good deal of mixture) resemble those of the Karens of Burmah.

The said state of Tsu, or Teru, gradually absorbed some twenty smaller states of different races. It grew progressively to an enormous extent, equal to, if not more important than, all the other states of the Chinese Confederation put together. At the end of the fourth century B.C., it had carried its sway over the border states near the sea in the east, the Ngu and Yueh; to the Nan-Ling mountains in the south; over the larger part of Honan on the north, and gradually extended westwards. The latter extension covered the E. of Setchuen, and the whole of Kweitchou provinces; it reached also the centre of Yunnan, and perhaps more south, under the name of T'ien or Tsen kingdom, which was severed from its suzerain country when the Ts'in of Shensi, then growing into the Empire, crossed the Yang-tze-Kiang in 279 B.C.

The name of Tien or Tsen, the only state which was maintained as a continuation of that of Tsu or Teru, when the latter was destroyed by its rival claimant, the Empire, the Ts'in in 224 B.C., has perhaps survived in that of the Shan state of Theinni, the Tsen-pho of the Siamese, and the Mu-pang of the Chinese. It is not unlikely that the concentration in the kingdom of Tsen or T'ien of many fragments of what had once been the great state of Tsu, led to a displacement of many populations which had assisted it; the result, which, indeed, was desired by the Ts'in emperor, must have been an exodus of some importance.

The rulers of the Tsu (Teru) state, notwithstanding the important position they held in the Chinese confederation, boasted "We are Man-y," that is to say, Southern Barbarians, and not Chinese. Their protracted sway, and the influence of the higher culture of the North, which through their channel was slowly impressed on all these populations, did much in the way of modification and absorption of many Chinese elements; but besides that, they have exercised a mischievous influence on ethnology, by the intermінglings, crossings, and recrossings which took place in consequence of the removal of many populations. It was their policy to displace subdued tribes, in order to weaken them or to get rid of their obstruction. It is, on the other hand, to their activity and concentration that the Taï Shan race owes much of its formation and existence.

***

We have now to consider the TAÏ SHAN race, the development of which is more modern than that of the Mŏn mentioned above. Their individuality as a race does not appear to have been evolved at so early a date, and the ethnological elements which, by their intermingling, produced the race, were still distinct for a long while. Their ancestors seem to have been, more than anything else, mere offshoots of the great

Mōn race, settled westwards, that is to say in the north of modern Setchuen, where their racial characteristics slowly developed.

An ethnological hypothesis which would make the Taï Shan race the outcome of an intermingling in irregular proportions of Mōn, Negritos, and Chinese, would not be objectionable in any way, linguistic, historical, or physiological.

As to the racial name which underlies the cognate appellatives of Shan and Siam, we have no hesitation whatever in dismissing, as inadequate to the exigencies of the case, the proposed etymology for *Siam* from the Sanscrit *çyâma*, "brown, or dark." The name is certainly older than this supposed origin would permit; and from its various appearances in the earlier seats of the race, where Sanscrit influences were not in activity, we cannot resist the conclusion that it is contemporaneous with the race itself. I am not indisposed to say that the *Shang* (*i.e.* traders) who overthrew the Hia dynasty and gave their name to the following one, were connected with the Shan race, and that their very name (or a form of it) is perhaps the antecedent of that of Shan or Siam. Many names much like these, such as Tchang, Siang, Shen, Sien, etc., etc., are met with in the nomenclature of native clans and tribes of the same stock in its earlier seats in Central China, and leave no doubt that they all represented one original name.

The great MUNG, or Ta Mung, are obviously of the

same race, in which we cannot fail to recognise the *Mung*,[1] the Shan. We hear of the Mung in the geographical survey which goes under the name of The Great Yü. They were in the region of the setting sun according to the *Erh-ya*, the oldest Chinese dictionary (fifth cent. B.C.), and their exact spot was in the western part of the Setchuen province. Their characteristic, as stated by the Chinese compilers, was sincerity; while the other populations of the eastern, southern, and northern borders were respectively benevolent, wise, or warlike. They formed the leading family of the Nantchao agglomerations as well as that of several others in later times.

The name of another branch of the same race appears very early, namely that of the PA, the transformed representatives of whom are the Pa-y, whose very numerous tribes are scattered from the south of Setchuen, throughout Yunnan and the south borders. We hear of them in 1971 B.C. when the Chinese ruler, K'i of Hia, is reputed to have sent to them his minister, Mang-t'u. They were subdued by the State of Ts'in in 338 B.C., and since that time have slowly advanced southwards. Their oldest settlements were

[1] It is necessary to remind the reader that the names of native tribes in Chinese books have arisen in a rather indifferent way; names of their chief's family, of their country or people, descriptive words of any of their characteristics, were equally suitable as an appellative; this appellative was written with a homophonous character, having almost always ideographically a punning sense.

in Western Setchuen. And not far from them were the LUNG of the same parentage.

We know more of the original seat of the LAO, or NGAI LAO, than of the others. The very spot which their traditions point out is the Lao Shan, *i.e.* Lao mountains, at the intersection of Honan, Hupeh, and Nganhuy provinces, whence they extended westwards in the Kiu-lung range, forming the boundaries of Shensi and Setchuen provinces. The fabulous birth of their ancestor Kiu-lung and his nine brothers, who intermarried with ten girls of another (Man ?) stock, is traced up to a *Lung* floating bamboo by which their mother Sha-yh, wife of *Te-mou*, became pregnant.

On the syncretism of this legend, we need not dwell, as it has reached us in several fragments; it is sufficient to notice the geographical location and the original intermingling which are there indicated.

We hear of a branch of the Ngai-Lao, in the third century B.C., when the Ts'in advanced in Setchuen. They appear again in A.D. 47, making raids on the Chinese territory descending the Han and Yang-tze rivers on bamboo rafts. In the year 69, Liu Mao, their general king, submitted to the empire with seventy-seven chiefs of communities, 51,890 families, comprising 553,711 persons. As they had extended over the whole western part of Setchuen and southwards, they were officially recognised by the Chinese Government in the east of Yunnan. In A.D. 78, having rebelled against the

Chinese officials appointed to represent the suzerainty of China, their king, Lei-lao, was defeated in a great battle, which caused many of their tribes to migrate into the present country of the northern Shan states. They soon recovered from this blow; and they developed and formed the agglomeration which became in A.D. 629 the great state of Nantchao, which afterwards extended in all directions. This state achieved for the Taï Shan race, in matter of unification, the work already begun by the state of Teru=Tsu followed by that of Tsen=Tien. Restricted to narrower limits, it continued from 860 A.D. to exist under the definitive name of Tali kingdom till its conquest by the Mongols.

An offshoot of the same stock had remained behind in the Kiu-lung mountains, whence they swarmed under the cognate name of Leao, and spread all over the south after 345 A.D. From the quotations in Chinese authors, their language was Shan with Tibeto-Burmese ingredients. They were exposed to a regular slave-hunting when the Chinese were able to take the offensive and to quash their successive rebellions. The result was to drive them southwards. An author of the thirteenth century speaks of them as having extended, in more than one hundred subdivisions, to fifty days' journey from the frontiers of the Ta-li kingdom.

Other branches were the Shen Lao, Ko-Lao, Po-Lao, etc.

In the vicinity of the Lao mountains was the easternmost branch of the race, that of the TCHAO in modern Nganhuy province. The meaning of the name indicates a nesting people, so called from their habit of building their houses on piles. It was among them (as a cognate tribe?) that the founder of the SHANG exiled Kieh, the last ruler of the overthrown Hia dynasty, in 1558 B.C. They extended southwards in Kiang-si and formed part of the Tsu kingdom, and were not dislodged from their seats before the 10th century of our era, when they were driven into Hunan, W. of Kwangsi and Kweitchou. Many of them migrated altogether from China at that time, but they are still largely represented by the Tu-jen, Tchung-Kia, and other tribes of Kwangsi and Kweitchou of the present day, speaking dialects much resembling the Siamese, of whom they are undoubtedly the elder brothers.

***

Several facts and some of the migrations to the South mentioned in the preceding pages, coincide with events related in Shan and Siamese traditions, though the dates, which are fixed on the Chinese side, do not agree. On the other hand, many new statements found in Chinese documents are a decided gain for the history of the Taï Shan. It was impossible in a survey of so many populations, of which we have only reviewed here the most important during two scores of centuries, compressed into so short a space, to supply all the information required for its complete proof; but it is given in my book on "CHINA BEFORE

THE CHINESE, the Aboriginal and non-Chinese Races of China," shortly to be issued at the Leadenhall Press.

The main conclusion of this Introduction is the unexpected disclosure, from Chinese sources, of the fact that the cradle of the Shan race was in the Kiu-lung mountains, north of Setchuen and south of Shensi, in China Proper.

TERRIEN DE LACOUPERIE.

UNIVERSITY COLLEGE, LONDON.

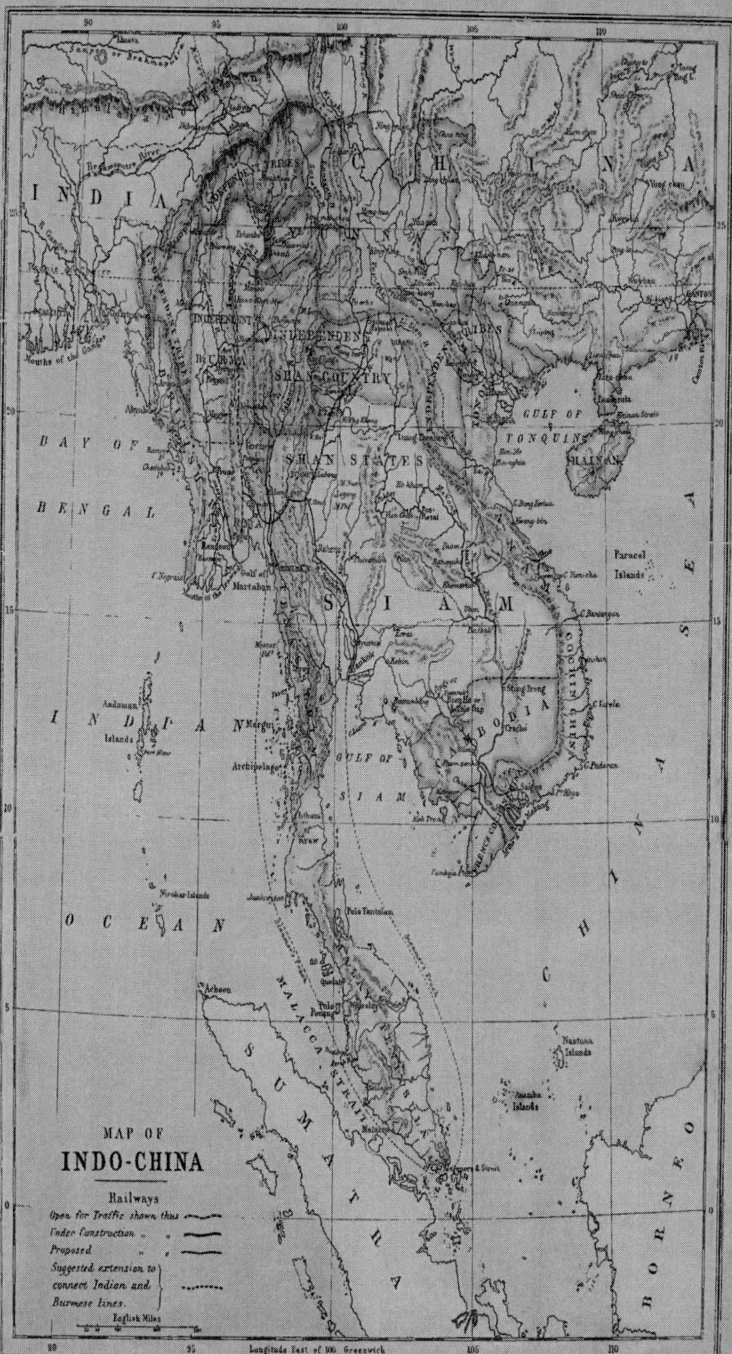
MAP OF
INDO-CHINA
Railways
Open for Traffic shown thus
Under Construction
Proposed
Suggested extension to connect Indian and Burmese lines.
English Miles
Longitude East of 100 Greenwich
London: Field & Tuer, Leadenhall Street.
INDIA
CHINA
YUNNAN
INDEPENDENT TRIBES
BURMA
SHAN COUNTRY
SHAN STATES
SIAM
CAMBODIA
COCHIN CHINA
TONQUIN
GULF OF TONQUIN
HAINAN
BAY OF BENGAL
INDIAN OCEAN
GULF OF SIAM
CHINA SEA
MALACCA STRAITS
SUMATRA
BORNEO
Mouths of the Ganges
Gulf of Martaban
Martaban
Rangoon
Akyab
Mergui Archipelago
Andaman Islands
Nicobar Islands
Paracel Islands
Natuna Islands
Anamba Islands
Acheen
Pulo Penang
Malacca
Singapore & Strait
Pulo Tantalam
C. Negrais
C. Padaran
C. Varela
C. Bantangan
Canton

CHAPTER I.

The golden country — Mineral wealth — Accounts of travellers—Golden pagodas—Khmer ruins—Their design — Enormous stones—Indian art—Indian migration to Cambodia—Advance of the Mékong delta—The French expedition—The Mékong or Cambodia River unnavigable—The French castle in the air—Tonquin as a base—M. de Carné's views—Little known of the country—Effect of slave-hunting—Depopulation of Vien-Chang—Population west of the Mékong—Richness of the valley of the Ménam—Importance of Zimmé—Railways proposed—Opening up China and the Shan country.—Mission.

A REVIEWER, in noticing the account of my journey through the South China Borderlands, sagely remarked, that the epithet "Golden" had been rather frequent in the title of travel books concerning the Far East. We had the River of Golden Sand, the Golden Chersonese, and lastly Across Chrysê—Chrysê the Golden of ancient geographers. The term "Golden," however, is not merely a hackneyed term when applied to the great arm that, stretching southwards from the eastern flank of the Thibetan plateaux, forms the whole of Indo-China, including the Malay Peninsula. This arm is veritably the gold-field of Asia. The reefs in India, which have drawn so much capital from England during the last few years, are merely outcrops of the formation which extends on the surface for thousands of square miles in this Golden Peninsula.

Gold is, and has been for centuries, washed in the beds of the Irrawadi, Sittang, Salween, Mékong, and Yangtsi-kiang, solely because these rivers have ramifications in this arm or in its immediate shoulder. The Lolos and Lawas finding gold in their hills, barter it for merchandise. Taxes are paid in gold, to the king of Siam, by tribes living in the hills to the east of the Mékong. In the Shan tablelands between the Irrawadi and the Salween, in the hills separating the Ménam from the Mékong, in their claw-like finish which grasps Cambodia, and in the vast range that terminates as a backbone to the Malay Peninsula, gold is washed for in the streams and even mined in places. Glance at the pages of any traveller through these regions, and the same story of their vast mineral wealth is told. Rocher and Dupuis have proclaimed the mineral riches of Yunnan and Tonquin; O'Riley, Richardson, Fedden, and others, those of the Salween-Irrawadi plateau; and Mouhot those of the Siamese Shan States, Siam, and Cambodia. Take M. Mouhot, for instance; he tells us of silver and lead near Bassac; iron at Stung Treng; gold mines at Kabin; gold and copper in the mountains between Bangkok and Korat; magnetic iron, antimony, argentiferous lead, copper, and tin to the northwards in the same range, and gold in the streams issuing from it; gold, argentiferous lead, zinc, copper, and iron, the latter two in abundance, in the Cambodian hills; and cannel coal and iron in the islands of the Gulf of Siam.

Precious stones are found in the plateau to the north-east of Mandalay, in the hills south-west of

RUINS OF KHMER TEMPLE AT ANCOR WAT.

Zimmé.[1] The region of Chantaboun, to the south-east of Bangkok, has been renowned for them for centuries, and only lately drew a large number of our subjects from British Burmah in search of them, many of whom returned well repaid for their labours.

The pagodas, resplendent with their gold-leaf covering, are the first objects that fix the gaze of the stranger on his arrival in Burmah or Siam. The spreading of the gold is the favourite act of the Buddhist devotees. The quantity that is used in Siam, the Shan States, Cambodia, and Burmah must be very great; and the amount that has been used during the many centuries that this custom has been carried on would, if it could be mentioned, seem incredible. That the practice is an ancient one may be seen by the decoration, not only of the images of Buddha, but of the ceilings, beams, and entrance pillars in the magnificent Khmer temples, the ruins of which are found to the east of the Ménam-Mékong hills, between the twelfth and sixteenth degree of latitude. These ruins have for some years been a puzzle to the antiquarian. Some of them have been built in terraces one above another, like the famous temple of Boeroe Boedor in Java, others are made of cross galleries; the terraces and the galleries, in each case, leading to a central temple, which is always a tower. The best design is that in which the two plans are seen in the same building, as in the famous temple at Ancor Wat. All the temples that have been examined, with

[1] Kiang-Mai, or Chiang-Mai.

the exception of those at Ancor Thom and Athvea, have their principal faces turned to the east.

The huge stones used in the buildings, often weighing from seven to eight tons, the distance they had to be brought, from eighteen to thirty miles, the immense size of the buildings, their wonderful design and artistic finish and ornamentation, bespeak not only the master-mind of an architect and artist, but that of an engineer. Well might M. Mouhot, on seeing one of these temples, declare it to be "a rival to that of Solomon, and erected by some Michael Angelo; it might take an honourable place beside our most beautiful buildings. It is grander than anything left to us by Greece or Rome."

The architecture of the ruins is evidently the outcome of Indian art. It appears from the records of the Tsin dynasty, in China (A.D. 265–419), that the early kings of Cambodia were natives of India; and that the people had books, writings, and treasures, and were noted for the practice of sculpture. There is likewise a tradition amongst the Cambodians that there was an immigration of natives of India into their country B.C. 254. It is therefore not unlikely that some of these temples were erected about this date. As Buddhism did not enter Cambodia until A.D. 422, this would account for the strange fact that images with from two to sixteen heads, and from four to thirty-two arms, the Indian Vishnus, as well as figures with wings, are found in the ruins, in company with those of Buddha.

At the time of the arrival of the Indian immigrants,

the delta of the Mékong is said to have extended no farther than the town of Pnompenh, which is situated at the junction of the outlet of the Great Cambodian lake with the river. An extension of a hundred and fifty miles in a little over two thousand one hundred years would appear incredible, were it not for the fact that the Gulf of Siam is still the area of volcanic action, and that there are many evidences of recent upheaval met with both along the coast and inland. For instance, M. Mouhot, when at Khao Khoe (a village to the north-east of Bangkok), which is situated at the foot of the hills a full hundred miles inland, noticed on all the neighbouring calcareous hills traces of the water which anciently covered them. He even found close to their base, under a stratum of soil, banks of fossil coral and sea-shells in a good state of preservation.

On the 5th June, 1866, the celebrated French expedition left Saigon in order to explore the country lying between French Cochin-China and the Chinese province of Yunnan. They embarked on the great Cambodia River with hearts beating high with the hope that this noble stream might prove, not only the means of floating them to the Celestial Country, but, in the future, a glorious path for their compatriots, whose banner they proudly hoped would soon float over the countries far, far to the north, and that the French might thus attain in the east an empire which would more than compensate them for that they had lost in India.

What pleasure there is in such ambitious schemes,

when life is as yet unsoured by rebuffs and disappointments, when our purpose is bent on performing great deeds, when we proudly think nothing is too fearful to be braved, and nothing within the range of possibility is too difficult for us to accomplish!

One cannot but feel sorrow for these Frenchmen on their journey; its very commencement was one of disappointment. Two days from their starting-point the river proved so impracticable that they had to abandon their gun-boat and take to canoes. By the end of December a sailor and French soldier, tired of the serious privations, stole some arms and refused to return to duty. A little later, on arriving at Ubone, it became indispensable to rid the expedition of the soldiers who composed the escort, as it was impossible to foresee what serious complications their bad conduct might bring about. There was, however, some excuse for the men; for even before they had left the frontier of Cambodia, all their barrels of brandy and wine had been pierced by legions of insects, and had run empty in a single night, and all their flour had been spoiled by the damp.

M. de Carné thus summed up the results of the first part of their exploration: "The difficulties it (the river) offers begin at first starting from the Cambodian frontier, and they are very serious, if not insurmountable. If it were attempted to use steam on this part of the Mékong, the return would be very dangerous. At Khong an absolutely impassable barrier, as things are, stands in the way. Between Khong and Bassac the waters are unbroken and

A BOAT ASCENDING A RAPID ON THE MÉKONG.

deep; but the channel is again obstructed a short distance from the latter. From the mouth of the river Ubone, which we had ascended, to Kemarat,—that is over a distance of two-thirds of a degree of latitude,—the Mékong is nothing more than an impetuous torrent, whose waters rush along a channel more than a hundred metres deep by hardly sixty across. The truth began at last to force itself on the most sanguine of us. Steamers can never plough the Mékong as they do the Amazon or the Mississippi; and Saigon can never be united to the western provinces of China by this immense river-way, whose waters make it so mighty, but which seems, after all, to be a work unfinished." The members of the expedition were depressed by the news of the Franco-German war. Sickness began with them before leaving the frontiers of Cambodia; and at Bassac, M. de Lagree, the leader of the expedition, contracted the fever, which brought on the liver complaint, from which he died at Tong-Tchouan, in Yunnan. The hardships with which they met were borne with patience, pluck, and resignation, although the heat and the rain through which they travelled must have tried them grievously.

Before reaching Siam-leap, after they had been forced to leave their canoes, the night closed in upon them whilst in the forest. It would have been impossible for them to continue their journey, so, although the rain was pelting down on them, each one made a bed of damp leaves and went to sleep in the clothes he wore, resigned to endure the water which poured from the sky. The penalty for this exposure was soon exacted. M. de Carné tells us: "During our stay at Siam-leap (their next stage), sickness had seized on our companions, like vultures on their prey. Leaving behind us, stretched on the mats of the pagoda, two officers and three men of our escort, unable to rise, we left with aching hearts, taking with us their baggage and their arms."

After coming to the conclusion "that Saigon is for ever separated from China by a long series of cascades and rapids," M. de Carné, who it may be here mentioned was the political officer attached to the French expedition, turned his hopes to Tonquin as a base for the extension of the French dominion over Indo-China, nor did his vista stop here, for in the conclusion of his book he says: "The force of circumstances, and the weakness of the Chinese themselves (this was during the Mussulman rebellion), enable us to foresee the dismemberment of that ancient empire. In the presence of such an eventuality, France should be prepared. Her part is traced out by the position which she already holds on the Anamite Peninsula. It is absolutely necessary that she should exercise a paramount influence at Tonquin, which is for her the key of China, and that, without hurrying by any impatience the course of events, she should show her flag to the people whose protectorate may some day fall into her hands." He goes on to state a little farther on: "Perspectives full of the deepest interest and attraction open from Saigon, beyond the mountains of Tonquin, over the fertile and healthy countries of Western China and Thibet. Fortune, which has so often made us pay for her favours of a day by lasting betrayal, appears to have become less cruel." These opinions of M. de Carné were published in 1872, and were most likely read with great interest by the Pekin Foreign Office; it is therefore not much to be wondered at that the Chinese Government strongly protested against the claim of the French to a protectorate over Anam and its province Tonquin under the treaty of 1874. We need not go farther than M. de Carné's pages fully to understand the hopes of the French and the objections of the Chinese.

Notwithstanding the journeys which have been made through Siam and its dependencies, but little is known of the country outside the routes taken by the travellers. The French, in their toilsome journey through the gorges of the Mékong, made but few detours, and gave us but little information about the extent of the population. The country to the west of the river, particularly in the lower portion of its course, seems to have been better peopled than that to the east. This may be accounted for by the shameful practice of slave-hunting which exists, the Anamites, Chinese, Cambodians, and Shans making a hunting-ground of the Mois Hills, which lie between Cambodia and Siam, and Anam.

As the French proceeded northwards, most of the hill-tribes were found to have accepted the Siamese rule, and were therefore safe from the incursion of their neighbours, and protected against the Anamites, who had been driven by the King of Siam across the hills which form a high and barren barrier between Anam and the Shan country. Some Anamite villages were, however, found whose inhabitants, at the time of the war with France and Spain, had sought protection in the valley of the Mékong from the forced enlistment of the King of Anam.

The province of Vien-Chang, one of the oldest Shan principalities in this part of Indo-China, they found had not fully recovered from the effects of its rebellion against Siam in 1827, at which time the capital was destroyed and the people removed to Ubone and to the country to the north-east of Bangkok. As in the olden days, the Shans from the north are still pushing down, and the Lau-Phun-Ham, or untattooed Shans, are being replaced by the Lau-Phun-Dam, their tattooing brothers.

M. Mouhot, in his remarkable journey from Bangkok along the hills which separate the Ménam River from the Mékong, gives more details of the population; the province of Korat, according to him, contains eleven towns, some of which have from fifty to sixty thousand inhabitants, besides a number of villages. In the two hundred miles to the north of Korat, he passed through sixty villages and six towns. When it is remembered that he journeyed along the high route used by the chiefs and the officers of the king, who are allowed to live at free quarters on their journey, and to use the people as carriers without payment, it is not likely that this was the most populous part of the country. The villages could

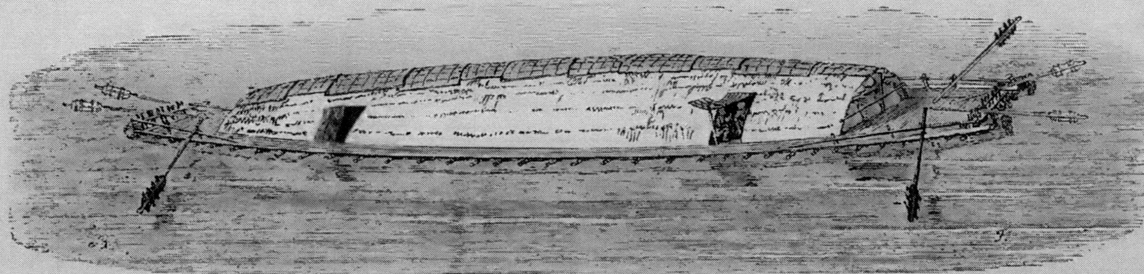

SPECIMEN OF A SHAN BOAT ON THE MÉKONG RIVER.

not have been very small, as he notes that they each possessed elephants, and several had as many as fifty or a hundred.

The population of the valley of the Ménam, in which Bangkok and Zimmé are situated, must be much more considerable than that of the country to the eastward. Herr Carl Bock, who recently travelled up the Ménam River from Bangkok to Zimmé, and thence to Kiang Tsen on the Mékong, found the country between Bangkok and Paknam-Po thickly peopled, the Ménam passing through a fertile alluvial plain; he says that the western branch of the Ménam, which joins the eastern at Paknam-Po, is rich and well peopled. The town of Zimmé, which, according to him, has a hundred thousand inhabitants, controls the trade of the Shan States and China with British Burmah and Siam. The whole country is extremely fertile.

After strongly advocating the construction of a railway between Bangkok and Zimmé, he goes on to say, not only would a railway bring Zimmé and the neighbouring Shan States into direct communication with the sea, but it would draw to itself the greater part of the trade of the Shan States and Yunnan, which at present finds an outlet full of difficulty towards the east at Canton, or a still longer and more costly way to the Yangtsi. It is a pleasure to find an authority like Carl Bock so thoroughly agreeing with part of my proposals. The connection of the British Burmah system of railways with Zimmé and Bangkok has for some time been advocated by me; and the further

C

extension to the borders of south-west China, and the permeation of branches throughout the Shan country, and indeed throughout China, is, I firmly believe, only a matter of time.

In 1879, owing to certain disputes between our foresters and the owners of the teak-forests at Zimmé, it was determined by the Government of India to send a mission to the King of Siam, in order to make arrangements for the meeting of a joint commission at Zimmé, which should settle all pending cases, and draw out such rules for the working of the forests as would be likely to prevent any future clashing between the rival interests.

Having proceeded to Bangkok, we were graciously received by the King, who proved not only willing but eager to insure the removal of all cause of friction between the chiefs, who were the owners of the teak-forests, and our subjects the Burman foresters. During our stay we were hospitably entertained by our consul, who did his utmost to insure our comfort and the successful termination of our mission.

CHAPTER II.

Leave Bangkok—Reach Maulmain—Our start for Zimmé—Arrive at Pahpoon—Mr. Davis—A famous dacoit hunter—Importance of Pahpoon—Moung Deepah—Mr. Bernard—Improved communications—Our mission—March to the Dahguin ferry—The Salween River—Catching timber.

LEAVING Bangkok in a gun-boat, a few days' run carried us to Singapore. There we changed to one of the local steamers, and, passing through the network of small islands lining the coast as far north as the mouth of the Salween, through coast scenery not to be surpassed anywhere that I know of, reached Maulmain after a voyage of ten days.

The *personnel* of the mission consisted of Colonel Street, who is now Commissioner of Pegu, as chief; Dr. Oswald Baker, as medical officer; Mr. McDermott, assistant superintendent, in charge of twenty police; a Burmese *myo-oke*, or assistant commissioner, who had a previous knowledge of the country; and myself, as personal assistant to the chief. We had thirty-two elephants in our suite, and a little army of followers, who were chiefly Burmese.

After gathering together our party and collecting the necessary stores, we started with a flotilla of native boats up the delta of the Salween River, to the mouth of the Yunzaleen, which enters the Salween in latitude

18° 6′ north. Proceeding up that river for ninety-five miles, we arrived at the town of Pahpoon, the head-quarter station of the Salween district, where we were welcomed by Mr. J. C. Davis, the officer in charge of the Salween hill-tracts, and of our diplomatic relations with the Siamese border province of Zimmé. This gentleman is renowned both as a police and district officer. Some years ago, when certain portions of the country were infested by dacoits, he employed his time for weeks in hunting them out of the precipitous country lying to the east of Thatone. So popular had he become amongst the quiet-loving people of the district, that he had no trouble in inducing them to join and aid him in freeing the country from these marauders.

His many daring feats are household words throughout the country; and he at length became such a terror to the numerous bad characters, that many plots were laid by them for his assassination. Timely warning, received from friendly villagers, enabled him to elude these attempts, and generally to punish the plotters severely, until the chief of the Toung-thoos—a hill-tribe of his district, whom he had been compelled to have removed from his post—concocted a well-laid plot for taking Mr. Davis's life, which nearly succeeded. One evening, when sitting after dinner in his bungalow, with the police officer and a friend who was paying him a visit, his quick ear recognised the sound of stealthy steps stealing along underneath the house, which is raised on posts some eight feet from the ground. Cautiously peeping over the verandah, he

THE GIANTS' BALUSTRADE AT ANCOR THOM.

saw a gang of armed men surrounding the house. Quickly re-entering his sitting-room, he told the police officer and his friend to guard the front entrance, and, looking for his arms, he found that they had all been removed. Stepping to his bedroom door, in order to secure the arms which he always kept at the head of his bed, he found it shut. Retreating a few steps to gain impetus, he rushed forward, and, forcing the door open, scattered the dacoits who were in the room pell-mell. Seeing a *dha*, or Burmese sword, which had not been removed, he at once secured it, but, in so doing, received a wound on the face, which would have destroyed his sight but for the rim of his spectacles. Quickly drawing his *dha*, he cut down two men, while the rest escaped, but were shortly after captured and transported for life.

Not long after this incident he was moved to the charge of the Salween district, where he has since done admirable work. Mr. Davis's wonderful aptitude in the acquirement of native languages, and his acquaintance with the manners and customs of the various tribes, make him peculiarly fitted for bringing turbulent districts into order; and his great tact and ability mark him out as the most suitable officer for frontier political service.

Pahpoon is situated at the junction of several im portant trade-routes to Maulmain from Karen-nee, the Shan States, and Zimmé, and is of great importance as the local headquarters of our foresters, who work the Salween and neighbouring forests. For many years it was kept in continued disturbance by Moung

Deepah, a celebrated leader of dacoits, and, on account of his depredations, trade through this district had been greatly hindered, almost entirely put a stop to. The ability and resolution of the district officers have made them so feared, that trade is now rapidly reviving, and dacoities are less frequent, and seldom pass unpunished. A road for pack-animals has lately been opened out from Pahpoon in the direction of Zimmé, the initial step in opening communications. The present Chief Commissioner of British Burmah, Mr. Bernard, is determined to facilitate the permeation of commerce throughout this part of the province, and is doing his utmost to improve the trade-routes and insure their being perfectly secure. The Yunzaleen River has been cleared of snags and other impediments, and police-stations have been placed at various points of the district in order to give additional security to trade.

After a few days' halt at Pahpoon, in order to get our unwieldy train into something like order, we set off on the 4th March, and, after crossing a range of hills, about two thousand five hundred feet in height, encamped on the banks of the Maythalouk stream, having journeyed for some nine hours along a track six feet wide, which had been cleared through the jungle. The Maythalouk stream was then only nine inches deep. In the rains it increases to a width of a hundred feet, and has a depth of seven feet, with a swift and headlong current.

The next day we proceeded along undulating and generally sidelong ground, until we reached a stream close to the thirteenth mile from Pahpoon. Continuing for some time down its narrow gorge, we reached the Toung-chyin *tsakan* (halting-place), having travelled some nine and a half miles, a short but tiring march. The following day the track led us up the hill-side, to a height of a little over two thousand feet above sea-level, whence we descended, first rapidly, and then gradually, to the Salween River, at the site of the Dahguin ferry. For the last four miles paddy-fields and *toung yas* (hill-cultivation) were met with, which were irrigated from the neighbouring waterfalls. The police-station at the Dahguin ferry is situated on the west, or British, side of the Salween; on the other side the Siamese have their station, both being stockaded. The hills on the British side are much higher than those on the Siamese. The current of the river, even at the time of our crossing, was running fiercely; many whirlpools and eddies were visible, and the depth in the centre was said to be great. Many rocks were seen cropping out, extending for some distance from the banks, and jutting up in places from the bed of the stream.

The Salween is one of the great rivers of the world. Its course extends through upwards of sixteen degrees of latitude and fourteen of longitude, rising in the west of the great central tableland of Thibet, and having a branch within one hundred and fifty miles of the head-waters of the Indus, Ganges, and Bramaputra. After proceeding nearly due east, from 83° 30′ east to 94° 10′ east, it makes an *S* curve, and then passing through a precipitous gorge, which sometimes widens into a narrow valley, continues through mountains towering from eighteen thousand to twenty thousand feet in height, as far as the twenty-eighth degree of north latitude. At this place, according to the Abbé Desgodins, the hills gradually lower their heads.

At the point where I crossed the Salween, on my late exploration from Canton to the Irrawadi, the pass over the hills next the Salween is only eight thousand seven hundred and thirty feet. The river is spanned by an iron suspension bridge four hundred and twenty feet long. The banks, at the bridge, are about two thousand five hundred feet above sea-level. The descent in the river-bed between twenty-eight degrees and the bridge—a distance of only three degrees of latitude—is said by the Abbé to be about three thousand five hundred feet. A fall of about fourteen hundred feet occurs in the next three degrees of latitude, where at the Soo-kat ferry the river is two hundred and forty feet wide, the flood rising in the rains no less than ninety-five feet. This enormous rise is caused by the contraction of the channel to eighty-five feet at a place lying between the Soo-kat and Takau ferries. At the latter it is seven hundred and fifty feet above the sea, the floods rising from forty to fifty feet. At the mouth of the Yembine stream, which flows into the Salween below the great rapid, which lies some distance down the Salween, below our point of crossing, Dr. Richardson found the width of the river to be only two hundred and fifty feet, by measurement. It is near this point I propose to cross my projected railway from Maulmain to Kiang Hung.

WHIRLPOOLS AT KENG KANIEN ON THE MÉKONG RIVER, CAUSED BY A CONTRACTION OF THE CHANNEL.

A short distance above Yembine, but below the *hat-gyee*, or great fall, a strong cable of twisted rattan is stretched across from bank to bank at a place called Kyo-dan, where the river narrows. The cable is used for the purpose of arresting the floating teak-logs coming from the upper regions. The owners of the timber proceed to Kyo-dan to claim their logs, which have previously been marked in the forests with a hammer bearing the private registered stamp of the forester. The logs are then collected, made into huge rafts, and taken down to Kado, the Government revenue-station, near Maulmain, where duty is paid and the timber cleared finally for export. The Salween is navigable for small boats as far as the rope-station, and it is believed that shallow-draught steamers could ply as far north as Shuaygoon, in latitude 17° 12′. The river at Maulmain is a mile wide, and bifurcates opposite that town, which is only separated from the sea by the narrow island of Beloogyoon, or "Devil's Island."

CHAPTER III.

Difficulties of crossing the Salween—In Siam—Pitching tents—Building huts in an hour—Sleeping in howdahs—Hmine Long-gyee valley—Population destroyed—White Karens—An oppressed people—American missionaries—A fruitful field—Mr. Bernard's report—Hmine Long-gyee—Large game—A vast breeding-ground—Slave-hunters—The Red Karens—A block to trade—Hmine Long-gyee—A Siamese official—Pain-killer—Kindness of the "town-eater"—Arrogance of the Burmese.

Our first attempt to cross the elephants of our party resulted in only four out of the thirty-two getting across; the remainder, not being used to such a swift and turbulent stream, at first refused to enter the water; when urged by their drivers, they became terrified, and, turning tail, rushed up the bank and stampeded up the mountain side, trumpeting wildly as they went. We had to take them to an easier crossing, where we managed to get them all over in safety.

The Salween forms the boundary between Siamese and British territory from the entrance of the Htoo River to that of the Thoungyeen. At Dahguin, on the Siamese side of the river, we found that the police stockade was garrisoned by thirty Siamese police, or so-called soldiers. Their arms were by no means formidable, consisting as they did of old flint muskets, which even a Burmese hunter would despise, and any one would have much hesitation in using. Their hair was dressed or rather cut in the usual Siamese fashion, short on the sides, and combed up in straight bristles, looking like a dirty clothes-brush rampant. The guard turned out, and politely saluted us as we mounted the bank.

Having lost a day in making the passage of the Salween, we left Dahguin on the morning of the 8th March, and proceeded up the May-koung-ku stream, which is a torrent about a hundred feet wide by eight feet deep in the rains, but reduced to a width of ten feet and a depth of one foot at this time. Following its banks, past many small waterfalls and over huge boulders, through a teak-forest, from which every tree of any size had been extracted, we passed through a gorge and stopped at Choungnaqua, where we pitched our tents with some trouble, owing to our having to superintend the work ourselves, as our Burmese followers, being unused to tents, were not handy at such a mode of camping. In Indo-China, as a rule, on arrival at the halting-place in uninhabited districts, small trees are cut down by them and fixed as posts for the erection of a hut, the branches being used for the floor—which is raised several feet from the ground—and roof scantlings; the whole is roofed over, as a protection from the heavy night dew, by the leaves of the eng, or other trees. So rapidly are these huts constructed, that it seldom takes more than an hour to run them up. They are far more advantageous than tents in the hilly parts of the country, as not only do they form a protection from wild animals, but they tend to raise you above the deadly miasma which exudes from the ground in many of the steaming valleys. Another enormous advantage is that, in a country where transport is difficult to procure, and scrub jungle or small trees are available, the saving of heavy and cumbrous baggage, such as tents, is a great consideration. In the pine forest, where no scrub jungle exists, and where the timber is too large to allow of being felled, and in the parts of the country where the trees are leafless for some months, use is often made, by the Siamese and Shans, of the elephant howdahs[1] to sleep in, and in their construction this purpose is borne in mind.

Next day, ten miles after leaving Choungnaqua, we topped the main range, and proceeding for about a mile over steep and broken ground, followed the Quay-bouk choung[2] to the Main Long-gyee[3] River, which at our point of crossing is a hundred feet wide and five and a half feet deep, with a very rapid current in the rains. The last mile of the distance was down a narrow valley until we came to the Hmine Long-gyee plain. The valley reaches as far as the eye can see, and is about three miles in width, consisting of grassy patches and rice cultivation. After crossing the river, we marched for about a mile across the plain to the town.

---

[1] A howdah is a seat placed on the back of an elephant, and is generally protected by a roof.

[2] Choung, Burmese for stream.

[3] Or, Hmine Long-gyee.

TYPE OF KAREN MAN.

Three-quarters of an hour's distance to the north-west lies the old walled city of Yunzaleen, which is now overgrown by large trees. The remains of the wall and a ditch of very considerable extent are easily traced. Yunzaleen was formerly a part of the old kingdom of Pegu; it was given at a remote period as a dower with a Talain princess to a chief of Zimmé. The chief of Hmine Long-gyee has the title of Myo-tsa, or "town-eater"; and his jurisdiction extends over the whole of the valley of the Ménium (or Hmine Long-gyee) River. In Dr. Richardson's time the whole of the inhabitants of this fine district, according to him, probably did not amount to more than two hundred families. This paucity of population most likely resulted from the fact that the Hmine Long-gyee valley lay on the route of invading armies from Zimmé, Siam, and Burmah.

The little outlying villages were inhabited by the Karen-pyoos (White Karens), a quiet, simple, timid race, who are rapidly being absorbed into Christianity, in consequence of the labours of the American missionaries. Their spirit had been broken by centuries of oppression, both from the Talain, Shan, and Burmese, whichever power happened to be in the ascendant. The Shans were, according to Dr. Richardson, esteemed by the people to be the most merciful, and the Burmese had the character of behaving in a most oppressive and cruel manner.

Even in 1836, the time of Richardson's journey, the Karens were so cowed that passengers easily obliged them to accompany their party through their jungles, to act as guides, clear the path, build huts at the halting-places, furnish provisions, and procure the necessary firewood and water; for all which services these poor people were not only in the habit of receiving no recompense, but considered themselves lucky if they escaped being plundered into the bargain. They were much surprised when they found that Dr. Richardson, according to the habit of English travellers, insisted upon paying for all supplies and services rendered him. Both men and women have nearly as fair complexions as Europeans, and the young people especially may be counted as good-looking.

The persecution of the Karens in our territory was put down by us with a strong hand on our annexation of British Burmah. Soon after taking Maulmain, the American mission determined to make the Karen country a field for their labour. So great has been their success under Judson, Mason, and other famous missionaries, that there are now no less than four hundred and fifty-seven Christian Karen parishes scattered about the country. Most of these support their own churches, their own Karen pastors, and their own school. So much are the people imbued with true Christian spirit, that considerable sums of money are subscribed by them for the furtherance of missionary work among the Karens, and other hill-races living beyond the British border. Mr. Bernard, the Chief Commissioner of British Burmah, has stated in his administration report for 1880, that the Christian Karen communities are distinctly more

A KAREN GIRL.

industrious, better educated, and more law-abiding than the Burman and heathen Karen villagers in their neighbourhood—an opinion which will be generally endorsed by all who have studied Burmah. The Karen race, and the British Government, owe a great debt to the American missionaries, who have wrought this beneficial change among the Karens of British Burmah.

The town of Hmine Long-gyee had increased from twenty houses, in 1836, to two hundred at the time of our visit. It is beautifully situated in the midst of gardens of pomegranate, cocoa-nut, papya, and guava trees. The surrounding fields are irrigated by Persian water-wheels, and laid out in terraces, two crops of rice being grown in the year. The hills to the east of the valley abound in tiger, elephant, elk, deer, wild cattle, and wild pig. The rhinoceros is found in the lower and grassy parts of the jungle, while monkeys and pheasants, as well as jungle fowl, are plentiful. The hills are covered with eng, saul, and small teak timber that has not been considered by the Burmese foresters worthy of extraction. The higher portions of the range and its spurs are covered with splendid pine-forests.

The river rises at Hmine Long-gyee thirty to forty feet during the rains, and many portions of the lower land in the neighbourhood of the town are at times inundated. Several villages dot the plain, and the whole country, excepting the rice-fields and garden land, is an enormous breeding-ground for cattle. As many as eight thousand a year used to be taken into the country of Karen-nee, and exchanged for slaves, horses, tea, and stick-lac. The cattle were purchased by the Karen-nees, or Red Karens, in Richardson's time, at an average price of one rupee for a cow, and two and a half for the very best bullock, or else bartered at the rate of seven bullocks for a pony, or its equivalent, a young man; while eight or ten bullocks were given for a young woman. The Karen-nees, like the Kachyens, their neighbours to the northwards, are renowned for their kidnapping propensities. At least one-third of the slaves are taken from the Burmese Shan States, and the remainder from the adjoining hill-tribes. The officers of the King of Burmah, when the Shan States were ruled by them, did nothing to protect the people, and even accepted presents from the Red Karens, as a bribe to stop their ears against all complaints. The country of these men-stealers extends from the Htoo River to the banks of the Salween, and is about thirty miles broad, by an average of fifty miles in length, and forms a block to all our traffic with the part of the independent Shan country lying to the west of the Salween. The traders fear to pass through the Karen-nee country, and either skirt it to the westward, through the nearly impassable land of the other Karens, who inhabit the western portion of Karen-nee, or else, crossing the valley of the Salween, proceed to our territory *viâ* the Hmine Long-gyee valley.

It is only from our having made a pact with the King of Burmah, by which it was agreed that neither of us would annex Karen-nee, that this lamentable state of affairs has been allowed to continue to the present day. If this small strip of country were brought into order, the increase of our trade with the now independent Shan States, lying west of the Salween, would be very great.

The men whom we met at Hmine Long-gyee were destitute of jackets, and apparelled solely in the *sarong*—a garment which is merely a waist-cloth, scarcely sufficing for the requirements of decency. The ladies are attired in what is known to the Burmese as a Zimmé *loongyee*,[1] which is simply a petticoat or skirt with horizontal stripes, ornamented with a border of dull-hued silver or gold. Sometimes a kerchief is thrown round the shoulders and over the bosom. The younger women are gradually becoming habituated to the wearing of jackets; this, however, is still looked upon as "bad form" by the elder ladies, who prefer to adhere to their primitive customs.

The streets of the town are kept clean by means of water raised by Persian water-wheels. The houses are comfortable, but have all steep roofs reaching down to within a few feet from the ground, thus rendering the interiors dark. This does not seem to be required from the rains being unusually heavy in these parts, for on inquiry we found that they were much lighter than in the countries to the westward. The entrance is made from the verandahs, at the end

[1] Burmese garment resembling our petticoat, but ungathered at the top.

of the houses, and stands of flowers are placed in front of the doorways, both to serve as a decoration and to baffle the gaze of too inquisitive eyes.

Only one *kyoung*, or monastery, exists inside the town, but outside there is a large cluster of them, surrounding a pagoda. Entering the one in the town, we found its walls covered with rough frescoes, bold in design and not without character. Some of them, which had been executed by an old *poongyee*, or monk, gave us no high opinion of his morality. One of these proved that, unlike St. Kevin, he had some idea of " what the wily sex can do," in the way of bringing men under their influence.

These poongyees, unlike those resident in Upper Burmah, do not prove ardent devotees of Buddha, although they take the same strict vows when they enter the priesthood. Their practice is even looser than that of the monks of old, as depicted by Froude. They are seemingly attached to all the so-called "gentlemanly vices," and are universally said to drink, gamble, and flirt in a most shameless manner. Their hold over the people is extinguished, and they are universally despised by the townsfolk. The people are generally quiet and orderly in their demeanour, and give but little trouble to the authorities.

In front of the court-house we noticed stocks, and perceived a few prisoners, who were heavily chained, straggling about. There are no carts in the district, and not more than half a dozen canoes were seen on the river; all the traffic is carried on by means of elephants, porters, and bullocks. The pack-saddle in use with the latter is rounded, so as to take the shape of the animal, and is of a better design than any I have seen elsewhere in the East. Some fifty police reside in this town, in order to preserve order in the district. Their main occupations appeared to be, judging by what we observed, betel chewing, smoking, and sleeping. A less disciplined squad I have seldom seen. A gong is used in place of a bugle, for their martial exercise.

The chief official of the place is appointed from Bangkok, and is blessed with only one wife. This is a most unusual circumstance amongst officers in these parts, but he compensates for his abstemiousness by the number of his female attendants. He wore an official costume, a strange olio, composed of a new German *pickelhaube*, a second-hand military jacket, a Siamese sarong, and French polished shoes. His gentility was further evidenced by the length of his finger-nails, which showed the impossibility of his having performed manual labour for at least a year.

In the bazaar we noticed, as is usual in the East, arsenic, vitriol, and other poisonous drugs lying in close proximity to more innocent medicines. One specific we found, though not in common use by the natives, was highly prized. It was locally known as *bangilla*. No specimen of it could be procured in the bazaar, and our worthy medico was much puzzled as to what this famous panacea could be. After much search, an empty bottle was found, when it turned out to be no other than the far-famed American "pain-killer."

The governor, or "town-eater," as such functionaries

are called by both Burmese and Siamese, proved hospitable in his way. On hearing of our approach, he sent five riding-elephants to meet us, but we preferred to walk. The howdah of the elephants has a curved roof, to shelter one from the sun and rain, and is far more comfortable for riding than that used in India. The governor supplied our larder during our stay, and did all he could to insure our comfort. Our Burmese followers appreciated this behaviour, though, much to our annoyance, they made no endeavour to hide the supercilious and arrogant contempt they had, or pretended to have, for the Shans. The intense conceit of the Burmese character, and the airs which the Burmans give themselves, are unparalleled by those of any people known to me.

TYPE OF SHAN VILLAGE ON RIVER BANK.

CHAPTER IV.

March to the Baw plateau—The water-parting of the Ménam and Salween — Lawas — Cultivation of cotton, indigo, sugar-cane, tobacco, and safflower—Preparation of cotton—Chinese purchasers—Iron manufactured—Women miners—Taxes of hill-tribes—Lawas—Lawa converts to Buddhism—Lawas called "Man-bears"—Singular custom—Difference between hill-races on the Anam and Shan mountains—Value of slaves—Highlanders of the Shan country.

After resting a day at Hmine Long-gyee, we left the town, and, following the banks of the May-tsaleen stream, proceeded for some six miles up gradually rising ground to our halting-place for the night. We were accompanied, in accordance with his instructions, received from Zimmé, by the "town-eater" in person. Our train was gradually growing; several ladies, in the airy costume of the country—which reminded one of that of mermaids—were in attendance upon him. We were the cynosure of their eyes, but being as yet unused to such extremely *décolleté* costume were too bashful to allow our gaze to rest for more than a casual glance in their direction. The pictures in the illustrated papers have, of late years, done their utmost to remove the fastidious objections entertained by Europeans to the aspect of the human form when partly unadorned—at least when accompanied by a dark hide.

The next day we continued our journey along the valley, which narrows in places to six hundred feet. Passing a steep granite cliff and many small waterfalls, we reached the Maysowan *tsakan*, which lies at the foot of the hill. The jungle, throughout this part, generally consisted of thitsee, or wood-oil tree, plantains, bamboo, and fine specimens of the tree-fern. Huge creepers and dense undergrowth made the jungle impassable, except where the path had been cleared. Pine-forest crowns the heights, and descends for a considerable distance down the slopes of the hills. Two miles from our last halting-place a steep ascent up the side of a spur commenced. After a continual clamber for about two and a half miles, we reached its crest, which is about three thousand five hundred feet above the level of the sea. At the very summit of this spur, which is about two hundred feet higher than the main range at Baw, we were surprised to find a small spring with a trickling stream. Descending the hill, we encamped upon the banks of the Mélaik stream, which enters the Hmine Long-gyee River, some distance south of the town. Following the Mélaik for a few miles, and then proceeding by an easy descent into a small open plain, where the pine-forest ceases for a time, we came upon a Lawa village of ten houses surrounded by rice cultivation in patches. A few buffaloes of very light colour were seen grazing near the village.

From this place we crossed another high spur, and

rested for the night by the side of the Métiu. This stream is the last met with that joins the Hmine Longgyee River, and it is up its course that I propose to carry a railway to connect Maulmain and Kiang Tsen. The high spurs crossed by us between Hmine Longgyee and this place will thus be avoided. The Métiu is the easternmost source of the Mélaik. The next day, an easy ascent of two miles brought us to the top of the Baw plateau. Thitsee and plantain trees had disappeared for some time, and we passed through a lofty pine-forest, with tall, straight trees free from branches for fifty or sixty feet from the ground. The wood, although of large growth, is full of resin, and therefore would not prove serviceable for masts or other purposes of naval architecture.

Baw is situated in a plain, which has the appearance of a clearance in the forest, some ten or twelve miles long, by five or six broad. This plateau forms the only elevation which has to be crossed between the Salween and the Méping, which is the western branch of the Ménam River, on which Bangkok, the capital of Siam, is situated. The height of this water-parting as taken by me, at by no means the lowest point, was three thousand three hundred and thirty-seven feet above the sea. This single barrier sums up the "stupendous" obstacles which, until our visit, were supposed to exist in the way of reaching the Shan country by means of a railway!

The inhabitants of the village of Baw are Lawas, who are said to be the aborigines of the country lying to the east of the Salween, from the borders of Yun-

E

nan to some distance south of Baw; they are still found in isolated hamlets scattered about the hills. McLeod, on his journey to Kiang Hung, passed through many of their villages. They are an agricultural race, cultivating cotton, indigo, sugar-cane, tobacco, safflower, chillies, cereals, and other produce. The cotton is grown in abundance on the sides of the hills and in the valleys. The seed is sown broadcast. The only preparation the ground undergoes is to have the old plants dug out and burnt for manure.

Their mode of separating the cotton from the seed is most expeditious, and is performed by one person. An upright wooden frame, consisting of two posts fastened in the ground, supporting in their centre a horizontal circular and smooth iron rod of an inch in circumference, which passing through the former on one side, is formed into a knee, and is fixed to a heavy wooden lever of about five feet in length, within six inches of the middle, causing one arm to be longer than the other, to give it an impetus when in motion. A wooden cylinder of about three inches in circumference is placed parallel to and in contact with the iron rod, and supported in the same manner; to this a handle is attached on the opposite side of the frame on the outside, and is turned by the hand. To the iron knee a string is fastened, which is conducted over a beam and brought down to a pedal, by which it is put into motion. The cotton is placed along the line of contact of the cylinders, which, revolving to each other, draw the cotton through, leaving the seed behind.

The cotton is pressed and packed by the Chinese,

who come all the way from Yunnan to purchase it. The pressing and packing is done in a well, into which the cloth for holding the cotton is introduced. After the cotton is well trodden down, the whole is bound tightly round with strips of bamboo. The bales are carried away on mules, the load varying from two hundred to three hundred pounds. Great care is taken to balance the packages equally, and to see that they weigh alike.

The Lawas we saw at Baw were not agriculturists, but iron-workers and manufacturers. The metal is found in a hill lying about half a day's journey to the north-west of the village, is a red oxide, and is worked solely by the women. It is brought to the village on elephants, and is smelted in such a rough way, that it yields only fifty per cent. of metal. The principal tax paid by the villagers to the Zimmé chief consists of elephant chains, spear-heads, cooking pots, and other ironware. Where iron is not worked in the other villages in the province of Zimmé, each household pays annually to Government a tax of ten viss (a viss equals 3·65 lbs.) of cotton, the same weight of chillies, and five of safflower.

The Lawas have flat noses and low foreheads. Their figures are short and ill-formed, their bellies are protuberant, but they are a strongly limbed and healthy looking race. Their complexions are much darker than those of the Burmese and Shans. The women are very ugly, and remarkably short and stout; their faces are large, their foreheads low, mouths particularly long, with thick lips, and eyes small and wide apart.

Their dress consists of a petticoat of white and red stuff, and a jacket which barely conceals their breasts. The people of Baw, though wretchedly poor in appearance, are reported to be rich, especially in elephants, of which we saw a considerable number near the village. The religion of the Lawas, and in fact of all the Mongoloid races, seems greatly to resemble the Shamanism of the old Tartars. Even their conversion to Buddhism does not free them from their belief in goblins, and they still continue to worship and fear their fetishes, even when accepting the ritual and moral code of the Buddhist religion.

It was amusing to find the dread in which the Lawas are held by both Burmese and Siamese. This is due to the fear of being bitten by them and dying of the bite. They are called by their Burmese neighbours the "man-bears." A singular custom obtains amongst these people, which may perhaps account partly for this superstition. On a certain night in the year, the youths and maidens meet together for the purpose of pairing. Unacceptable youths are said to be bitten severely if they make advances to the ladies; while, on the contrary, the more favoured swains are received with blandishments and kisses, if the caresses of this part of the East can be called by such a name. Burmese travellers, hearing of this custom, are reported on one occasion to have attempted to take unfair advantage of it. The treatment they received from the Lawa damsels is said to have taught them a lesson which has given good grounds on which to base the tradition.

The Shans look upon the Lawas and Karens as one race, and, notwithstanding their fear of them, hold them in very poor esteem, counting them as mere savages. The members of the French expedition ot 1868, on their way up the Mékong, noted the great difference in bearing and character of the hill-tribes who live among the Shan mountains from those they met with when journeying in the hills lying to the east of the great river. These seem to have been timid to excess, having, according to De Carné, been, previous to their submission to Siam, hunted incessantly and carried off as slaves by the Siamese, the Anamites, and the Cambodians. When at Attopeu, the French explorers noticed that several of the tribes living between the Mékong and the crest of the main Anam range (the boundary between Anam and Siam) had submitted to the King of Siam, and paid him a light tribute. For this they had received substantial advantages, for they need no longer fear the incursion of the slave-dealers, who still drive a flourishing trade amongst the independent tribes.

The slaves who are captured become slaves in the fullest sense of the word; they are carried off, with no hope of deliverance save death or escape. Trapped by ambush, and driven off after capture, like fallow-deer, by the man-hunters, they are torn from their forests, chained, and taken to the chief places of the Shan country, Siam, and Cambodia, for disposal. At Pnompenh, the new capital of Cambodia, now under French protection, they are in especial demand, and are of a higher value than Anamite or Cambodian slaves. According to De Carné, they are worth eight hundred francs each; while a Cambodian is hardly worth five hundred francs, and no more than two hundred francs is given for an Anamite. The main feature which determines their value is the degree of confidence which the master can place in their uprightness, which varies according to the race to which they belong.

The Anamites on the one hand, and the Shans and Cambodians on the other, give themselves up to this shameful trade. The French narrate how, on asking the chiefs the worth of the principal articles of merchandise in their villages, they never failed, after mentioning rice, cotton, or silk, to add the slaves, whose value fluctuated like that of other things, according to the law of supply and demand.

The life of a slave is not that of the southern plantation type; for although usually employed in agriculture and domestic work, they are treated with the greatest kindness. They live so intimately and familiarly with their masters, that but for their long hair, and different physiognomy, they could not otherwise be recognised by a visitor. Prisoners of war belong to the chief, and their children are born slaves; they are either used as soldiers, as in Siam, or distributed amongst the petty chiefs. Besides the above, there are bond-slaves and slaves by judicial confiscation for theft and other crimes.

The hill-people on the Shan range (Western Siamese mountains), and throughout the hills between the Ménam and the Mékong, and those to the north of Zimmé, are

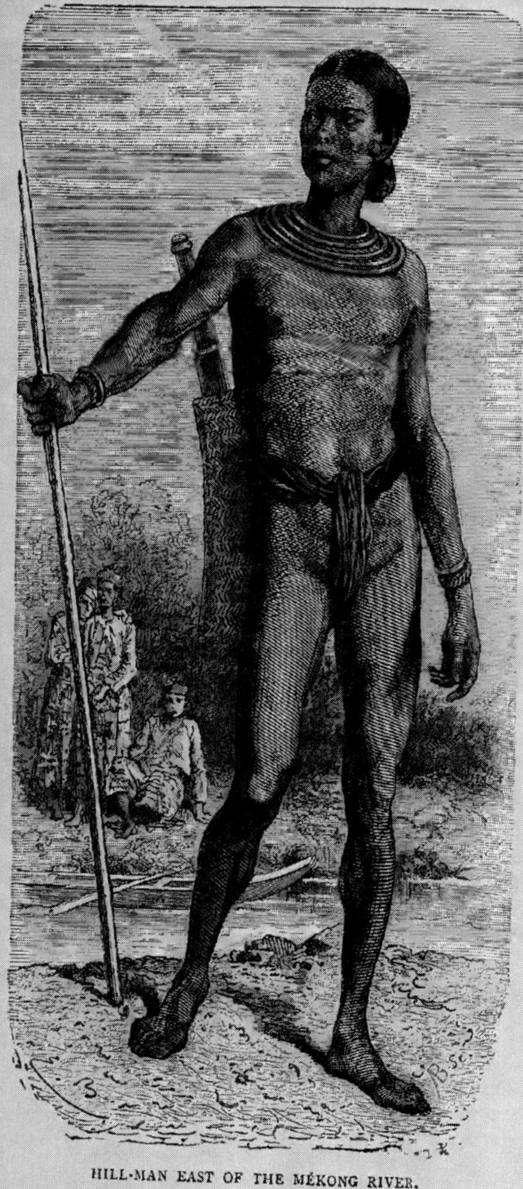

HILL-MAN EAST OF THE MÉKONG RIVER.

by no means a timid race. At the various markets throughout the country, they hold themselves like free men. The finest herds of cattle belong to them, their villages are substantially built, they are admirable husbandmen, and the manner in which they irrigate their fields is remarkable. It is not because they are driven to seek a home in the hills, but from choice, that they select these uplands as their habitat. Their character is generally the same as that of those hospitable aborigines whom I met in my late exploration through Yunnan. Their costumes present a great variety of rich and picturesque designs, and they are noticeable for their fair skins.

CHAPTER V.

Sources of information—Karen habitat—Orang-outang—Lawas and Kachyens—Ka-kuis—Ka-kuas—Ka-koi—Independent Lawas —Red Karens—Sacrificing to nats—Offerings—Divination by fowls' bones—Marriage feast—Divorce—Funerals—Karen-nee —Mineral wealth—Dress—Language—Slaves—Slavery on our border—Mutsa—Si-sun—Kapin—Kadams—Palongs—Yins— —Toung-thoos—Motsoos—Shan-Tayoks—Yendalines—Let-htas—Karens—Sgaw—Sho—Pye-ya—Three clans of White Karens—Ma-nee-pgha—Pa-koo—We-wa—Pie-do—Koo-hto—Shoung—Ha-shoo—Ka-roon—Pye-ya—Bghai-ka-tew—Bghai-ka-hta—Pray—Ma-noo-ma-naw—Tshaw-kho—Karen language —The La-la—Yem—Kali—Putai—Kaláu—Ka-káu—Other tribes.

THE sources of information regarding the other tribes of the heart of Indo-China are few and far between, owing partly to the extreme difficulty experienced by travellers in acquiring information, but more still to the fact that but little exploration has as yet been accomplished, especially in the regions bordering British and Upper Burmah, and those west of Tonquin.

Among other tribes mentioned by various travellers —McLeod, Richardson, O'Riley, Watson, Sconce, Anderson, Cushing, Mason, Spearman, Cameron, and Mouhot—as living west of the Mékong or Cambodia River, are the Karens, Lawas, Karen-nees, or Red Karens, Kachyens, Ka-kuis, Ka-kuas, Ka-koi, Mutsa, Si-sun, Kapin, Kadam, Paloungs, or Polongs, Yin-nees,

Yin-nets, Yin-bans, Yindalines, Yondalines, Let-htas, Padaungs, Yeins, Dummoos, Dunos, and Toung-thoos, and various Karen tribes.

The Karens are found throughout the hills, to the west of the Ménam, as far south as the eighth degree of north latitude. There they are replaced by the Orang-outang, not our ancestors, although some would-be funny people in Singapore assert that they are the possessors of caudal appendages. The Orang-outang are divided into several tribes, which seem to differ considerably, not only in their physiognomy, but in their hair, which is met with straight, curly, and woolly. Their stature seldom exceeds five feet; their body and limbs are neatly moulded, but the former has the appearance of being too heavy for the latter. Their eyes are small, well set, and not sunken. Their nose is low in the face, and shows no sign of a bridge; and their forehead is slightly retreating. Their mouths are large, with thick hanging lips, nearly devoid of muscle. Their head is small, and their expression is open and frank. The whole of the hill-tribes in the Malay Peninsula are said not to number more than eight thousand people. Their religion is similar to that of the other wild tribes. The Lawas, or Lewas, and the Kachyens, reside in the mountains lying east and west of the Salween River.

The Ka-kuis[1] amount to from forty thousand to fifty

[1] Ka, or Kha, is the generic Shan term for hill-people,—Ka-kuis means a hill-people called Kuis. In the same way the Anamites use the term Moi, and the Cambodians Phnom, or Penom. The names given by different travellers are very confusing; each race calls the

thousand. They are a short, ugly, and dirty race, much given to ardent spirits, as is usual with most of the hill-tribes. Their dress resembles that of the Shans, the head-dress of the women being ornamented with beads and strips of bamboo, of which the ornaments worn by them round their necks, and in their ears, are made. They have no idea of a Supreme Being or a future state, but worship *nats*, or spirits, in the same way as the Lawas and other hill-tribes do. They have no written language. They bury their dead, and all belonging to one family are placed in the same grave. An aperture is left near the head, into which food is daily placed for the use of the corpse. They cultivate grain, tobacco, chillies, and cotton, and are said to pay no taxes, but make presents of mats, cloths, and other articles to the chiefs, and supply them with rice when they travel, as well as carry their baggage.

The Ka-kuas resemble the Ka-kuis generally in their habits and dress, but are considered more civilized. They wear their hair like the Chinese, with a tail. The married women only wear a head-dress, which is not made till they are entitled to adopt it; they will not part with this on any consideration, and it is buried with them at their death. This race is much afflicted with goitre. The Chinese maintain that the Ka-kuis and Ka-kuas came originally from Uncian of Marco Polo, Yung-chang of to-day. The dress of

others by different names, which often refer merely to some peculiarity in their dress or customs; thus one and the same tribe is often described under various names. Again, the spelling of the names is apt to vary—Charai and Giraie, Chiamese and Tsiamese, and so on.

the Ka-koi women consists, according to Cushing, of a very short petticoat of dark blue fastened about the waist, and a short jacket quite tight-fitting and ornamented with seeds. The head-dress is formed of a series of bamboo circlets, two inches broad, which are suspended from the coil of the hair behind, into which a small bamboo frame has been inserted. From the opening behind dangle paper streamers of various colours, and the bushy tails of some animal resembling the fox. In front, the hair hangs over the forehead, and is cut off where it meets the eyebrows. The fore part of the head is covered with bunches of beads made from the seeds of a plant abundant in the hills west of Kiang Tung, where these people reside.

The independent Lawas, who are said to number about eighty thousand, are chiefly cultivators of cotton, and are found in the high mountainous country to the northward and westward of Muang Lem; they wear their hair short and uncombed, and their sole garment is a small waist-cloth. They hold little communication with their neighbours, and never willingly permit a stranger to penetrate into their mountains. The Chinese caravans are often robbed by this tribe. The Lawa villages consist of from four hundred to five hundred houses, and are ruled by independent chiefs, who are frequently at war with each other. The heads of the conquered are very much prized, and serve to decorate the warriors' houses. Heads are in requisition, for the purpose of propitiating the nats (genii) of the woods and hills, and insuring good crops. The men obtain the heads by inveigling unsuspicious travellers into an ambuscade; when secured, the heads are passed from house to house, with much ceremony and rejoicing. From this habit they are termed the "goung-pyat," or head-cutting-off Lawas. Some of the tribe, who live near Muang Ma, or Kiang Ma, a town to the north of Muang Lem, on the borders of China, are said to give gold, which is found in the hills, in exchange for cattle, betel nut, salt, and silver.

The Red Karens, or Karen-nees, who live on the west of the Salween and close to our northern Tenasserim boundary, are called Niang and Yang-aing by the Shans, and Yang-tsa by the Chinese. They are said to be a part of a Chinese force who overslept themselves, and were left behind by the main body, when obliged to retreat from want of supplies. They are reported still to have the Chinese seal amongst them.[1]

Dr. Richardson, who visited them in 1837, describes their mode of sacrificing to the nats, who are extremely numerous; every tree, hill, river, stream, rock, in fact every object, natural or artificial, has one. Their children, wives, and the men themselves are believed to be liable to be seized by the evil spirits when passing through the jungle for firewood or water. How they are seized they cannot very intelligibly

[1] This most likely occurred in the Mongol invasion of Pa-pe si fu in A.D. 1300, when the Emperor Timour-han, or Tching-tsong, sent an expedition into the country to the south of Yunnan. The Mongol armies were often formed of hill-tribes who had submitted, and it is not unlikely that the Red Karens are of the same stock as some of the tribes to the north of Yunnan.

explain; but it appears that some obscure feeling of illness grows upon them, or some vague fancy, arising from a morbid imagination, portends some approaching calamity.

A sacrifice then becomes necessary; they accordingly consult the fowls' bones, the leg bones in preference; and if the augury requires it, the sacrifice is made. For this sacrifice, as many as eight or ten bullocks or buffaloes are sometimes killed at a time, a great part of which is left to decay. When one beast is killed, the head is put down, with the tips of the fore feet on each side of it, the hind feet a little behind, and the tip of the tail a little farther back between them; all the most worthless portions of the animal are thus bestowed on the nat,—the rest is taken home and eaten. A small portion of the dressed victuals is brought out and added for the nat.

Sometimes sacrifices are made and prayers offered up for a continuance of health; but generally they are only used to propitiate evil spirits who have already inflicted some illness or misfortune. If a sacrifice is not indicated by the fowls' bones, none is made, even if the person is dying. In a large village three or four days seldom pass without a sacrifice, at which times large quantities of a vile arrack of their own manufacture is consumed. This spirit they drink habitually, and always carry with them, if they leave their houses for a day. They do not, however, eat or smoke opium, or gamble. The women manufacture the clothes for the family, and the men make gongs.

Their religion consists entirely in attempts to propitiate by sacrifice the malignant nats, by whom they suppose all sickness and misfortune is inflicted, with no other view than to obtain the sacrifice of some animal or other; they endeavour to find out what, by a peculiar method of divination, with the leg or wing bones of fowls, holding two parallel between the finger and thumb, with the holes for the transmission of the blood-vessels upwards; they choose one for the person, and one for the diseased, or for the business to be undertaken, and introducing a small piece of bamboo into the holes, they judge by signs, only known to the initiated, what is proper to be done.

They have neither priests, lawyer, nor physician, and use no medicine in illness; but a sacrifice of a buffalo, bullock, pig, or fowls, as indicated by the bones, is made to the nats. If the patient gets worse, it may have been from a wrong sacrifice, and another of a different animal is made; and should he die, it may be either that the sacrifice has been made of the wrong animal or to the wrong nat.

Marriages are early amongst them, and are not binding unless the female has been given away by her parents. At the marriage, a pig or a bullock or two is killed, according to the wealth of the parties, and a feast is given in the village, in which arrack is always an attractive feature. Divorce is easily obtained, if there are no children; but should there be one child, the parents are not permitted to separate. Before marriage, great license is allowed.

Their funerals are more simple than those of the White Karens; the body is merely interred, and money, valuables, paddy, yams, pumpkins, in short everything used by them in life, is interred with it, in greater or smaller quantities, in proportion to the wealth of the individual. A horse is often let loose (if the person possessed one) on the occasion, with some distinguishing mark; and he is never reclaimed. If the deceased was a person of substance, sometimes as many as five or six bullocks are slain near his grave; the heads, feet, and tails are left for the nat, and the rest consumed by his friends and relations. For the poorer individuals, a pig or a fowl or two is sacrificed in a more humble way.

Although great slave-hunters, the Red Karens do not make slaves of any villagers who pay them blackmail, and they tax very lightly the Shans who take refuge in their country to escape from the brutal oppression of the Burmese. The Karen-nee country is therefore very thickly populated, and even the slopes of the hills are terraced for cultivation, the terraces being faced with stones and earth frequently five or six feet high.

The country of Karen-nee, like the neighbouring Shan country, is highly metalliferous. Mr. O'Riley, when there in 1864, discovered ores of bismuth, galena, and manganese, and was informed of the existence of those of copper and silver (argentiferous galena). Tin is also mined in the country, and was at one time largely exported. The soil of the plateaux, hills, and valleys is highly productive.

The dress of the Red Karens is a short pair of breeches, generally red, with perpendicular, very nar-

F

row, black or white stripes ; sometimes white with black or red stripes, drawn by a string tight above the hips, and reaching one-third of the way down to the thigh. In warm weather, this, and a handkerchief round the head, forms the whole of their dress ; in cold weather they wrap themselves in coarse cotton sheets of their own manufacture, and wear a bright red turban. The women wear a cloth about the same length as the men's breeches. This forms the whole of their dress in warm weather ; in winter they have an oblong piece of coarse cloth, once white, but which is seldom or never washed, the corners tied in a knot over the right shoulder, the rest of it hanging free reaches to the knee, the left arm covered up, the right naked and at liberty ; sometimes two are worn, with a knot on each shoulder. They also wrap themselves in sheets like the men, in the cool of the morning and evening.

Those who can afford it are absolutely loaded with paltry small white, red, and green beads, wearing an immense roll round the ankle, round about the calf, the waist, the neck, and the head. Their language is peculiar to themselves, differing altogether from that of the natives by whom they are surrounded, and appears to be a dialect of the same language as that spoken by the White or common Karens, who inhabit the hills south of them.

The Red Karens are called Karen-nee by the Burmese, Kara and Pra-ka-ra by themselves, Bghai-moo-hte by the other Bghai, or Pye-ya, the Karen tribe to which they belong. They are very ferocious,

HILL TRIBES IN THE INDEPENDENT SHAN STATES.

preying without mercy on their neighbours. Those who have emigrated into British territory require to be regularly watched, as they commit dacoities and robberies whenever they can. There are six clans of Bghai—the Bghai-moo-hte, Bghai-ka-tew, Bghai-ka-hta, Pray, Ma-noo-ma-naw, and the Tshaw-kho.

About one-third of the inhabitants of Karen-nee are slaves or serfs. The chief cause of this, according to O'Riley, lies in the prevalence of indebtedness throughout the community. Debt is incurred originally by the heads of families, to meet some casual expenditure attending their superstitious ceremonies, and increased by the exorbitant interest they have to pay. When this remains unpaid at the period of the death of the borrower, and no effects are available for repayment, in accordance with the terms of the agreement, one or more members of the family become bond-slaves, and subsequently, from incapacity to liquidate the original debt, with its large accumulation of interest, become permanently the property of the lender. Although bound to assist in the cultivation of their masters' lands, the bond-slaves are not debarred from other pursuits from which to derive a means of eventual emancipation; but this is of rare occurrence, and the state of indebtedness has become an integral portion of their social system, as well as of that of Upper Burmah, the Shan States, Siam, and Cambodia.

The other by far more iniquitous and remorseless state of slavery in its worst features, which prevails with this race, has its existence in their kidnapping propensities; no one single individual of them but is ready on all occasions to avail himself of the opportunity to seize the person of any one of the Karen and Shan tribes which occupy the country in their vicinity.

In most of the Karen-nee villages, "Shan-yangs" of the Karen tribes, Yendalines, and Padaungs, of the mountain-ranges to the north-west, are found, all doomed to a hopeless state of slavery, into which, priced like beasts of burden, they are sold to the Zimmé Shans, by whom they are re-sold to the Siamese. This traffic is, however, decreasing. To the more depraved Shans and Toung-thoos of the neighbouring States, the Karen country affords a means of selling into slavery any member of their own community who may have incurred their enmity, and acts of the most inhuman kind are constantly enacted.

As an instance of these, O'Riley stated that, while at Nyoung Belai, a poor woman with two children came to him with a very pitiful story. She said that her husband, a Toung-thoo, residing at Nyoung-ywai, had fallen into difficulties, and had induced her to accompany him to Karen-nee, where he had sold herself and children to one of the chiefs, then present, for the sum of £6. By the above means O'Riley says about 1,200 souls were annually captured and purchased by the Karen-nees.

The people of Mokmai, or Mokmé, a Shan State lately tributary to Upper Burmah, make no secret of their fear and weakness, and tell many tales of the Red Karens' skill in kidnapping; amongst others, of three Karens who came on a party of six of their people, and seeing they were weaker than their intended prey, waited till night, when, making a large bundle of bamboos, interwoven with thorns, they threw them over the Shans as they slept, and, standing on them, with their spears pricked them out one by one, tied their hands, and marched them off.

The Mutsa villages are found throughout the hills to the north of the Siamese boundary, between the Salween and Mékong Rivers. Their dress is said to be like that of the Ka-kuas. These people are nat-worshippers, bury their dead, and polygamy is only allowed if the wife is barren. Their dialect is described as a mixture of Burmese and Chinese; some of them can write Chinese, but they have no distinct writing of their own, and their language has more Burmese than Chinese words in it. Most of the Si-sun are under the rule of China, and dress like the Chinese. They cultivate opium, worship nats, speak a distinct language, have no written character, and pay tribute to .China and Kiang Hung. The Kapin, who reside on both banks of the Mékong, worship nats. The head-dress of the women is said by McLeod to be peculiar, but he gives no description of it; the men dress like other mountain tribes. When burying a friend, those who have lately lost their relatives, take money, and request the corpse to receive charge of it, and deliver it to their departed relatives, who are supposed to stand in need of some purchaseable comforts in the other world; the money is accordingly buried with them. They practise polygamy. Tribute is paid by them to Kiang Hung.

The Kadams, like the civilized Lawas, are partially converted to Buddhism, and monasteries and temples exist in most of their villages. They are not a numerous tribe, but speak a distinct language, which has been reduced to writing, the Shan character being used. They are of middle size, have broad faces, large noses, thick lips, rather small eyes set wide apart, and their hair is rather curly, like that of the Orang Benua, the aborigines of the Malay Peninsula. They are not polygamists, believe in metempsychosis, drink spirits, like all the other hill-tribes, and are said to be a very quiet race. They are much afflicted with goitre.

The Palongs, or Poloungs, are darker and smaller than the Shans, but otherwise there seems to be little difference between them. They cultivate tea in the northern part of the Muang Lem district, and opium in the hills about Maing-kaing, a town to the north of Ledea. They are also found in south-west Yunnan. The race of Yins[1] are said to be very numerous, and are said to be similar to the Toung-thoos. They consist of three tribes—the Yin-nees, Yin-nets, and the Yin-bans—and are found in the Shan States west of the Salween, to the north of Ledea. The women of the Yin-nees have broad bands of wire round their waists; and as these are fastened very tightly over their dresses, a change of clothes must be a rare occurrence with them.

[1] Rens, or Rins: the Y is used by the Burmese of Pegu the R by the Arakanese and Northern Burmese.

HILL-MAN, SOUTHERN FRONTIER OF YUNNAN.

74

The main body of the Toung-thoos reside in Thatone, an ancient town in the Martaban district, and the hills to the northwards. In A.D. 1007, many of them were removed to the Shan States west of the Salween by A-naw-ra-hta, who reigned in Pagan at that time. The descendants of the latter are still found as a distinct people in Northern Karen-nee, and on the Shan plateau to the north of it, but little is known of them. Some Motsoos were met by Captain Watson at the Oo-noung Bazaar, on the Salween. They had come from a place about a fortnight's journey to the north-east. Their dress is very becoming, consisting of a black cloth jacket, embroidered at the cuffs and collars, black Shan trousers, and a very gaily coloured turban. The slopes of the hills to the west of Thai-nee are cultivated by the Paloungs, Kachyens, and the Shan-Tayoks, or Chinese Shans. The soil is very rich, even high up in these hills, and the white poppy is grown extensively. In the glens large plantations of sugar-cane exist.

The Yendalines are reduced to four hundred souls in number, and differ widely from any of the other Karen races surrounding them. From the waist upwards, the women, from infancy to old age, remain uncovered. These people are unrestrained by any code of morals such as usually binds man and wife. The female can at any time desert her husband for some one else, without question; and it is rare for any woman of this tribe to arrive at middle age without having a family by two or more husbands. This absence of morals has gradually produced a great deterioration in the people, who are more stunted in their form, and far below the other Karens in their qualities. They are described as passive, enduring, and obedient, and gain their living by working in the teak-forests of Karen-nee.

The Let-htas are found not far from the home of the former tribe. Their hair is worn short, with a pendant lock from each temple, no head-covering being worn by them. The unmarried youths are profusely bedecked with red and white bead necklaces, wild boars' tusks, brass armlets, and a broad band of black braid below the knee. Their language is more guttural than that of the Shans, Toung-thoos, or Karen-nees, and distinct from either. The heavy eyelid, nearly closing the eye, the retreating forehead, and the elongated shape of the skull, is said to resemble the wandering tribes of the Kirghish. The youth of both sexes are kept with strictness in separate houses. These people are said to have absolutely no belief in a future state, but their religious ceremonies are similar to those of the Kayos, another hill-tribe. The sacrifices made by them are confined to fruits and flowers principally, which are placed on rude altars of bamboo, on the highest pinnacles of their mountains. They have no laws or rulers, and the Karens say they do not require any, as the Let-htas never commit any evil among themselves or against any other people. The sense of shame amongst this tribe is so acute, that on being accused of any evil act by several of the community, the person so accused retires to a desolate spot, digs his grave, and strangles himself. Such occurrences are not frequent, and the reason most likely is that they abstain from intoxicating liquors. They possess no slaves, nor are any of their race sold into slavery.

Karens of various tribes are found southwards of Luang Prabang, throughout the range of hills which separates the Mékong from the Ménam Rivers. They are most numerous, however, in the Shan mountains to the westward of the Ménam, and in the continuation of those mountains which run as a backbone down the Malay Peninsula, and in the hills to the west of the Thoungyeen River. The Karens are divided, according to Spearman, into three tribes—the Sgaw, Sho, or Pwo, and Pye-ya, or Bghai, and these again into clans distinguished by their dress and dialect. The Sgaw, who are called White Karens by the English, are in three clans—the Ma-nee-pgha, Pa-koo, and the We-wa. The Ma-nee-pgha are by some considered a portion of the Pwo tribe, on account of the nasal sound of their dialect; unlike most of the Karens, they possess other domestic animals besides fowls and swine. Owing to the labours of the American missionaries, the majority of them have been converted to Christianity.

The Pa-koo dialect is closely allied to that of the Sho, but wants the final consonant. Like some other tribes, these people, in their heathen condition, keep stones in their houses, which they believe possess miraculous powers; these stones are supposed to cause the death of any enemy whose footprint is struck by one. The dress of this people consists of a white tunic or blouse, without stripes, and with a narrow border of embroidery at the bottom, the patterns differing in every village. Over two thousand of them have embraced Christianity.

The We-wa have primitive costumes, which is caused by their having been in such a low stage of civilization until lately, that the women did not know how to weave. Their dialect is similar to that of the Sho, to whom they are in many ways alike. The Sho, or Pwo, are in five clans—the Pie-do, or Pie-zaw, or Plaw, the Koo-hto, the Shoung, the Ha-shoo, and the Ka-roon. The Pie-do have two or three different dialects, and hence the different names, all calling themselves by their term for man. They sacrifice a black bullock to the lord of the earth, and their morality is very strict and stern. Their dress is a white blouse with red perpendicular lines. Many of the men have become Christians.

The dialect of the Koo-hto bespeaks them of the Sho tribe. They are not warlike, but are given to quarrelling among themselves. The men shave the head all but a long tuft of hair, which is left on each temple. The women wear short togas and brass coils above the knee, besides the coils below the knee and round the neck, worn by some of their neighbours.

The Shoung were employed by us as border-guards, before our annexation of Pegu, and were exempted from all taxation, on condition of their keeping watch against the incursions of the Red Karens. They wear white trousers with radiating red lines at the bottom. The Ha-shoo, or Ha-shwie, are a tall, slender, active, and warlike race; the women are ugly, ignorant, and degraded. They resemble the Shoung tribe. The Ka-roon, or Gai-kho, used to bury a slave with every deceased slave-holder or elder, but the custom is dying out. They are fierce and savage, and consider themselves as superior to all other Karens. The men are stout, tall, and muscular, daring in adventure and warlike in disposition. The women are large and fair, and often have ruddy complexions. These people hate ponies and elephants, and not only will not allow them to enter their villages, but will neither provide nor sell fodder for their use. Their trousers are of silk, and often handsomely embroidered; they are marked with red lines at the bottom, radiating like the rays of the rising sun.

The Pye-ya, or Bghai, include the Kara, or Karen-nee, who are called by the English Red Karens, and have already been described, the Bghai-ka-tew, the Bghai-ka-hta, the Pray, or Bree, Ma-noo-ma-naw, and the Tshaw-kho. The Bghai-ka-tew wear white tunics with perpendicular red stripes. The Bghai-ka-hta are gradually becoming civilized. Their dress consists of white trousers, with red radiating lines worked in them at the bottom. They are partial to dog's flesh, and eat it without salt. The Pray are the Ishmaelites among the Karens, go about almost naked, and are savage, treacherous, and ignorant. The Ma-noo-ma-naw are little known; they dress in trousers. The Tshaw-kho wear white trousers ornamented with red or black stripes.

The Karen language is monosyllabic, and has consequently no inflections, but is amply provided with suffixes and affixes. Dr. Mason says that there are affixes for number and gender. The case is distinguished, in some instances by position, as the nominative and accusative; in others by affixes, as the vocative; and in others by prefixes, as the dative and ablative.

To the east of the Mékong River and to the north of the Siamese boundary, McLeod mentions the following tribes:—The La-la, Yem, Kali, Putai, Kaláu, Ka-káu, Kama, Kamet, Tsen, Thin, Nga, Ka, and the La. All that is known comes from McLeod. The language of the La-la is different from any of the others; they have no written character. These people bury their dead, worship nats, are addicted to spirits, and permit polygamy. They are tributary to Kiang Hung, and dress like the other mountain tribes. The Yem speak a different language, and dress like Shans; their manners and customs are similar to those of the La-la, and they have no written language. The Kali reside on the south of the Chinese border; the same remarks apply to them as to the last two, only they dress like Chinese, are opium planters, and are tributary to China and Kiang Hung, I believe. The Putai dress like Shans, worship nats, bury their dead, are addicted to spirits, and permit polygamy. They pay tribute to Luang Prabang and Siam. The Kaláu are tributary to Luang Prabang and Kiang Hung. The Ka-káu do not permit polygamy, and generally dress in white. The maidens of this tribe twist their hair on each side of the head, so as to

A HILL-MAN AT PAK BEN, NEAR THE EAST SOURCE OF THE MÉNAM.

resemble the horns of a buffalo. They are tributary to Kiang Hung and Luang Prabang. The other tribes are either tributary to China, Kiang Hung, or Luang Prabang. In conclusion, it is worthy of notice that the hill-people surrounding the delta of Tonquin, and called by the Anamites Muangs, or Muongs, are of the Shan race.

CHAPTER VI.

Leave Baw—Beautiful scenery—Dulness of natives—Muang Haut—Silkworms, fruit, and vegetables at Muang Haut—The Méping—Karen villages—Looms—Glutinous rice—An extensive plain—Railway to Bangkok—Worked-out teak-forests—Inundation—Bastard sandal-wood—Stick-lac—India-rubber—Kiang Tong—Herds of half-wild elephants—Our train—Elephants necessary for travel in the rains—Elephants grazing with cattle—Difficult to re-capture—Motherly affection for baby elephants—Mahouts as footstools—Kind Karen drivers—Elephants rising in price—Catching and taming—White elephants—Strange beliefs concerning white elephants—Elephant-artillery.

Leaving Baw, for the first nine miles our route ran by an easy descent through a magnificent pine-forest. The views obtained were indescribably grand, and the air was bracing, adding spring to our step and making me feel as if once more back again in the highlands. At various points of our march through the dark pine-forest, panorama after panorama opened to our view. The brilliancy and clearness of the atmosphere enabled us to trace the crest of the mountains lying far away in the distance, and forming the water-parting between the Ménam and the Mékong Rivers. The intermediate country seemed to be a sea of hills, without any recognisable scheme or direction.

The towns and villages could not be seen, but their

positions were marked by the clumps of palms and other trees by which they were surrounded. The variety of the timber, the different hues of the foliage, and the peeps which we had at the Méping trending its silvery course through the grassy plains, increased the charm of the scenes. As view after view, each seemingly more glorious than the last, was disclosed, exclamations of surprise and delight constantly broke from us. Our followers could not understand what we saw to admire in the noble vistas. A deer on the hillside, or the opening of a whisky flask, would certainly have interested them, but the beauties of nature were absolutely unintelligible to them. As for our native guard of Madrassee Hindoos, their thoughts never could range beyond food, women, and pay.

After leaving the pine-forest the gradual descent continued for a mile, when for about three miles the path became more steep, passing through small tree-jungle, until we reached the banks of the Kwaybabee stream, where we encamped for the night. The whole of next morning we followed a track winding over undulating ground through the jungle, and passing two pagodas, which had been built on conical-shaped hills, of which there are about ten in the neighbourhood, we reached the village of Muang Haut, which is called Main [1] Wut by the Burmese. The road for the last few miles before arriving at the

[1] Main, or Maing, is the Burmese equivalent for the Shan word Muang; they mean province, state, or principality. Kiang is the Shan word for city, and Kaing, or Kain, the Burmese.

village runs through bamboo clumps and small irrigated rice-fields. A small distance from Muang Haut is a stream in which, according to Dr. Richardson, rubies are sometimes found.

Muang Haut, although containing only two hundred houses, is called a town, and is included among the fifty-seven townships[1] of Zimmé. It is situated on the western side of the Méping, surrounded by plantations of cocoa-nut, palmyra, plantain, and other fruit-trees. The mulberry-tree, grown in all villages in the neighbourhood, is a mere shrub. Silkworms are reared by most of the villagers. Radishes, onions, sessamum, and other crops are grown by the women; and cucumbers, pumpkins, and gourds are cultivated on the sandy islands of the river. At most of the villages throughout the Méping valley, oranges, pummaloes, pine-apple, mango, palmyra, cocoa-nut, guava, and other fruits are abundant.

The Méping is here seven hundred and forty-seven feet broad from bank to bank. The current at the time of our visit was only about two miles an hour; but owing to the many shifting sand-banks, large boats are unable to ascend higher than Yahine. The country in parts is subject to inundation in heavy floods, which at times drive the people from the river-banks. The valley of the Méping varies from ten or twelve miles to sixty or eighty in breadth; the soil is a rich sandy loam, apparently, judging from the sections shown by the river-banks, of great depth.

---

[1] Or principalities.

In the neighbourhood of the village are several White Karen villages, in which the people speak a widely different dialect from that on our side of the frontier. They are pleasant and frank in their manner, and appear to be well made, and have the character of being docile and orderly, giving little trouble to their rulers. All their wants are supplied by themselves. Their dresses are made at their own looms. The silk is the produce of their worms, and the cotton of their fields. It is amusing to watch them squatted on their elephants, consuming the contents of their pot of a glutinous kind of rice, looking as happy and free from care as children. They are a harmless, simple, and kindly people, the very opposite in their disposition to the Red Karens.

The inhabitants of Muang Haut, as well as of all villages and hamlets along the banks of the Méping, are Shans. The valley opposite the town is several miles broad, and only requires an access of population to develop its fertile soil. The ordinary breadth of the river, for some distance above Muang Haut, is about six hundred feet. The hills on the east of the river cease near Tapin, a village some miles to the south of Muang Haut, and a vast plain extends southwards past Yahine (Raheng). Through this plain it is proposed to carry the railway to Bangkok. Between this part of the Méping and the Salween, the teak-forests are nearly worked out, and the timber that is left is small and of poor quality. Notwithstanding the great rise in the value of teak of late years, it no longer pays the Burmese contractors, whose fathers made fortunes in this district, to continue to work the forests. Every stick worth floating away has been recklessly cut down and removed. No fostering shelter has been left for the young trees, nor have any been replanted. In the nine principal forest-tracts hitherto worked—the Zimmé, Hmine Long-gyee, Thoungyeen, Dahguin, Mé-gu, Phonmezé, Nanpa, Monepégyee, and the Salween—but little timber remains worthy of extraction. Good forests still exist, notably that of Lagon, which lies south-east of Zimmé; and those in the neighbourhood of Kiang Tsen.

Being in haste to reach Zimmé, we did not halt at Muang Haut beyond the time necessary for refreshment. The headman pressed us to stay, and had prepared a house, in the verandah of which we found a huge pile of cocoa-nuts ready for our consumption. The amount of cocoa-nut milk that we imbibed so frightened the head-man that he warned us to place reins on our deep potations. The ill-effects, however, were avoided by our taking a dash of whisky, which was much relished by the Shan official. Leaving the town, the road skirts the foot of the western hills on the right bank of the Méping, over bare sandy soil with occasional clumps of bamboo, and trees generally free from brushwood, and some of them bearing a clearly defined flood-mark. The bastard sandal-wood abounds here, but is not made use of by the Shans. The pouk-byin, from which the stick-lac is gathered, is seen everywhere, and the *mimosa catechu*, or india-rubber creeper, abounds in the woods throughout the valley. In the evening we encamped on the banks of the Mé-kin, or Mé-tchin, a branch of the Méping, the road throughout having been very good.

For the next two days we continued along an equally good road, through the same description of country, until we reached the cultivated rice-fields which mark the vicinity of the town of Kiang Tong. In the jungle neighbouring Kiang Tong, about two hundred elephants were roaming in a wild state, having been freed from labour, let loose, and devoted to the pagoda in that town. At the time of our visit they had become a terror to the people and a cause of devastation to their fields. Owing to their religious servitude, or rather emancipation, they were not allowed to be recaptured, and had become as fierce as those roaming wild in their native haunts in the wilder parts of the valleys of the Salween and the Mékong. While on the subject of elephants, I may mention that we had by this time sixty of them in our train; for, as the mission progressed, we were joined by local officials, and our camp presented a truly imposing appearance. The elephant is an absolute necessity during the rainy season throughout the mountainous districts of Siam and the neighbouring Shan country to the north, the rivers and streams being without bridges.

In the dry season, owing to the greater part of the trees on the plateau-land having shed their leaves,[1] and to the absence of shelter from the sun, travelling is

[1] On which the elephants feed.

better performed by means of ponies and mules. Even in the forests elephants are seldom worked between the hours of 10 a.m. and 3 p.m., and eighteen miles is generally the longest distance which they can accomplish in one day with an ordinary load, ten or twelve miles being the usual daily distance when on a protracted march, of say a fortnight's duration. Their load is seldom greater than that of three small oxen, and does not exceed from two hundred and fifty to three hundred pounds. If forced to push on, owing to want of forage in the hot weather they fall ill, and, becoming emaciated, have to be left for several months in order to rest and recruit. They are used throughout the Shan country and North Siam, not only for dragging timber, but for the carriage of all agricultural produce.

At all the towns we passed, it was a strange sight to see the number of elephants grazing together in the fields with the bullocks and buffaloes. Their feet are generally shackled with ropes of twisted cane; should the shackles break, the animals have often to be tracked for days through the nearly impenetrable jungle before they are captured.

It is amusing to watch the females when accompanied by their young on the line of march. Not only does the mother take peculiar care of the little one, but in the case of any accident, such as slipping down a *khud*, or ravine, all the other females at once leave the track, and rush to render their assistance. The tender consideration of the mother for its offspring is shown in its constant watchfulness, even

VIEW OF THE MÉKONG, NEAR PHON PADANG.

when mounted and in use; and never for a moment is the young one left to roam out of sight, and even the iron goad of the cruel driver thrust into its head will not prevent it from attending to its young one.

While crossing the hills between Pahpoon and Main Long-gyee, some of the places passed by the elephants were alarmingly precipitous. It was interesting to see the manner in which they cautiously clambered up a broken hillside, or slid down, belly almost touching the ground, the opposite declivity, always slippery and frequently approaching the perpendicular. When crossing a stream or swampy ground, they sounded the depth before each step was taken, literally feeling their way, with their trunks thrown forward. Their instinct seemed to approach almost to human judgment and discretion, and astonished us greatly. When crossing an unfordable river, like the Salween, the body is usually completely under water, while the trunk is just sufficiently elevated to enable them to breathe. The *mahout's*[1] position is anything but enviable, as, in case of the animal suddenly losing its presence of mind, it is apt to seize the driver with the trunk and thrust him under foot, so the Shans say. The Siamese elephant is generally smaller than the African species. We seldom saw them of a greater height than nine feet; but were told—what seems improbable—that they are sometimes found twelve and thirteen feet in height, near the Mékong River. The Karens are much kinder drivers than the natives

[1] Elephant driver.

of India, Burmese, or Shans, and their charges seem more compliant to their soft words, signs, and coaxing, than to the cruel hook-hammer used by the others.

Ten years previous to our visit, good elephants could be purchased in the Shan country for from three hundred to four hundred rupees; but, owing to the great demand for them in the teak-forests and timber-yards, the price has risen to eight hundred and even a thousand. They are now chiefly procured from Muang Nan, Muang Phé, and, what is called by the Burmese of Zimmé, Lao Myo, a name loosely employed by them for the Shan country north-east of Zimmé, or strictly the region east of the Mékong. They are *said*[1] to be caught, as many a young gentleman is ensnared, by the fascinations of the softer sex. An elephant in love must be an exceedingly comical sight. The female enters upon her task apparently with all the keen delight which that sex seems ever to experience in captivating the heart. She is taken to the edge of a jungle where a herd is known to be roaming, and at once proceeds, in *insouciant* fashion, to cultivate their acquaintance and friendship. So skilfully does she use her blandishments that she rarely fails to attract a number of admirers, whom she triumphantly leads back to a strong *kraal*, or bamboo stockade, which has been prepared for the purpose of their capture and subjection. After entering this the hunters close the entrance, and remain masters of the

[1] According to the accounts given to us by the Shans and Burmese foresters, for which I do not vouch, however.

males she has enticed. The poor captives are kept on extremely low diet, and are alternately cruelly ill-used and coaxed until they feel themselves to be powerless against the will of man. They are then gradually turned out ready to be sent to market. The female elephant, having very short tusks, is of little use in manipulating timber in the forests and yards, and is therefore of less value than the males.

According to M. Mouhot, the Siamese, who, like all Buddhists, believe in metempsychosis, think that the soul of some prince or king has passed into the white elephant, and their belief is the same in regard to white apes and other albinos. They therefore hold all these in great respect. A white elephant is thought to bring good luck to the country. So much is this the case that they have often proved the cause of a war between Siam and Burmah. The well-known belief that Gaudama's soul inhabited an elephant of this colour, during his last appearance on earth before he became Buddha, is likewise a reason for the great reverence in which it is held.

Although the elephant is a formidable-looking animal, its skin is easily excoriated, and hence a sore back is the inevitable consequence of an ill-fitting saddle. The sores being difficult to heal, the doctor who was with us had the dangerous task of attending to a wound on the leg of one of our elephants, which had through neglect become full of maggots. To prescribe was easy enough, to apply the remedy was a totally different task. A large syringe being filled with a lotion, every one gathered round with bated breath, in expectation of what would happen. Taking good aim, the doctor squirted with all his force, and the contents went home. The animal was fairly astonished. Raising his injured limb as high as he could, he swayed about as if he would topple over. Fortunately, however, he did not lose his temper nor his balance, nor yet attempt to break loose and hurt any one. When future applications had to be made, he behaved like a human patient, and seemed to be aware that the doctor was his friend, and in a week he was well again. The result of this cure was that the doctor's reputation spread far and wide throughout the country.

Elephants were used as a means of transport by the Siamese and Burmese armies in great numbers. One branch of the army consisted of an elephant service, the animals being trained to carry two jingals and four men each. The artillery was never fired over the animal's head, its tail being turned to the enemy before the piece was discharged from its back.

To journey on foot is considered to be undignified, and the Shans were fairly astonished that we—who were officials, and therefore dignitaries in their eyes—used our legs by preference whenever the road permitted us to do so.

CHAPTER VII.

Rest-houses provided—Hospitality—Paying for presents; foolish scruples—Kiang Tong—Boats—Boat-women—A friendly official—Bathing incident—Curiosity of Shan ladies; *contretemps;* modesty triumphant—Pagoda serfs—Cities of refuge—Monasteries—Chinese ornamentation of monasteries—Shameless priests—Lost in the forest—Kindness from villagers; good-natured curiosity; white all over?—Primitive modesty—"The shameless people"—Water-wheels—Rural life during harvest—Fertility of the Méping plain—Two harvests—Sugar-cane—*Toung-ya* or Hill cultivation—Fishing hamlets—Balachong—Nga-pee—Siamese Northern Shan States peopled by the Burmese Shans—People of Vien-Chang removed to Bangkok and Zimmé Shans to Mokmé—Return of descendants as slaves.

THROUGHOUT our journey to Kiang Tong, and indeed along the whole line of march to Zimmé, houses had been erected for our accommodation by order of the king of Siam. They were roomy and well-built bamboo structures, with raised floors and verandahs supported on stout bamboo posts. We were hospitably received everywhere, presents being brought for ourselves and followers; and we had the main supplies, such as rice, vegetables, fruit, and firewood, provided always with great promptitude along our route. Finding that these provisions were supplied by the people at their own cost—which is usual in the country when officials are concerned—we made a point of paying for everything used by ourselves and retinue.

Our Burmese followers laughed heartily at our foolish scruples, and told us that we were furnishing a bad precedent for the future.

Kiang Tong is a clean and well-built town, consisting of some three hundred houses, and has a prosperous air. A great quantity of bamboo grows in the neighbourhood, which is extensively used both for building the houses and for roofing the shallow-bottomed boats, now numerous on the river. The boats are formed of single trees, opened out by means of fire until they are nearly flat; a broad plank is then added to each side. Nails are nowhere used in their construction, the fastenings being pegs and rattan. When complete, the boat is coated with *thitsee* (wood-oil), which is equal to any calking. The bottom is generally of *thingan*, a wood heavier than water, and the sides of teak. The boats are usually about sixty feet long and six feet broad. At Zimmé we saw a number being made on the banks of the river, and it forms there quite an industry. The boats are "poled" along the stream by women, the "lords of creation" confining themselves to the lighter and more agreeable task of steering. We saw a number of boats near Kiang Tong, and never once saw a man at work, except at the stern of the boat. Soon after our arrival the *puniah*, or head local official, paid us a visit. He was a pleasant, fat-faced old gentleman, with a merry twinkle in his eye and a very friendly manner. He presented us with a number of cocoa-nuts, which were very grateful after our weary march.

TYPE OF A SHAN VILLAGE, ON RIVER BANK.

In the evening we went to a neighbouring stream for a bath, undressed, and were swimming about, when, turning back, we saw, to our astonishment and dismay, that a number of Shan dames and damsels were congregated close to our clothes, and were watching us with intense interest and amusement. They were neither shy nor diffident of strangers. In this dilemma we naturally felt abashed, but they were painfully the reverse. In vain we hoped that their modesty might incline them to retire on our displaying the intention of making for the bank. Not a bit of it! Go they would not. We were all getting chilly, and, after a council of war, resolved to make a feint of landing, hoping that they would withdraw for very shame's sake. Vain were our hopes, for our manœuvre was only received with shrieks of sustained laughter. The leader of the band of these merry nymphs should have known better than cause us such cruel embarrassment. She was the wife of a young *chao*, or chief, who had been appointed to meet and accompany us; this added to our perplexity. At last we could stand it no longer. Shivering with cold, and notwithstanding the volleys of laughter which greeted us, we made a rush for the bank and our clothes. Our worthy medico was unable to conquer his native propriety. The lady was stern, and would not budge an inch. It was now getting dark, and being her dinner-hour, she at last consented to retire, and the shivering disciple of Æsculapius was able to come ashore, chilled to the marrow, but proud in his consciousness of modesty triumphant.

In Kiang Tong, the *bonzes*, or Buddhist priests,

have a stronghold, the place being entirely inhabited by *phra-gyoons*, or pagoda serfs—people who have been dedicated to the service of the pagoda. These serfs are generally either criminals who have escaped to the pagoda, as the Jews did to cities of refuge, or they are the descendants of captives in war, who have been dedicated by the chiefs to the pagoda. There are three or four such towns, or villages, in the Zimmé territory. The phra-gyoons have to present tithes of all they produce for the use and maintenance of the pagoda and its priests—not a hard servitude. In every town there is a monastery, generally situated in a picturesque site. Compared with Burmah, there are but few pagodas scattered about the country, and these are of a peculiar design. The base is square, and the building runs in rectangular terraces for about one-third of its height. The upper part is circular, and of the Burmese type.

The *kyoung*, or monastery, at Kiang Tong is a fine, teak-roofed building, the interior pillars of which are handsomely decorated with gold. The general ornamentation of the building bore a strong resemblance to Chinese art, being very rich, but fantastic in design and gaudy in colour. The statue of Buddha was solemnly enthroned in the background, and surrounded, as is usually the case, by a number of Shan statuettes and tawdry knick-knacks, which would seem more in place in a London curiosity shop than in a temple devoted to Buddha.

The temple gardens were beautifully kept, well stocked with fruit and other trees, and evidenced great care on the part of the custodian. The old priest came to greet us with a cordial air of genuine welcome, and seemed pleased to pay us every attention, and show us over the monastery. Imagine our disillusion when, on parting, he asked us point-blank for a present of money! On our refusing this most unpriestly request, his suavity disappeared, and he became very rude in his behaviour, belabouring us with his tongue until we were out of earshot.

The priests are in bad odour with their flocks, because of their evil lives and their rapacity. They have retrograded from the observances required from the priesthood still further than the Maha-gandee sect in Burmah. Not only do they take money openly, but, in opposition to all their vows of abstinence from all cravings of the flesh, they covet and vociferously beg for everything that they think can be acquired by begging. Far from turning their eyes aside or looking down, as is the custom of their *confrères* elsewhere, when a woman is present, their morals are, to say the least ill of them, not of the strictest. They have, however, the merit of being good handicraftsmen, and work with a will at carpet-making, carving, painting, and other arts. The monastery cells in which they live are by no means ascetic, but extremely comfortable.

The hospitality of the people, as often shown to us, appeared to be intuitive, and not to arise from any constraint. One day, proceeding ahead of the main party, two of us lost our way, and, after a wearisome tramp of four or five hours, found ourselves, as *Punch* once had it, "five miles from everywhere." We were thoroughly wearied in body and mind, and were rapidly attaining a state of ill-humour, when we stumbled on a small village. We were at once cordially welcomed by the people, who had probably never seen a European before. They conducted us to a cool verandah, brought us cocoa-nuts, and quickly supplied us with refreshments, which we so much required. Their curiosity, which was natural, was evinced in so good-humoured and courteous a manner, that it was impossible to be offended at it. Nevertheless, it at length proved unpleasant, as it tested our sense of decorum severely. After examining all our belongings, including my watch and aneroid, which they could by no means comprehend, the ladies were bitten with the same desire as the Siamese chief's wife and her attendants had previously shown during the doctor's dilemma. They seemed to think that only our hands and face were white, and the police officer, my companion, was asked to convince them upon this point. He accordingly accommodated them so far as to take off his coat, and bare his arms for their inspection. This, however, did not satisfy their curiosity, and they proposed that he should still further divest himself of his clothing, so that they might be certain that we were quite *white all over*. On his refusing their request, loud shrieks of laughter greeted his too oppressive propriety.

Modesty is a comparative quality, and varies in different climes, but according to Western views it is little understood by these primitive people. I feel uncertain to this day whether they do not believe our skins were

A STREET IN A SHAN VILLAGE.

as dark as their own, and that the fairness of our faces and hands was by some means artificially produced. While on this subject, I may mention that the Burmese who have visited the Shan country tell wonderful tales of the utter indecency of the poorer class of its inhabitants; and, indeed, go so far as to call them "the shameless people." The bazaar at Zimmé was described to me, before leaving Burmah, by an epigrammatic Burman as "a mile and a half of nudity." This proved to be a mere traveller's tale, as, though the garments worn are not superfluous, they are modestly worn, and all that the climate requires.

The village, like others we passed through, is pretty, and inclosed in a small plantation of trees, consisting chiefly of cocoa-nut and palm. The houses were surrounded with neatly kept pieces of ground; the gardens were carefully tended and very well stocked. Water is supplied to the villages by means of large Persian wheels, about seventeen feet in diameter, having some sixteen spokes and twenty paddles, each paddle being four feet long and one broad. They are let into bamboo weirs thrown across the river. The increased velocity caused by the damming of the stream gives the necessary power for driving the wheel.

The people, as a rule, are agriculturists; and as a good deal of land belongs to the chiefs and officials, at the time of the harvest these often proceed to their fields and live there, superintending the work-people. The towns at this season resemble London in the autumn,—it may be said there is no one in town.

But so sparse is the population as compared with the extent of land, that only one-twelfth of the available ground is cultivated. The land throughout the Méping plain is generally fertile, and can be cultivated in the rains, or by irrigation from the streams during the dry weather.

The principal rice-harvest is in November; another crop is ready in July. The cultivation is carried on by the serfs of the chiefs and officials, and by those dedicated to the pagodas, as well as by freemen. In some districts sugar is extensively grown, and the more disreputable portion of our following found constant employment in making raids on the plantations, notwithstanding our frequently punishing them for their depredations, which they considered harmless. The ground is prepared for the cane in what is called in Burmah the *toung-ya* fashion. Trees are cut down and burnt, and the cane is planted, the first year's harvest generally covering the cost of production, the second crop being better than the first, and the third the best of all. The old roots are then sometimes dug up and new canes put in. Generally, however, the ground is forsaken, and a new part of the forest is fired and similarly treated, as before. The *toung-ya*, or hill-gardens, are precisely similar to those met with in Burmah and Siam amongst the hill-people, and this system of cultivation is also common in different parts of India, probably wherever the hill-tribes exist. They are found in Mysore and the central provinces, where they are called "dhaiya," and in Assam, under the name of "jhoom."

The system is extremely wasteful, and is only possible amongst a people not very numerous, and for whom a large extent of unoccupied land is available. It is the *bête noir* of the officers of the forest department, in whose reports may be read many a denunciation of this pernicious method of cultivation. The slopes of the hills are seen dotted here and there by these patches of *toung-ya*, the most favourable spots being chosen. Having selected the side of a hill—the more thickly covered with bamboo and forest the better—the cultivator and his family set to work in April and fell everything, the stumps being cut away as close to the ground as possible without grubbing up the roots. After a couple of months' drying—this being the hot season—the fallen trees and dried brushwood are set on fire, and burn for several days—some of the larger logs even for weeks, the ashes fertilizing the soil. In the Shan country in suitable localities an ingenious method is adopted in order to facilitate operations. The work of felling is commenced from the bottom of the hill-slope; the lower trees are only cut slightly on the upper side, the woodman, as he ascends the hill, cutting deeper and deeper, until he at last completely fells the trees. In this way they fall on those below, turn them over, and this continues to the bottom.

Rice is planted on the round tops of knolls, or on the steep slopes, with little attempt at levelling the surface. After the first fall of rain, the soil is slightly broken up with a kind of hoe, and the ashes mixed with it; the seed is then sown broadcast. From this time onwards the principal labour is in keeping down the weeds and roots which spring up again and invade the rice-fields. It would be unwise to dig the ground deeply, for the diluvial rains would carry away the soil with a rush when no longer kept in its place by the roots. In the hills of the Shan country the usual crops are a glutinous rice unlike that of the plains, cotton, and sessamum. The rice and sessamum are reaped in September or October, and the cotton is picked from December to April. The *toung-ya* is then abandoned. The obstacles offered by nature seem to develop the energy and activity of the hill-tribes, and endow them with manly qualities and an independence of bearing which the inhabitants of the plain lack.

Some of the hamlets near the river-bank are exclusively inhabited by fishermen; and every man, woman, and child, from October to June, is at work with net, rod, line, or the baskets which are worked at every weir, situated next the fisher hamlets. A condiment of salted fish is much in use, not only in Burmah and the Shan country, but in the Straits Settlements, where it is known to Europeans as balachong. The Burmese have three varieties; namely, nga-pee goung, "whole nga-pee"; toung tha nga-pee, "pounded nga-pee," or fish paste; and tsein-tsa, "raw eaten," so named because it can be eaten uncooked. The "whole nga-pee" is eaten roasted, fried, or curried, the fish being, if possible, kept whole by the cook as well as by the manufacturer. The large fish are scaled by hand, but the smaller ones by means of

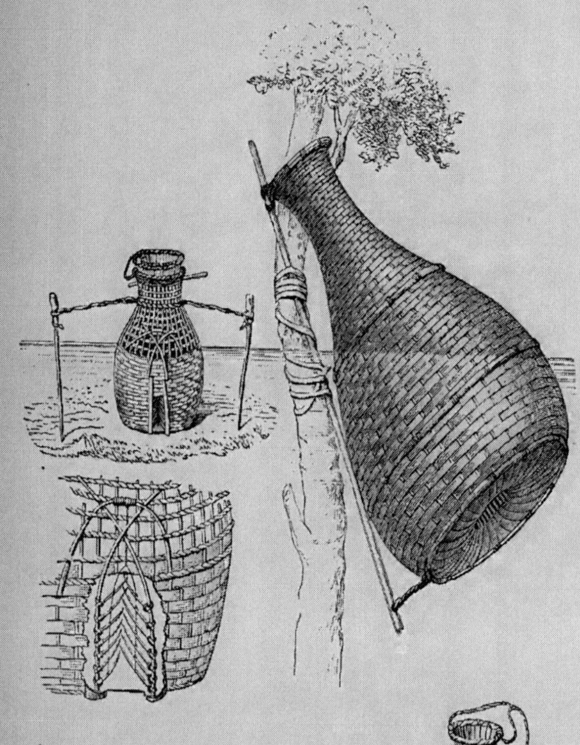

FISHING UTENSILS.

a bamboo, the end of which is split up and made into a kind of stiff brush. This is worked amongst a mass of fish thrown together, almost alive, into a wooden mortar. The fish are then cleaned, and the head, fins, and tail of the large ones are removed. They are then well rubbed with salt, carefully packed in bamboo baskets, weighted down, and put away for the night, the liquid draining through the baskets. Next day they are carefully taken out, again rubbed with salt, and spread on a mat in the sun, and the day following are packed away in jars, with alternate layers of salt, and then left in a cool place. Gradually the liquid rises to the top and evaporates, leaving a layer of salt on the surface. In about a month they are ready for sale. Sometimes the supernatant liquid gets full of maggots before completely drying, in which case it is removed and more salt added.

"Pounded nga-pee" is made only from small fish and shrimps, which are spread out for two days on mats in the sun, without any salt, and uncleaned. When they commence to turn putrid, they are pounded in a wooden mortar with salt. The mass is heaped up in a shed, and several hollow bamboos inserted into it. Through these the liquid escapes. The nga-pee is then dug out and shovelled into boats to be taken away. This is the offensive-smelling nga-pee, known best to all residents in Burmah, and alluded to in books on that country.

The "raw eaten" variety is made entirely from shrimps, and principally at Mergui and Tavoy. The colour of the shrimp paste is either red or brown, accordingly as it is made from a red or brown-coloured species of shrimp. The smaller kind are exposed to the sun immediately they are caught, and, when they are half dry, salt is added; the whole is then intimately mixed into a paste by hand three times a day for three days, being left in the sun in the intervals. It is then ready for use, and is put into pots. The larger sort are exposed in the same way, but are pounded with salt once a day for three days.

The inhabitants of the Méping valley are chiefly the descendants of the Shans who were driven from the now independent Shan States whilst they were under the Burman rule. Not only is this the case, but the majority of the Shans found in the country between the Méping and Luang Prabang come from the same quarter. Many villages occupied by them are likewise found on the backbone of hills separating the Ménam from the Mékong River, an unknown part. Before the migration of these people the country was occupied by another branch of the same race, who were called Lau-Phun-Ham, or "white-bellied Laos," —a name given on account of their not having adopted the custom of tattooing. The tattooed Shans, who came from the upper country, the now independent Shan States, are called Lau-Phun-Dam, or "black-bellied Laos."

Even in the time of McLeod, when he visited Zimmé and the Shan country in 1836, settlers were found in the country from Kiang Hung, Kiang Tung, Muang Niong, and Kiang Tsen, and many other places to the north. Having left the Burman Shan States

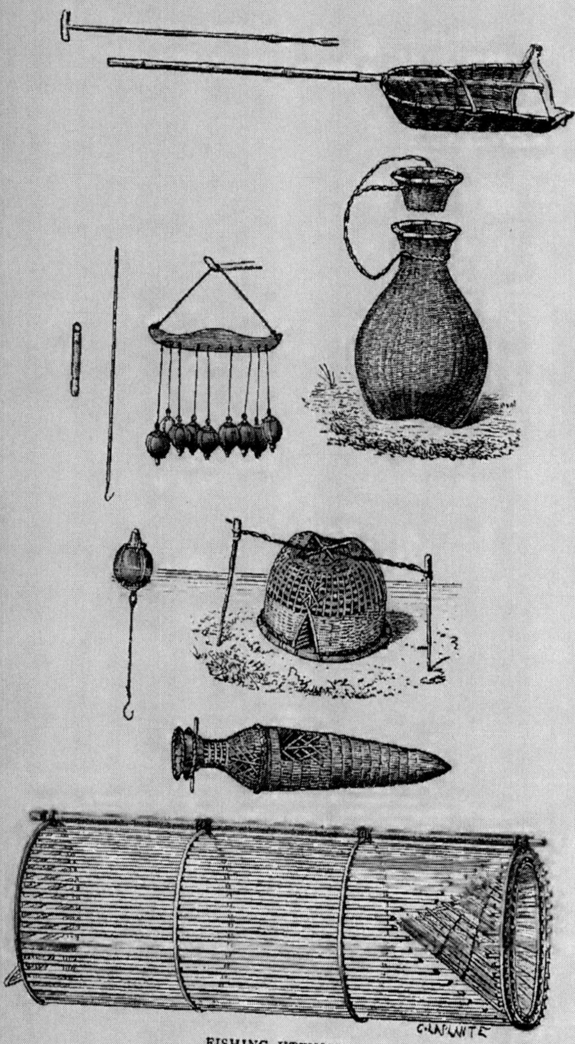

FISHING UTENSILS.

about the beginning of the century, they had been distributed by the Siamese authorities in the five towns of Zimmé, Labong, Lagon, Muang Phé, and Muang Nan. Together with the Talains, who had escaped from Burmah,[1] they comprised more than two-thirds of the whole population of the country. On the destruction of Vien-Chang by the Siamese in 1827, the inhabitants of that part of the country were taken away and settled at Bangkok. The people of Zimmé had mostly been removed in 1777 by the Burmese to Mokmé, or Mokmay, a town in the Burmese Shan States. At the present day these Mokmé Shans are often kidnapped by the Karennees, and sold as slaves to the Zimmé Shans, a very uncomfortable way of returning to the land of their fathers. From the foregoing we see the strong connection which exists between the present inhabitants of the Siamese and the independent Shan States. The Northern Siamese Shan States may, in fact, be said to be colonized by Shans from the now independent States to the northward.

[1] It is alleged that 200,000 left Burmah for Siam and the Siamese Shan States between A.D. 1772 and 1814. Another emigration occurred under Meng Kyaik in 1824.

CHAPTER VIII.

A chief—Shaking hands—Entry into Zimmé—A *cottage orné*—Siamese commissioner—King of Siam's kindness—A Yunnanese cook—Zimmé—Large households—Bazaar—Women conservative—Shan costumes—Home manufactures—Distance from Bangkok—Dyes—Fair complexions and rosy cheeks—Quiet as Quakers—Cattle-thefts—Frogs a delicacy—Chained and unfed prisoners—Punishments—Rule-of-thumb law—Palm-oil—Barbarity—Even-handed justice—Death for theft—Punishments for adultery.

AFTER an interesting journey of seventeen days from Pahpoon, we arrived within one day's distance of the town of Zimmé. We were met by a chao,[1] called Myintha, or Prince, by our Burmese followers—one of the thousand chaos with whom the place abounds. Four ponies decorated with glaring and cumbrous trappings were waiting our use. The chao insisted on shaking hands, which was not altogether pleasing, as his were not of the cleanest. Hand-shaking, it may be noted, is a custom imported from Bangkok, and all the chaos we conversed with insisted on our complying with it, more to show that they were conversant with the *convenances* of society than for any other reason.

---

[1] A Shan and Siamese title, meaning prince or chief. "The title chao in Nan-Chao is said by a Chinese author (Pauthier, p. 391) to signify King in the language of these barbarians." *Vide* Yule's "Marco Polo," vol. ii. p. 59.

The following day we made our entry into Zimmé, looking a somewhat sorry lot—dirty, unkempt, and travel-stained. Our procession, however, was imposing, consisting as it did of such a variety of people and animals. The inhabitants thronged out in great numbers to see the strangers, but were quiet in their demeanour, and formed a great contrast to the often turbulent and rude crowds of the Chinese cities. Their manner was fully as courteous as that of Burmese, who behave well, under similar circumstances. We entered the town by the north-eastern gateway, and were conducted to—what was a great surprise to us —a charming little residence, in the shape of a *cottage orné*, which had been built for our reception. Here we were cordially welcomed by a dapper, wizened, little old gentleman, who was evidently used to holding intercourse with Europeans. He informed us that he had come from Bangkok, and was holding office in Zimmé as resident commissioner of the King of Siam. Having served us with wine, coffee, and other refreshments, he grew more communicative, and we learned that we were the guests of one who had visited London, knew Paris by heart, and loved it, especially, I fear, the not altogether too proper *quartiers* of that city. His opinions were expressed in brief but graphic language: "too much plenty work in London; plenty pleasure Paris." Although he had quite forgotten his knowledge of the French tongue, he still retained his love and admiration of France and French things.

The cottage, which had been prepared for us by the

express command of the King of Siam, was furnished with all sorts of Parisian knick-knacks, a practice much affected by the court officials at Bangkok. The cookery was a strange travesty of the European art, in the French style. When we learnt who the cooks were, our astonishment ceased ; the *chefs* were Yunnanese. Notwithstanding our wish not to hurt the old gentleman's feelings, we were compelled to fall back on the bread and excellent Chinese tea which were provided.

Our host did all he could to make us comfortable, and the transformation in our surroundings which had taken place within a few hours was great. A day or two before we had been dwellers in tents in the primeval forest, seemingly hundreds of miles away from all civilization, while here we found ourselves in an excellently built little house, adorned like some Parisian *café*, and with every appliance of home-life surrounding us. A large supply of European tinned provisions, and wines, which had been ordered by the king to be sent for our use to Zimmé, did not arrive in time, owing to the delays on the river in the upward journey. The consideration shown by His Majesty the King of Siam in the arrangements ordered for supplying our wants made both our journey and our stay at Zimmé pleasant.

The town of Zimmé, Kiang Mai, Tsching Mai, or Zama-pada-pur-there-nagara-nawara-raza (its name according to the Labong Chronicle), is situated on the right bank of the Méping, at a height of about eight hundred feet above sea-level. It is the largest place

A SHAN BULLOCK CART.

in the Méping plain. There are fields between the river, which lies on its eastern side, and the town, which is said to have been built A.D. 1294. Northward and eastward is a large swamp or tank; to the north-west broken ground and garden land; to the westward the old Burmese fort and cultivated fields; and southward one large sheet of cultivation, mainly rice. In the dry season the river is fordable in several places near the town, the depth at the crossings being some three and a half feet. A wooden bridge, built substantially of good teak, some two hundred yards in length, spans the river near the north-east corner of the town, over which large droves of cattle and crowds of foot-passengers pass. Carts are mentioned by McLeod and Richardson as existing at Zimmé and Labong, but during our visit we did not observe any. Some of the chaos, when visiting Maulmain, have, however, purchased carriages; and I have little doubt that on my next visit this will have led to a great improvement in the roads about the town.

There is what is called an inner and outer town, each surrounded by fortifications. The inner town, where the *tsobua*, or chief, and other chaos reside, is an oblong, six thousand feet from north to south and four thousand eight hundred from east to west. Each face has a gateway in the centre, except on the southern side, where there are two, placed five hundred yards from the angles; the gates are defended in the same way, with a small bastion at the sides. These, as well as the walls, have embrasures for guns, at varying heights, but we nowhere saw any trace of guns, except in the centre of the town, in an open space near the chief's palace, where they lie half buried in the ground and surrounded by heaps of rubbish. The walls are inclosed by a ditch, some fifty feet in width, which is filled at the north-west angle by means of a canal leading water from springs in the hills. The depth of the ditch, originally some fifteen feet, is hardly anywhere now more than six or seven feet. At first strongly built, the walls are, from continued neglect, fast falling into ruin, and great portions are to be seen lying toppled over and half buried, while only here and there has any attempt been made to patch up the fast crumbling structure. Although at one time, no doubt, a formidable place to the undisciplined forces of the Burmese and Siamese, it would present no resistance to European artillery of the present day. The outer fortifications, which reach from the north-east to the south-west, are curved, and about two miles in length. They are built partly of brick, the remainder being merely a wooden stockade, with a ditch outside, which is nearly dry.

The town has some nine hundred houses inside the inner fort, but there are many more than that number in the portion of the town inclosed by the outer fortifications and in what may be termed the suburbs, which are built along the banks of the Méping River. The population must not be judged from European examples of the average number of the household, or even from that found in neighbouring countries, such as Burmah. In Zimmé the household often contains thirty, or even fifty, people under one roof at night.

WOMEN SELLING AT BAZAAR.

The inner fort is supplied with water by small channels intersecting it in different directions, and the roads are kept clean and neat. The houses, as a rule, are built of teak-wood, and have a substantial look. The palisading, about ten feet high, surrounding the compounds, gives the place the aspect of a prison. The extent of a compound varies with the wealth and position of the owner: a big chao has a big garden, an ordinary freeman a more limited space. All the gardens are well stocked with a variety of fruit-trees. The morning after our arrival, we got up early and strolled down to the bazaar, which consists of long rows of booths lining one of the main streets. It was a pleasant sight to watch the market-women, carrying their loads on their heads, quietly filing through the town. Many of them must have been up long before dawn, as some of the villages from which they came are situated at a very long distance from Zimmé. The market for edibles opens at 6 a.m. and continues for about three hours, when the sellers, who number about fifteen hundred, return home. The stalls in the vegetable, fish, and meat markets are occupied solely by women; whilst those where miscellaneous articles and piece-goods are sold are tended by either sex. The dress of the women is, as is usually the case, far more picturesque than that of the men; besides which the ladies at Zimmé are more conservative than their male folk, and still adhere to the costumes worn by their race previously to leaving the Burmese Shan States for these parts. Unlike the Siamese, they wear their hair long, tie it in a tasty knot on the crown of their head, fasten it with a handsome gold pin, and twine a gold chain around it. The only other ornaments worn by them are gold bracelets, and sometimes gold ear-rings. Their petticoat is either of coarse silk or of a particoloured cotton fabric; it is fastened below the breasts by twirling and tucking one of the ends in. The lower portion of their dress is decorated with a border worked in silk or gold thread. The young women wear pink kerchiefs, and the older ones have a dark-blue cotton scarf, thrown over their shoulders, which is generally drawn across their bosom.

The men wear a *putsoe*[1] tied round the loins, a sash of red cotton material round the waist, and sometimes a huge turban of the same material and colour as the sash. Their hair is dressed in the usual Siamese style, "*à la* cock's comb," well greased, and cut close at the sides. The holes in the lobes of their ears are decked with flowers, of which both men and women seem to be very fond. Their jackets, which are generally of a dark blue, are often bordered with tinsel, a large quantity of which is imported from China. The garments worn by both sexes are generally the manufacture of their own looms—the silkworms are bred in the villages, and the cotton is grown in their fields. English piece-goods are gradually entering the field, notwithstanding the present cost of carriage. They are brought up from Bangkok, taking forty-five days on the journey of about five hundred miles, and from Maulmain in British Burmah.

[1] Burmese name for a waist-cloth worn by men.

Their dyes are of local manufacture, similar to those in use amongst the Burmese. Saffron is generally used for yellow; green is produced by dipping threads that have been dyed yellow in a boiling decoction of the leaves and twigs of the creeping *Marsdenia tinctoria.* Indigo, which grows wild as well as in a cultivated state, is used for blue, the mordant being the bark of a kind of *Eugenia.* Stick-lac, the fruit of the tamarind, and various woods, give red. The safflower yields yellow, and, when mixed with other ingredients, red. Jack, the root of a species of *Garcinia*, the flowers of the *Butea*, and the leaves of the *Memeclyon*, give different tints of yellow. Black is produced from the *Diospyros mollis, Terminalia chebula,* and the *Jatropha curcas.* Orange from the seeds of the *Bixa orrellana.*

The people struck us as fair for Easterns, and some of the women even had rosy cheeks. It was quite pleasant to see a people who could blush, or rather whose blushes could be discerned. Their countenances, on which good-natured frankness was stamped, were of an even more Tartar cast than those of the Burmese, at least so it seemed to us. The nearly dead silence which reigned in the bazaar was only broken by an occasional half-suppressed but genial laugh. This was a great surprise to us who had so lately left Burmah, where the haggling, chatting, and vociferation in the markets is nearly deafening. Here the people were as quiet as Quakers; business was carried on without people being importuned to buy, and even the necessary chaffering was done in undertones, which only made more noticeable the strange quietude of the scene.

The principal meat sold in the market is pork, which is plentiful and good; no pig is allowed to be killed until it is brought before a *dine*, the Burmese name for a superintendent, who is appointed by the chief. Pork being a monopoly, a tax of about three shillings is levied from the Chinese butchers on each animal before it is allowed to be slaughtered. Pig's fat, when properly reduced, is the cosmetic generally in use at Zimmé, and, being unscented, gives anything but an agreeable aroma to the hair of the people. Very little gingelly, castor, or cocoa-nut oil is found in the town. Owing to the frequent cattle thefts which used to occur, special inquiries are made before cattle are allowed to be killed; this accounts for the scarcity of beef in the market. Fish, although plentiful in all the streams, particularly to the north, is rather scarce in the town, most likely because the principal part of the people, being Buddhist, are therefore adverse to taking life. All fishermen are looked upon here, as in Burmah, as outcasts.

Vegetables, such as Karen-potatoes, onions, and chillies, were abundant, as well as cocoa-nuts, plantains, mangoes, and other fruit in considerable variety. A great number of frogs are seen tied up on strings in the food bazaar, and are esteemed a great delicacy by the Shans. Most cases of snake-bite which occur here and in Burmah happen during the torchlight hunts after the frogs. The snakes naturally object to men poaching upon their preserves, frogs forming the chief article of their food.

As is the case amongst all Indo-Chinese races, the servants of the chiefs and high officials have the privilege of providing for their masters' requirements without payment to the stall-holders. This custom might be made a source of great oppression were it not for the force of public opinion. The prisoners, who are allowed to roam in their chains about the town, their relations and friends being responsible that they do not escape, seem to be allowed the same privilege, but this may arise from the kind-heartedness of the people, which is undoubtedly great. These prisoners have an iron collar rivetted round their necks, from which are fastened the heavy irons which keep the arms and legs in bond so far as rapid exercise is concerned. There is no Government allowance for their food, so they are entirely dependent upon the stall-holders and their relations for their diet. The term of their imprisonment seems to depend very much upon the ability of their friends to pay the fines which are imposed for all crimes but murder.

In cases of debt, the debtor is imprisoned, or rather put in chains; and if unable to satisfy his creditor, he and his family are sold for the creditor's benefit. For crimes, the principal part of the fine goes to the aggrieved person, the remainder to the chief and court officers. If a theft is proved, three times the value of the article is decreed to the owner; and if not paid, the offender, after suffering imprisonment in irons, is made over with his family, to be dealt with as in cases of debt. No inquiry is made until the prosecutor lodges, or gives security for, the amount of the value of the property stolen; and if he fails in proving his charges, he forfeits the amount, which is given to the accused. The fines for assaults and abuses vary greatly, according to the rank of the party complaining. The cases are decided according to the judgment of the officers who try them, and not from any fixed code of laws. The litigants are obliged to provide the officer with refreshment whilst the case is pending. Palm-oil is said to be very efficacious in some cases; for example, one poor wretch, on the occasion of our visit, had been tied up for some hours in a broiling sun preparatory to being flogged. We were informed by a bystander that he could easily have escaped the punishment had a little blandishment in the shape of hard cash been bestowed on the jailer in charge. This latter individual was a fat, cheery fellow, quite a wag in his way. He chuckled hugely at the good joke he was about to enjoy in thrashing the miserable wretch who was tied up ready for the lash. The reason for the flogging was that the culprit had the previous night attempted to commit suicide by drowning himself in the river. When I suggested the cruelty of tying him up in the sun, as he was evidently suffering from fever, the jailer laughed immensely, and remarked merrily, "The heat of the sun will take last night's damp out of him."

One of the prisoners was the son of the chief of Labong. The punishment of his offence would probably commend itself to the disciples of Sir Wilfrid Lawson. The young scapegrace had run wild, and one evening consumed a large quantity of country

A SHAN GIRL.

spirit, a sort of *sam-shu*, and when in his cups had insulted some ladies, who reported the matter to the chief of Zimmé, by whose order he was detained in chains as a punishment for his disorderly conduct. The law is not always equally applied to the nobility and peasantry in these parts, however. A part of the prison—a dirt-begrimed den—was set apart for *chaos*, or nobles. It is only in recent years that the chaos have thus had justice meted out to them; this is owing to the more just administration of the law, enforced by the Siamese officers deputed by the Government to be resident at Zimmé. The floggings are severe, and consist of thirty stripes laid on with all their might by three strong men, each giving ten lashes to the writhing wretch, who is tied up to a framework of bamboo in a public place. The punishment for theft in the Shan States lying west of the Salween, when they were under Burmese rule, used invariably to be death, a great contrast to the clement rule of the Zimmé and independent Shans.

At a trial for adultery, witnessed by the French expedition in one of the Shan States on the Mékong, the two offenders were tied one at each end of the same bar, and forced to look each other in the face, meanwhile striking two sonorous bamboos together to attract public attention. The woman was fined some fifty shillings, and her paramour four pounds. Husbands in such cases are allowed to divorce their wives, but, if they do so, are not allowed to take them again for ten years. The fine levied on the woman is paid to the husband, that inflicted on the man is pocketed by the judges. Formerly the punishment was more severe. A woman convicted of adultery became her husband's slave, and could not be redeemed. In Tonquin at one time it was still more rigorous. A husband was then authorized to cut off his wife's hair, and lead her in that state before the mandarin, who caused her to be thrown to an elephant which was trained to be the public executioner. A still more barbarous punishment is said to have been in force formerly in Burmah. The peccadilloes of the husband are never interfered with by the law in the Shan country.

CHAPTER IX.

The Sooptip pagoda—Burmese forts—An aqueduct—The Méping valley—A gigantic bell—A nest of monks—Entrance of Buddhism into Burmah, China, and Cambodia—Shamanism—Absorption into Buddhism—The Tha-tha-na-paing; its former powers—Monasteries for the lazy—"Pure from infancy"—Burmese monks; respectfully treated—Temples and monasteries at Zimmé—Dissolute priests—Character of schools—Two bad to one good—A light of Buddhism—Ruined pagoda—A nat's temple—Human sacrifice—Religion of the Steins—Shamanism the fount of nat worship.

A RANGE of hills with peaks, some of which are two to three thousand feet in height, lies about three miles due west of the town. On one of these peaks is the far-famed Sooptip pagoda, a favourite resort for the religious, and a building of great sanctity. The road to it leads through the ruins of a small square fort about half a mile distant from the western gate of the town; the fort was built by the Burmese, who, when they last invested the place, in A.D. 1766, had numerous works all round Zimmé.

After passing the fort, the road continues through fields to a village at the foot of the hills, where the ascent begins. The ascent is at first very gradual, but latterly very steep. The road is in tolerably good order, and an aqueduct fed by one or two very fine springs is carried alongside, conveying a plentiful supply of excellent water to the town. A fine row of pines is planted on each side of a long flight of steps leading immediately to the pagoda on the hill top. From the top of the platform, about two thousand feet high, is seen a magnificent panorama. The Méping flows from the north-westward, and, bending at the town, trends away to the south-west. Its banks are darkened by trees, concealing scattered houses and small villages, and one or two large tanks are visible to the northward not far from the town. The country beyond is, in fact, one sheet of fields, with numerous topes of trees marking the position of as many villages. The valley here, from ten to fifteen miles broad, stretches away to the south, until it loses itself in the fine deltaic plain in which Bangkok, the capital of Siam, is built. On the outside of the platform is a great bell, highly prized by the Shans, which was presented to the pagoda by the late chief, weighing, according to the inscription which has been chiselled on it, one hundred and fifty-six thousand Shan viss, or about one hundred and eighty-three tons!

Zimmé is a perfect nest of *poongyees*, or Buddhist monks; I should think there must be at least five hundred of them inhabiting the seventy-five monasteries in the town. Their religion is the Buddhism of Ava, and almost all the *zedi*, or pagodas, both in and out of the town, were erected by the Burmese while they held the place. Whether Buddhism first entered Zimmé and the neighbouring country from Thibet, Burmah, China, or Cambodia, is unknown.

SECTION OF A KYOUNG, OR MONASTERY.

Gaudama is said to have become Buddha in B.C. 588, and the Buddhist era dates from B.C. 543. Buddhism entered Thibet in B.C. 313. In B.C. 90, the Buddhist scriptures were reduced into writing in Ceylon; and about B.C. 241, the time of the third and last great Buddhist council, Thawna and Ootara, two missionaries, landed at Thatone, a town near the gulf of Martaban. From this place the religion is supposed to have spread up the valleys of the Sittang and the Irrawadi; it does not seem to have become the national Burmese religion for many centuries afterwards; for Na-ra-pa-dee-tsee-thoo, who was king of Pagan, an old capital of Burmah, in A.D. 1191, is described by the native historians as a religious monarch who did much toward firmly establishing Buddhism in Burmah and the other adjacent countries. The date of its entry into China is given as A.D. 66; and it is said to have been brought from Ceylon to Cambodia in A.D. 422. The Mongols at the time of their conquest of China were Shamanists; and Buddhism, according to Col. Yule, became practically extinct amongst them after their expulsion from China, in A.D. 1368, when the old Shamanism revived. It was not until A.D. 1577 that the great reconversion of Mongolia to Lamaism began.

It may be here noted that Shamanism, or nat worship, is not only the sole religion of most of the hill-tribes in Indo-China, but has been absorbed into the worship of the followers of Buddha. A capital example of this is given by "Shway Yoe," in his very able and interesting book "The Burman," where the inscription on a bell, presented by two Buddhist peasants to a pagoda, amusingly jumbles the two religions. The Soola-gandee sect in British Burmah, and the Tha-tha-na-paing, or "master of religion," who resides in Mandalay, are doing their utmost to purify the religion and to enforce obedience to its rules on the monks, but with little effect, so far as one can judge. In the present day the power of the Tha-tha-na-paing is merely nominal; the effects of his jurisdiction are scarcely felt beyond his own neighbourhood. Such, however, according to Bishop Bigandet, was not the case in former times. Spiritual commissioners were sent yearly by him to examine into and report on the state of the communities throughout the provinces, amongst which Zimmé was included whenever Burmah could get the upper hand. They had to inquire particularly whether the rules were regularly observed or not, and whether the professed members were really qualified for their holy calling or not. They were empowered to repress abuses; and whenever some unworthy brother was found within the inclosure of a monastery, he was forthwith degraded, stripped of his yellow garb, and compelled to resume a secular course of life.

Unfortunately for the welfare of the order, these salutary visits take place no more; the wholesome check is done away with, and, left without superior control, the order has fallen into a low degree of abjectness and degradation. The profession of *talapoin poongyee*, or monk, is often looked on now as one fit for lazy, ignorant, and idle people, who, being anxious to live well and do nothing, put on the sacred dress for a certain time, until, tired of the duties and obligations of their new profession, they retire and betake themselves once more to a secular life. It is not very common to meet, even among the Burmese Yahan, men who from their youth have persevered to an old age in their vocation. These form rare exceptions. They are very much respected and held in high consideration during their lifetime, and the greatest honours are lavished upon their mortal remains after their demise. They are often designated by the honourable denomination of *Ngay-hpyoo*—"pure from infancy."

No member of the laity could formerly enter the priesthood without becoming a mendicant, bidding adieu to the world and entering a monastery, subjecting himself to a life of self-denial, and spending his days in the strict observance of restraining rules, however galling he might find them. In Burmah the priests, or rather monks, are represented by the yellow-clad poongyees, dwelling in monasteries scattered over the face of the country, living upon alms, possessing no property, receiving their food morning after morning from the townsfolk of their quarter or the inhabitants of their village, all in strict silence, the eyes fastened on the ground and without even looking a request. Passing slowly down the street in single file, each one carries a pot, which he opens on the approach of a donor and receives the gift without a change of expression, movement of the head, or a word of thanks. They are held in the highest respect by all ranks of people, from the sovereign on the throne to the beggar in the street. Their dress, their mode of life, their renunciation of the world and its pleasures, draw on them the admiration and veneration of the laity.

When they appear in public, they are the objects of the greatest deference; all people, whatever may be their social position, give way before them. The visitor, who seeks them in their monasteries, prostrates himself before them three times with joined and upraised hands, both on entering and leaving their holy presence. On standing up, he must fall back to a convenient distance, as it would be highly indecorous to turn the back on so saintly a personage, and, wheeling slowly to the right, he may depart. Throughout British and Upper Burmah, the respect paid to the members of the order is everywhere apparent, in the liberality with which their wants are supplied, the size and beauty of the dwellings built for them by the laymen, the respectful language in which they are addressed, the submissive attitude of those who appear before them, and in the pomp displayed on the occasion of the solemn cremation of their mortal remains after death.

The temples at Zimmé are of brick, consisting of one hall, varying from sixty to a hundred feet in length, and thirty to fifty in breadth, at the end of which a large image of Gaudama stands on an elevated platform, surrounded by smaller ones. The floors are raised about three feet, and bricked, and generally smeared over with *thitsee*, or wood-oil; the sides of some are closed, with the exception of the doorway,

A MUSICIAN, MASQUERADER OR MUMMER, AND TWO HILL PEOPLE, AT BASSAC, ON THE MÉKONG.

while in others the wall is built only half height. The roof over the centre of the building, being raised higher than the covering of the sides, is supported by very fine lofty posts of teak, and tiled, and the whole adorned with carved wooden ornaments, and a small *pyathat*[1] over the centre. The insides of the buildings are painted with subjects taken from their sacred writings, principally from the five hundred and fifty *zats*,[2] and are by no means badly done; the pillars and roof are highly ornamented and gilt. The interiors of most of these buildings, which are numerous in the town, are rich and handsome, and are kept remarkably clean and in good order.

The monasteries of the priests are similar in size to the temples, but not ornamented; the interior is partitioned off into small rooms for their accommodation, rendering the building very dark. The numerous trees about these religious buildings render them cool and pleasant; and the grounds, which are surrounded by a low brick wall, are kept very neatly swept and are evidently well looked after. We soon became convinced that the priests are by no means as strict in the observance of their duties as the Burmese priesthood. They are seen at all hours, and in every direction, loitering about idly, mixing with the people, sitting in the bazaar, conversing with women, even entering private houses at night, riding elephants, eating after the sun has passed the meridian, devour-

[1] A spire, with successive tiers of diminishing roofs (3, 5, or 7).

[2] Accounts of the previous existences of Buddha.

ing flesh, selling what is given for use in the monasteries, and bowing to the chief and his wife, according to native report. Many of them indulge in spirits and cock-fighting, go about with unshod feet, wear gold and jewellery, "convert" bad stones, supposed to be precious, into a resemblance of good ones; mix themselves up, to use a Burmese expression, in the affairs of women; and, in fact, do many things that they are strictly enjoined by their rules not to do. During their Lent, which is supposed to be observed for forty-eight days, they receive grand offerings, selling most of the articles received for the highest prices which are obtainable. *Pwais*, or plays, some of them by no means moral, are constantly given by the people in Lent; and the priests themselves, directly against their vows, indulge in music, every *kyoung*, or monastery, being well supplied with flutes, cymbals, and drums. On the whole, we were forced to the conclusion that the majority of these priests were idle, good-for-nothing, illiterate, and dissolute men. To use McLeod's words, the yellow robe, in fact, appears to be the emblem of idleness, ease, and debauchery. Their only literature consists of a few Pali manuscripts, and copies of the pwais usually performed.

The poongyees are supposed to supply the educational wants of the people; but, as a matter of fact, they do nothing of the kind. They are merely teachers, by their example, of apathy, laziness, and downright vice; and every year finds them farther on the downhill road which must end in either the dis-

UTENSIL FOR HOLDING CONSECRATED OIL.

establishment of the monasteries or the curbing of the priests and enforcement of decent order and living amongst them. The present King of Siam has taken means in Bangkok, his capital, to purge the monasteries and curb the licentious behaviour of the monks by closing several of the worst-conducted monasteries and forcing their inmates to return again to civil life. A high official of Zimmé told me, in the course of a long conversation held with him on the subject, that there were good and bad priests and good and bad monasteries here as well as everywhere else. He had, however, to confess that the Zimmé priests were decidedly below par, or, as he put it, "Well, there are here two bad for one good, I think." We learnt that as for strong drink, the priests no longer make so much as a pretence of abstaining from its use. One day, while paying a visit to one of the dignitaries of the place, my host produced some capital European refreshments, and as we sat in the verandah indulging in them and smoking our cheroots, the head priest, a sort of bishop, and a most venerable-looking old man, was introduced. He had just returned from a long journey, and had hastened to pay his compliments to my entertainer. Greatly to my surprise, this light of Buddhism was immediately offered a glassful of rare French brandy. He drank it with the greatest gusto, and then begged that he might be supplied with another.

Previous to the investiture of a poongyee as head of the monasteries in the State, the *tsobua*, or prince, asks him if he will obey his lawful orders; and on being answered in the affirmative, he makes over to him the authority over all ranks of the priesthood. The high priest then asks the tsobua if he will listen to his intercession in favour of criminals condemned to death, when it shall appear to him that the punishment is too severe for the offence; to which the chief has to yield assent.

In the centre of the town are the ruins of a large pagoda much higher than any of the others. It has a square basement of considerable size and height, and appears to have been arched; the whole of the wall, and upper part, has fallen down. In the same inclosure, near the eastern gate, is a small building of brick, said to be the abode of a guardian *nat*, or deity of the place; it is kept locked, and only opened once a year, when offerings and sacrifices are made and left within the building. It is said that human victims were immolated at his shrine formerly, but now pigs and bullocks are substituted. Every house in the province is obliged to contribute towards this festival. Human sacrifices are, according to Mouhot, still offered up by the Steins, who are worshippers of nats, living to the east of the Mékong River in Cambodia. These people have neither priests nor temples, yet they recognise the existence of a supreme being, to whom they refer everything, good or evil; they call him "Brâ," and invoke him in all cases. They believe also in an evil genius, and attribute all diseases to him. If any one be suffering from illness, they say it is the demon tormenting him; and, with this idea, make night and day around the patient an insupport-

A STEIN WOMAN.

able noise, which they keep up until one of the party falls in a kind of fit, crying out, "He has passed into my body; he is stifling me!" They then question the new patient, asking him, first, what remedies to give the sick man, and how the demon can be made to abandon his prey. Sometimes the sacrifice is a pig, or an ox is required, often a human victim; in this latter case they pitilessly seize upon a slave and offer him up to the evil genius.

I have previously described the nat worship amongst the Red Karens, which is similar to that of the other hill-tribes occupying Indo-China. The strong resemblance it has to that of the Steins, who inhabit the south-east of Indo-China, amongst whom M. Mouhot dwelt for some time, shows that the religion of the aboriginal tribes throughout the country is virtually the same, and so similar to the Shamanism of the old Tartars as to leave no doubt that it must have been derived from the same fount.

CHAPTER X.

Buddhists browsing in the missionary fold—Anamite converts—The last, best gift of France—An ugly race—The Giao-chi; a distinct race; character—A purgatory for missionaries—Hunting a tiger—The Steins—An opening for missionaries—Ancient belief of the Aryans, Chinese, and Jews—Shanti worshipped by the Emperor of China—Missionaries at Zimmé—Voyage up the Ménam—Difficult navigation—Bangkok—Its population—Sir John Bowring's mistake—Population of Siam—Census not published—Need of further exploration—Siam an unknown country.

It is the experience of both Protestant and Roman Catholic missionaries that it is very difficult to convert a Buddhist; indeed, some of the latter priests [1] have told me that, although they had gathered in many Hindus and hill-people to their flock, whom they might truly count as Christians, yet the Buddhists were as goats amongst their sheep, and jumped in and out of their fold as it suited their convenience. They had merely joined them for the sake of browsing, for some little temporary advantage, and could never for a certainty be counted as part of the flock.

[1] The American missionaries at Bangkok told Sir John Bowring that twenty-two missionaries had been sent out, and that the number of native Church members was thirty-four.

It is true that there have been many converts amongst the Anamites, but then their religion can hardly be called Buddhism; it is a curious compound derived from many sources, and they have so little zeal in any one particle of the said olio that it is really difficult to know what to call them. M. de Carné, who would naturally speak well of what was when he wrote the last, best gift of Fortune to France, asserts that they are all freethinkers. Anyhow, they seem to be an unpleasant people to study, much more to have to live amongst.

According to Père Legrande de la Liraye, the Anamites are the worst built and ugliest race in Indo-China. Their skin is coarse, of a dirty yellow colour, less dusky than that of the Cambodians, but of a deeper hue than that of the Chinese and Shans. Their heads, rather flat at the top, are broad at the sides, particularly behind. Their faces, flat, bony, and angular, have prominent and high cheek-bones, the smallest and flattest noses in Indo-China, and mouths not only large but adorned with thick and fleshy lips which protrude equally from the face. They have little pig-eyes, with eyelids like those of the Chinese. To finish off the picture, they are shorter, smaller, and less vigorous than any of the neighbouring races, have bowed legs, and strut about like turkeys. Natural selection can hardly be said to have improved this race, if this account be true. What distinguishes them most from other people is the distance that their big-toes are separated from the next ones, hence the flippant Chinese call them

Giao-chi,[1] or "Bifurcated toes." This general deformity indicates their having been a distinct race for a very long period, and very few of their neighbours, most likely none who could avoid it, have been crossed by them. The peculiar big-toe, according to Garnier, is, however, found amongst some of the hill-people near Bassac, and is sometimes met with among the yellow race in parts of Yunnan. The Anamite traditions extend to the time of the first dynastic emperor of China, that wonderful engineer Yu, who "controlled the waters," in whose time they were denizens of Tonquin and the region lying between it and the Yangtsi-kiang.

The description given by Abbé Gagelin of the character of this hideous and uncouth race is quite as displeasing as their appearance. He says, speaking of his own Christian servants: "All sensibility appears deadened amongst them; they are very proud, and great cheats. There is so little affection among them, that the nearest relations never think of embracing; even a child, returning to his parents after a ten years' absence, would not think of such a thing. Among brothers and sisters it would be considered almost a scandal. They will not permit us missionaries to caress a child, not even a baby. This coldness is not confined to their domestic relations; under

[1] Or Kiao-chi, written with Chinese characters commonly translated as above. The oldest name in Chinese books, according to Terrien de La Couperie, is written with different characters, which mean "Intermingled basis." Yule has surmised ("Marco Polo" vol. ii. p. 101) that "the syllables were originally a phonetic representation of an indigenous name which has no such meaning" as "crossed toes."

an ardent sky, which should warm the imagination, they, in their stupid *sang-froid*, will not tolerate in a preacher the slightest movement or gesture." Could Dante have invented a purgatory more complete for the torture of ardent French missionaries!

M. Mouhot, who had not suffered exile amongst them for years, as the afflicted missionary had done, thinks him rather hard in his judgment of a people who had often sheltered their pastors in times of persecution at the risk of their lives. Let us see how he himself paints his Anamite lily,—his description is not altogether encouraging:—"They are lively, adroit, intelligent, and courageous,"—that is not a bad beginning,—but there seems to be a question as to the courage of the ordinary Anamite, for there are discrepancies in the accoúnts of travellers which lead one to think that they, like the generality of people, are only courageous in facing dangers that they are in the habit of constantly encountering. Take, for instance, M. Mouhot's account of hunters attacking a tiger, and compare it with M. de Carné's description of a tiger surprising an Anamite. M. Mouhot says: "The tiger of Anam is terribly savage, and his strength is equal to his ferocity. Often, however, a couple of men will go alone to attack one, armed merely with pikes. As soon as they see the animal, the more powerful or more courageous of the two lowers his pike; the tiger hesitates for a moment, and sometimes, if not pressed by hunger, turns and disappears with the rapidity of lightning; but at other times he will make a spring at the hunter, when, if the force of the leap does not carry him right over the man's head, he falls upon the pike, which the hunter then elevates by pressing the handle on the ground. The second hunter now comes forward, and in his turn pierces him, and, uniting their strength, they both hold him down till he dies." Now let us turn to M. de Carné; according to him an Anamite, surprised by a tiger, treats him like a great mandarin; gives him the very respectful title of grandfather, kneels, and beats the earth with his forehead, and meets the fate of little Red Riding-hood, whom her grandmother ate.

Returning to the character of the Anamites, having heralded all the good points he can think of, M. Mouhot goes on with his description as follows: "But they are obstinate, vindictive, dissemblers, liars, and thieves; slow to get into a passion, but terrible when they do. Their dirtiness surpasses anything I have ever seen, and their food is abominably nasty. Rotten fish and dog's flesh are their favourite diet."

It is quite refreshing to turn from the Christian Anamites to the less repulsive, if heathen, hill-tribes. Even life in the fever-stricken haunts of the so-called "savage" Steins would be more in accordance with one's spiritual requirements; for although their superstition does sometimes lead them to vary their sacrifices of pigs and oxen with that of a slave, they are yet gentle in their dispositions and very hospitable. Amongst them a stranger is certain of a welcome; the fatted pig or fowl is at once killed, the loving cup produced, and bamboos handed round,

A STEIN CHIEF.

M

to be used as we use straws with sherry cobbler. A follower of Sir Wilfrid Lawson would find himself in a predicament at such a feast, for not only is it etiquette to eat all that is set before you, but the refusal of a suction bamboo is considered as a piece of great rudeness. Bowie-knives, or their equivalent, are in vogue in this part of the country, and more than one savage has paid for such an insult with a knife-thrust.

The Steins display their hospitality still further by spilling a little rice before each meal, for the benefit of the souls of their ancestors; and every day some member of the family goes to the graves and sows a few grains of rice, so that the dead may have something to eat. Offerings are likewise made to their ancestors in the fields and other places that they were in the habit of frequenting. At the end of a long bamboo, which is planted in the ground, they suspend plumes of reeds; lower down are fastened smaller bamboos containing a few drops of wine or water; and, lastly, on a slight trellis-work raised above the ground is laid some earth, in which they stick an arrow, and on which they throw a few grains of cooked rice, a bone, a little tobacco, and a leaf.

In the account of my travels through the South China Borderlands, I called attention to the promising field there was for missionaries amongst the mountaineers of Yunnan and the Shan country lying to the south of it. These people are being, by the same gradual process that has acted upon the inhabitants of the plains, slowly absorbed into Buddhism. Many of those in the independent Shan States have already embraced that religion, or rather added it to their own. No time should be lost by our missionaries in entering the field and rescuing these people from the atheistical tenets of Buddhism. Many of them already have a faint idea of a supreme being; the Steins call him Brâ, and invoke him in all cases; the Shans call him Phya Then; the Chinese, Tien; and the Karens, Tie.

The religion of the worship of Shanti, or Tien, is the oldest recorded in China. A temple is said to have been erected to him B.C. 2697, and his attributes, according to Père du Halde, are very similar to those of the Jewish Jehova. It is indeed interesting to find indications that the most ancient religions of the Aryans, Chinese, and Jews were really one and the same. Shanti is still worshipped by the Emperor; his temple is said to be the finest in China, and there are no traces of idolatry in it. Either the remembrance of this worship, handed down from generation to generation, or else their later contact with the Mahomedans, who have been settled for many centuries in Yunnan, or perhaps the neighbourhood of the Mussulman Malays, who have been in the Malay Peninsula[1] ever since their first settlement there at the end of the thirteenth century, may have given the Karens this vague belief. Any of these assumptions seems more likely than that of certain writers who

[1] Karens extend as far south as 9° north latitude in the Malay Peninsula.

NAVIGATION IN INUNDATED FOREST LAND, MÉKONG DELTA.

have asserted, and still urge, that the Karens are no other than the descendants of the lost tribes of Israel.[1]

The good work that the American Baptist Mission, which was established by Dr. Judson in Burmah in 1815, has done, has already been alluded to; and I was pleasantly surprised, on reaching Zimmé, to find two missionaries and their families established there. One of them had been in residence for fourteen years, and the other, who was a qualified physician, for about four, happy in their Shan home. These worthy people had come to Zimmé by boat from Bangkok, and described the journey as most tedious. Channels had to be dug through the shifting sands, sometimes as often as half a dozen times a day, and so false was the bottom that work done by a boat's crew in the morning was useless to craft following a few hours after. There were no less than thirty-two rapids passed where the river leaves the mountains below Muang Haut, and some of them had so great a fall as to be dangerous. The boatmen had behaved very well, and shown great courage, coolness, and judgment whilst running the rapids.

The difficulty of navigating the river perhaps accounts for the fact that the inhabitants prefer travelling by elephants, ponies, or even bullocks, to any sort of water conveyance. One can hardly believe that they are the same race who are seen at Bangkok,

[1] A few Jews who claim descent from the tribe of Asser, and say that they reached China during the Han dynasty (B.C. 206 to A.D. 264), are still found in the Chinese province of Honan, and are called the Blue Mahomedans.

where the inhabitants form mainly a floating population, the chief thoroughfares are the canals, and the people may be said, without exaggeration, to live upon the water. A great number of the houses are actually built on rafts, and can be moved about as their occupiers may desire. The place has been so frequently described by travellers that I made no particular notes during my stay there. The population in 1856 was given by Bishop Pallegoix as four hundred thousand; and the Catholic missionaries with whom Sir John Bowring conversed generally concurred in the accuracy of the bishop's estimate. Owing to the great increase of the inhabitants, arising from the immigration of Chinese, and other causes, it is now generally allowed to be between five and six hundred thousand. It is a very difficult matter, indeed an impossible one, to compute the population of Indo-Chinese kingdoms from the official returns, even if they were procurable, for no one is inscribed in the census lists except the regular taxpayers. According to Garnier, this class does not include any one over the age of seventy or under the age of eighteen; neither does it include the chaos (or ruling class), their families, or their slaves, and this latter class forms from one-tenth of the population in the large provinces to one-fifth in the small ones. The tributary tribes pay by the village, and therefore do not have their names inscribed; besides which, no direct tax is raised from Chinese, Peguans, and other strangers who have not been born in the country.

On inquiring at the Siamese embassy, I was told

CHINESE CULTIVATOR IN THE SHAN COUNTRY.

that none of the inhabitants of the provinces of Zimmé, Luang Prabang, or Kiang Tsen was ever put on the inscribed list. Prince Prisdang assured me that Sir John Bowring had made a great mistake in taking the list of those who were liable to be called out for military service as the gross population of the kingdom; and that if that list were multiplied by five, it would give a nearer approximation to the population. M. Mouhot says that a few years before 1862 the native registers showed, for the male sex (those who were inscribed), two million Siamese, one million Laotians (or Shans), one million Malays, one million five hundred thousand Chinese, three hundred and fifty thousand Cambodians, fifty thousand Peguans, and a like number composed of various tribes inhabiting the mountain-ranges. Taking these statistics and multiplying them by five, which Bishop Pallegoix allows is a fair way of computing from them, we should have a population of twenty-nine million nine hundred and fifty thousand. To this would have to be added the Chinese and Peguans who had not been born in the country, and were therefore not among the inscribed; also the hill-tribes that were merely tributary, and therefore paid by the village; as well as about one-seventh of the total of the above for the ruling classes, their families and slaves. This total would give at least thirty-five million inhabitants for Siam Proper, to which would have to be added about three million for its dependencies, Zimmé, Luang Prabang, and Kiang Tsen. The gross population of the Siamese dominions previous to 1862 would therefore be about thirty-eight millions, instead of from four and a half to five millions, as was stated by Sir John Bowring.

The manner in which Sir John Bowring got his figures is curious; he takes the statistics given by Pallegoix, states that Pallegoix says that "with reference to the official census, neither old men, nor women, nor children are ever spoken of by the Siamese. To all questions as to the number of the inhabitants, the reply is, so many men. The number should therefore be estimated at five times the amount shown in the record." He then takes the record, but, instead of multiplying the six millions shown in it by five, so as to arrive at the approximate number of the population, he not only forgets to do so, but assumes that the six millions is an exaggeration, and diminishes it as I have just shown.

How the statistics quoted by Pallegoix and M. Mouhot managed to leak out is a mystery to me; for Sir John Bowring says, "The records of the census are regularly made to one of the high functionaries, who is restrained from communicating the particulars to any but the king and the ministers"; and this is still the case. The need of further exploration in the country is self-evident, as at present we are absolutely in the dark as to its true state away from the main lines of travel. Native statistics and information are unreliable, and European observation is required. That Siam is a land-locked country without roads and bridges, with its rivers impracticable for any distance for large craft, owing to rapids, fierce currents, and quicksands; that it is very fertile, and has a large population in the valley of the Ménam, and by no means a sparse one in other parts; that it contains about two hundred and sixty thousand square miles of territory, and is very rich in minerals and in teak-forests, the greater part of which is unworkable for want of good communications, is about all that we know at present outside the immediate neighbourhood of the capital and of the tracks followed by the few travellers who have traversed interior Siam.

CHAPTER XI.

Burmese contempt for the Shans—Theatres as schools for manners—Matrimony in Burmah—Madras women sold in British Burmah—Value of slaves in Cambodia, Siam, and French Cochin-China—Laws of slavery—Slaves from gratitude—Voluntary slaves—K'ai fak and K'ai kat—Wives and children for sale—A lesson for servants—Forced marriage—Wives purchasing each other—Wives and husbands mutually responsible—Bond-service not slavery—King's slaves—Debt-bondage—Heavy interest—Compound interest not allowed—Mortgaging one's person—Debtors in chains—Consent of slave required before he can be sold—Can change his master—A bill of sale—Slaves kindly treated—Heavy taxation, gambling, and improvidence—Government in Siamese provinces—Small pay, and exactions, of officials—One-third of the people slaves—Clans—Chiefs and vassals—Danger of feudal power—Weakness of Siam—Railways required—A nation of slaves—Effect of slavery—Chinese traders—France is taking advantage of Siam's weakness—Enlightenment of the present rulers—Fear of France—Siam at present our market—French jealousy and intentions—Intended annexation—M. Blanscubé's programme—The French railway—Siam's helplessness—The French toils—France's action depends upon us—Our stake—The protection of Siam vital to British Burmah—Friendliness of the king to the English—Peace on the frontier—Eagerness for our alliance—The French a cause of disturbance in Indo-China—A warning given by *The Times*.

In a previous page I remarked upon the arrogance and intense conceit of the Burmese, as evinced in their supercilious contempt for the Shans. This arises, strange to say, not from mere ignorant boast-

A LAOS, OR SHAN WOMAN.

fulness, but from the knowledge that the Shans are their inferiors in the art of politeness, indeed mere boors in comparison with themselves. Their feeling is analogous, in fact, to that of a public-school boy towards all wearers of corduroy breeches at home. From their very babyhood they have sat out, for days and nights in succession, long dramas, in which practised performers, or, as is frequently the case, people of their own village or town, have displayed the manner in which kings, queens, princes, princesses, and other perfectly polite people, act and speak, under all circumstances. There can be no doubt that this schooling has imparted to the manners of the Burmese, particularly to the women, a polish which is seldom met with elsewhere outside the highest circles. Their language and their behaviour towards the *poongyees*, or monks, their rulers, strangers, and each other, is full of gracious consideration, refinement, and high-bred courtesy. Even their seeming abasement before the monks, and their superiors, is looked upon as etiquette, to omit any particle of which would be deemed ill-manners of which the culprit should be heartily ashamed.

The same sort of plays are acted at times both in Siam and the Shan States, and there can be no doubt that they have influenced the manners, thoughts, language, and habits of the people. Anything that tends to increase the courtesy of people to each other must render life more enjoyable, must raise them in the social scale, and, by giving them a better opinion of themselves, make them more manly, and

N

in time shame them out of the indolence which leads so many of the Siamese to prefer living the life of serfs, dependent upon others, rather than as free men, who must battle with the world and face the consequences.

It is rather a hackneyed saying that any one treading on British soil becomes free; it is true that in such a case a slave can claim his freedom, but it is still the fact that not only are their daughters sold into matrimony by the poorer Burmese in British Burmah, but natives of India bring women over from the Madras coast and sell them to the highest bidder. In the case of the Burmese it may be said that the option of accepting a husband lies with the daughter, yet custom is strong, and few elopements occur. This custom of expecting a dowry from the would-be husband is considered only a just remuneration for the expenses incurred in the daughter's bringing up. On the other hand, with the Madras women, middle-men are employed, who pay the expenses of the voyage, and expect to be remunerated handsomely before they part with their dark bargains. The traffic in Madras women is, of course, carried on *sub rosa*, and, unless married, any woman can claim her freedom whenever she chooses; but such is their ignorance that very few cases of this are known to have happened.

We have seen that in Cambodia, which is under French protection, slaves vary in value from two hundred to eight hundred francs, or from £8 to £32.[1] In Siam the value of a man is from £10 to £20, a

[1] M. de Carné.

woman from £7½ to £12½, and children from twelve to sixteen years of age from £5 to £7½;[1] slaves by birth in the latter country can claim freedom, on reaching manhood, by paying £6. Some of the laws of slavery in Siam give one such an insight into the character and customs of the people that they are worth while quoting.

"Laws of Slavery.[2] There are seven classes of slaves, viz. :—

1. Bought with money. 2. By birth. 3. Left by legacy. 4. By gift. 5. Those who become so from gratitude. 6. Voluntary slaves in time of famine. 7. Prisoners of war.

These seven classes may be claimed and compelled to work.

The following six classes cannot be compelled to work :—

1. Manumitted slaves. 2. Those slaves whom the master has allowed to become talapoins.[3] 3. Those whom their masters have given to the talapoins. 4. When the master himself has become a talapoin. 5. Those who come to live round the man's house. 6. Those who live upon his lands.

Slaves bought with money are subdivided into three classes :—

1. Those slaves who are free by payment of the

[1] Vincent says that thirty dollars, about £7, is considered a high price at Saigon for Anamite girls.

[2] Bowring's Siam, vol. i. p. 195.

[3] Bonzes, poongyees, or monks.

debt. (These must have a security, and are classed as 'K'ai fak.')

2. Those who are bought irredeemably. (These have no security, and are classed as 'K'ai kat.')[1]

3. Those who pay interest instead of working.

Husbands may sell their wives,[2] parents their children, masters their servants.

When children are sold under the full value, they must not be beaten till they bleed.

When slaves *K'ai fak* take their master's place in prison,[3] half their money must be remitted; but if they are *K'ai kat*, no part is to be remitted.

If a man sell a slave, and after receiving the money refuse to give up the man, he shall pay twice the price —three-quarters to the buyer, and one-quarter to the Government.

If a buyer disapprove of a slave before three months have elapsed, he may claim back his money. If a master strike a slave so that he die, no claim can be had upon the security, and the master shall be punished according to law.

Anything that the slave shall break after the money has been paid shall be added to the redemption money paper.

[1] This class is not numerous; they are chiefly young girls who are sold by their parents. There is no redress for the purchaser if the girls abscond, as they frequently do.

[2] A husband may sell a wife that he has purchased, but not one who has brought him a dowry.

[3] It is a very common occurrence, when masters have been arrested for debt, to make their slaves take their place until the masters can collect the money to pay with.

If, in minding cattle, he should be negligent, and they be lost, he shall pay; but if more be given him than he can possibly look after, he shall pay half. But if robbers *bind* him, and steal the cattle, he is not liable.

Any claim against the slave must be made before he is sold to another master.

If a master insist upon a female slave marrying against her will, half her redemption money must be remitted.

If a slave go to war in lieu of his master, or by the king's command, and fight there, all his redemption money must be remitted; if he do not fight, half must be remitted.

If a slave be placed to plant rice, etc., he cannot leave until the season be finished.

If a master sell a slave, and then re-purchase him, if the master dies, only half can be demanded for the slave.

If, when rice is dear, a slave sells himself below the standard price (£6 for women, and £7 for men), when rice gets cheap, his price shall be raised to the standard.

If a slave injure himself when at work, compensation shall be allowed according to the amount of injury.

If a slave die in defence of his master, nothing can be demanded from the security.

In case of any epidemic, and the relations of the slave who is ill with it attend him, nothing can be demanded.

If a merchant have a slave who has been in the habit of collecting accounts and selling goods for his owner,[1] and that slave abscond with money received on his master's account, his master cannot claim.

If a man have several wives, the smaller selling themselves to the higher wives, no interest can be claimed, as they are all considered sisters.[2]

If a master wishes to get rid of a slave, and cannot, he can take him to the judges, and if they cannot sell him within three days, and another person buys him after that time, he must be *K'ai kat*.

The children of slaves who are the relatives of the master are free.

If a slave run away, the money expended in apprehending him must be added to his account.

Slaves having children, the children must be charged for according to age.

If the parents' price is below twenty-four ticals each, their children are not considered slaves.

If a slave quarrel with his master, the judges will not receive his complaint until he has paid his money, unless it is a serious charge.

If a slave makes money while in service, at his

[1] The Shans who come to Burmah with ponies and cattle are generally slaves or serfs; but though they could escape from their servitude by breaking their trust, I have not heard of a case of one doing so.

[2] The wife who has been the object of the marriage ceremony *khan mak*, takes precedence of all the rest, and she and her descendants are the only legal heirs to the husband's possessions.

HILL-MEN NEAR STUNG TRENG ON THE MÉKONG.

death it goes to his master; but if he had money before, it goes to his relatives.

If a slave accuse his master of capital crimes falsely, he has his lips cut off; but if the charge is true, he receives his freedom. Children always accompany the mother.

Two slaves, husband and wife, having their names on the same paper, if one of them run away, the other can be charged."

The above are generally literal translations of the most important laws.

Slavery is hardly the term that should be used for the bond-service that is found in Burmah, Indo-China, and the Malay Peninsula. Prisoners of war, who are called king's slaves, are paid whilst serving in the army or navy, and get their rice as well. They have to serve during three months of the year, receiving ten shillings a month as soldiers and one pound as sailors; the remaining nine months they can employ as they like. Although the male children of king's slaves are classed with their father, the parents are allowed the same privilege of selling their daughters that the Siamese have.

The debt-bondage arises from the heavy rate of interest that is given for loans; as much as six per cent. a month is sometimes charged for the first three months, after which time the rate is reduced to three per cent. Compound interest is, however, not allowed; and there is often no interest required when cattle, carts, or other articles which can be used beneficially by the parties to whom they are pledged, have been given as a security. If the party borrowing has not sufficient goods to cover the value of the loan, he pledges his own person; and should he not pay the interest, he is handed over to the ruling powers, and has to wander about in light chains, working on the public works by day, and linked to the other prisoners by night, until he is released by his friends paying his debt, or until somebody will do so and accept his labour in lieu of the interest, in which case he becomes a bond-slave until the principal is paid.

The principal class of slaves in Siam are slaves by purchase, and redeemable. These have either been sold by their parents, or, when free, have sold themselves. No one can sell a slave without his own consent, and any slave can change his master by borrowing from another man and repaying his master his manumission money. Every slave has his paper, the ordinary form of which is somewhat similar to the following:—

"Wednesday, the 7th day of the waning moon of the 11th month of the year 1217 of the little era. I, Know, the husband, and Nu, the wife, sell our son Pau to L'uang Lurassakon, for the sum of one hundred ticals (£12½), our son being the slave of no one else, nor of the king. For the truth of which I hold myself responsible; and if the said Pau should run away, I hold myself responsible for him."

Bishop Pallegoix, who had been many years in Siam, was of opinion that slaves are as well treated in Siam as servants are in France; and Sir John Bowring

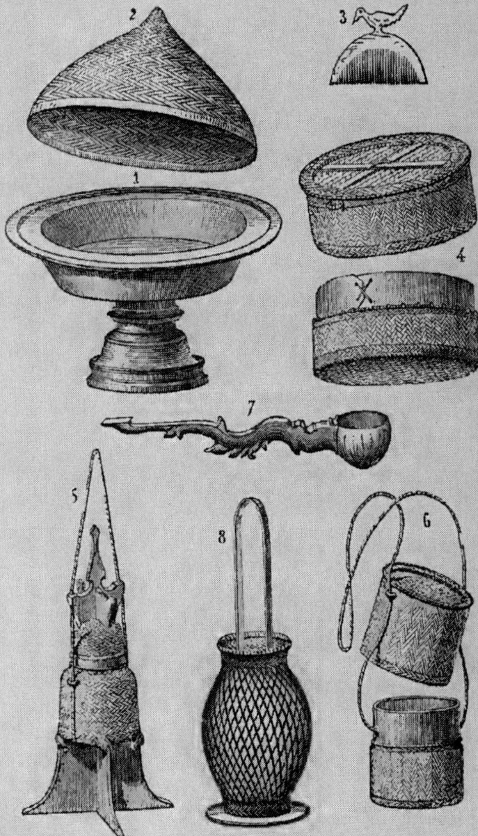

DOMESTIC UTENSILS

1, 2. Dish of lacquered bamboo, with plaited cover. 3. Wooden comb. 4, 5, 6 Utensils for holding cooked rice. 7. Ladle for water. 8. Bamboo lantern.

informs us that they are treated so kindly that, whenever they are emancipated, they always sell themselves again.[1] Garnier, in alluding to those in the Laos provinces, says that even savages who are captured and sold as slaves are treated so kindly that, to a stranger, if it were not for their physiognomy and long hair, they would seem part of the family of their masters. The same kind treatment of slaves is in vogue, according to Dr. Anderson, even amongst the Kachyens, the wildest of the wild hill-tribes.

The indebtedness of the people, which is the principal cause of more than one-third of the population of Siam being in bondage, arises from three causes—heavy taxation, gambling, and indolent improvidence. The taxes of men,[2] from eighteen to seventy years of age, on the inscribed lists in the Laos provinces,[3] are a head tax of 10*s.*, a land tax of 266 pounds of rice, and manumission from *corvée* labour £2. Assuming the value of the rice to be 6*s.*, about half what it would fetch at Rangoon, we have a gross taxation of £2 16*s.* a man. The *corvée* money is generally appropriated by the governors, there being no check to show whether the people work for the three months on public works, or pay in lieu of doing so. This abuse is sanctioned to some extent on the ground that the pay of public functionaries is inadequate to their support.

[1] According to Sir John Bowring, the Christians in Siam treated their slaves worse than the natives do.

[2] Garnier.

[3] Not including Zimmé or Kiang Tsen.

The cities and towns of Siam are ranged under four classes. The capital, and every city in which a tributary prince resides, are *Muang ek.* The provincial capitals are denominated *Muang to,* and are governed by a *phaja.* The towns of the third order, called *Muang tri,* have a *phra* for a ruler; and those of the fourth class, called *Muang chatava,* are governed by a *luang.* Every village throughout the country has a mayor, called a *kamnan.* The provincial governments are composed of the governor, his *balat* and *jokabat, i.e.* lieutenant and deputy-lieutenant. A dozen of the principal people form a council, called *kromakan,* which meets daily, and settles all affairs of local importance. At the end of November the principal officers receive their pay. The princes receive £200; the phajas from £120 to £20, according to their rank; the phra and the luang from £15 to £7½; while the pay of subaltern officers is from £5 to £2.[1] Is it a wonder that complaints are heard of the exactions of officers residing far from the central authority and who are so badly paid?

In the provinces, not only are one-third of the population said to be slaves,[2] but whole clans are dependent, much as the Highlanders of Scotland used to be, upon the *chaos,* or chiefs. When the taxes are collected, should the vassal be unable to pay them, he is frequently helped by the chief, who, on failure of the vassal to repay the principal with interest, can sell him as a slave. Many of the chaos, instead of taking

[1] Sir John Bowring. [2] Pallegoix.

extreme action, are satisfied with tribute from the vassal in the shape of presents and extra services to themselves and families. It is self-evident that the growth of such feudal power must be very dangerous to a State like Siam, which has had so frequently to put down rebellions on the part of its tributary States. Its true policy should be gradually to reduce the power of the chaos, and to replace them by a service similar to that with which we govern India. At present it may not be strong enough to govern the outlying bulwarks of the kingdom without their aid; but, if railways are made, and communication thus facilitated, the king will be able to take a firmer grasp of his dominions, to repress ambitious revolt before it can show its head, and, by rendering the taxation of the people equal and therefore more bearable, do away with the fearful indebtedness which is rapidly turning all his subjects into slaves, giving the trade entirely into the hands of the alien Chinese, and rendering them the only free men in his dominions.

Slavery is a canker which saps the manhood out of a people, encourages them in indolence, prevents them from enriching themselves and the State, keeps them backward in civilization, poor in spirit, and unfit, and perhaps unwilling, to cope with another race that will not bear the yoke. It corrupts the nature of the masters, who, wallowing in sensual indulgence, lose all zest for vigorous action, and at length become as unfit to govern others as they have become to control their own unruly passions. "He that loves pleasure must for pleasure fall," is one of those lessons that history is never tired of repeating. The Chinese are everywhere rapidly increasing in Siam; the whole trade of the coast is carried on by them; and the Chinese, and other Shans from the north, have for centuries been permeating through Upper Burmah and Siam, carrying away the cotton, tea, and other produce in return for the salt and other merchandise that they bring down. Our Burmese subjects and the Chinese, with the Northern Shans, bid fair soon to have the whole trade of the country in their hands.

France, seeing the weakness of the Siamese, is already coveting the country. The King and his family are enlightened, having received a European education, and it is his earnest wish to raise his people in the social scale. The difficulty is to begin. At present he advances inch by inch, and falters on his course; would fain lean upon England, but is afraid of the jealous anger of France; is afraid lest England should fail to aid Siam in any way when France advances with a threatening air. We know that our merchandise is found in all the bazaars of the country; our Burmese pedlars were met by the French vending our goods at Ubone, at Luang Prabang, at Muong Line, and other places. De Carné found our rupee was a redoubtable rival to the Siamese tical at Luang Prabang, and was accepted at the same value, although it is really worth sixpence less. He says: "The Burmese offer the public English stuffs, cotton checks, printed calicoes, woollen fabrics, buttons, and needles." Korat, he acknowledges, is "a vast entrepôt, where a

A FRESCO IN A SHAN MONASTERY.

O

great many Chinese have settled, who go out from it in all directions through the Siamese territories, and carry the English cotton checks through every part of Middle Laos." In the concluding chapter of his "Travels in Indo-China" he exclaims: "It will be recollected that his (the chief of Luang Prabang's) States border on Tonquin; that they are inhabited by a vigorous and pushing race (the Northern Shans); and that we found in his capital a considerable commercial activity, evinced by a daily market, the only one, probably, which exists in Siamese Laos. On the day when our advice, given with prudence, and firmly pressed, shall have effected a union of subjects by curbing the ambition of their princes, Anamite merchants, replacing the Burmese pedlars, will start from the banks of the Tonquin (the Songka River) to carry to Luang Prabang, and thus to the greater part of the middle and lower valley of the Mékong, the tissues and other manufactures of Europe, at present introduced almost exclusively from Bangkok." These were the views of no ordinary Frenchman, but of the officer of the political department who was deputed to accompany the French Government expedition in its exploration of the country lying to the north of French Cochin-China. In another place he says: "I know well that we are not established at Tonquin (M. de Carné died in 1870; this was therefore written some years before the French treaty of 1874 with Anam, by which they got their footing in Tonquin) as we are in Lower Cochin-China; I am, moreover, far from being convinced that it would be a real advantage to us to take immediate possession of the direct government of this country; but it is necessary that the Emperor Tu Duc should consent to tolerate our presence in it, to protect attempts at any agricultural, industrial, or commercial establishments which may be made by our compatriots. When the voice of the Governor of Cochin-China plays a greater part in the councils of Hué, it will not be long before it makes itself heard at Luang Prabang."

The acquisition of Tonquin, Anam, and the Siamese province of Luang Prabang, however, was no bound to his ambition. In an earlier part of his book he indicates the policy of the French towards the south-eastern portions of Siam: "Nature herself seems to have marked out the field we have to clear in the lower part of the Mékong valley. On both sides of the Mékong, the Se-mun, or Ubone, and the Se-don bound the zone within which our influence behoves us to prevail. On the right bank, the ancient Cambodian provinces I have just named seem to be inexhaustibly fertile. Their productiveness, stimulated by new markets, by the opening of roads which the geological structure of the country makes easy, will increase the exports of Saigon." It will be remembered by the reader that Ubone is one of the places where he found Burmese pedlars selling our goods. The influence of England is well portrayed by him: "Now that we are finally settled in Indo-China, it behoves our honour that the population of the interior should learn to know our name, as that of

SHAN PRIEST WITH DRUM AND GONGS.

the coast has already, and that England should no longer be imagined by these ignorant people to be the only Western power. At Ubone, this title of English, which they persisted in giving us, procured us more consideration than we should otherwise have met." The policy of M. de Carné has all along been that of the French Government in Cochin-China—the acquisition of the whole valley of the Mékong, which forms three-fourths of the dominions of Siam, and the ousting of English influence and commerce, to be replaced by that of France. M. Blanscubé, the French delegate from Cochin-China who brought in the Bill for sanctioning the present expedition to Tonquin, has taken up the mantle of M. de Carné; his voice is listened to with trustful eagerness by the French nation. This diplomatist has been good enough to let us have a peep at his policy. At a public meeting in Paris he remarked: "The mountains which separate the basin of the Ménam from that of the Mékong divide this vast peninsula (of Indo-China) into two parts almost equal. All the western part belongs, directly or indirectly, to England; the eastern portion must belong to France." This is frank language. Nothing could be plainer than this programme of M. Blanscubé's; it sums up part of the proposals of M. de Carné, and clearly defines the hope of Admiral de la Grandière, the late ambitious Governor of French Cochin-China, that "France may resume in Indo-China the place she has lost in India."

The Government of Siam is not wanting in astuteness; it fully understands the hopes and the designs of France, is aware that Tonquin is desired as a base for the conquest of the northern part of its dominions, and that a railway is even now being pushed up the valley of the Mékong from Saigon, in order to aid the French in their intended conquest of the south-east provinces. This is the railway that M. Blanscubé alluded to when he said: "Once at Luang Prabang, the railway will bifurcate: one branch will go to Tonquin and the other to Yunnan, and all the products of the peninsula and of China will flow to Saigon." Siam, without exterior aid, must be unable to resist the encroachments of France; in its present weak condition it might be vanquished with ease by any European adversary. France could force a protectorate upon it, which means very surely but the first step towards absorption. France could crumble it up and devour it by morsels, as it is doing Anam. Siam has had Cambodia already torn from its flank, without our even protesting, and feels that it is useless to cry, like a whipped child, "Don't, don't, please don't!"—that would not stop France in its career. Without our help it would have to lie down, like M. de Carné's Anamite, who, when faced by the tiger, called it his grandfather, and submit to its fate. At present, in default of an understanding with us, Siam, feeling its inability to resist, has to crouch to its would-be oppressor, affects a leaning towards France, and dare hardly turn to us, until sure that she may rely upon our aid, for fear of rousing the anger of France and leading her to action. The French are spreading their toils around Siam; only the other day a French man-

VIEW ON THE MÉKONG RIVER IN FLOOD.

of-war went to Bangkok to force a convention on the King of Siam. It is true that it only concerned the demand that French *employés* on the Siamese telegraph line should not be dismissed without the consent of the French consul at Bangkok—still it was the thin end of the wedge. If France is allowed to think that we should only grumble at her annexation of Siam, as we do at the rapid approach of Russia to our north-west frontier of India, she will certainly dismember Siam. If she succeeds, not only will our way by land to China be blocked, our trade with Siam and the Shan States stifled, but endless complications will arise, which will end in the dismissal of either one or the other of us from the finest granary of the East—Indo-China.

Although our stake in Siam is not at present large, it is infinitely greater than that of France. If the valley of the Ménam is opened up by railways and connected with the British Burmah system, our trade would rapidly increase. Even in the last year, owing to a few more police-stations being placed on the frontier, our land trade has very nearly doubled. The protection of Siam is vital to our trade and our agriculture in British Burmah; cattle plague ravages the herds in the latter country, and our chief source of supply lies in the enormous number that are bred in Luang Prabang and other parts of Siam. If we could not replenish our stock, our rice cultivation would be brought to a standstill or seriously diminish. Siam is the breeding-ground for the elephants that are required for our military commissariat, our teak-forests, and our timber-yards. Our teak-forests, and those of Upper Burmah, are rapidly being exhausted, and many of our foresters are now working those of Siam. If the country is opened out by railways, the large forests existing between the seventeenth and twenty-second parallels of latitude will become easily available and be a valuable source of supply. Siam is a friendly power; it has opened its provinces to our trade; our subjects, when trading, are certain of protection; at our request it has abolished all monopolies but that of opium;[1] our commerce is but lightly taxed; both criminal and civil suits, where our subjects are defendants, are heard by our consul; our provinces have been linked to it by telegraph lines; our missionaries are protected, and their converts are allowed to live in peace. The King and his relations have received a European education; fine schools have been founded in Bangkok; not a soldier is required on the Siamese frontier, although it bounds our territories for more than six hundred miles; a postal service is being organized throughout the kingdom; no complaints are ever made by our frontier officers of incivility or officiousness on the part of the Siamese governors, who, in conjunction with us, do their utmost to prevent all dacoities and theft on the frontier.

The King is eager for a friendly alliance with us, and is aware that such an alliance means safety to his kingdom, and is the only aid that he can rely upon in

[1] A monopoly of spirits exists in Zimmé.

order to save his kingdom from annexation by the French. Ever since the Franco-Spanish war with Anam in 1858, when Turon was occupied by the French, they have been a cause of disturbance in Indo-China. *The Times* did well in reminding them, a few months ago, that on no account would we accept them as neighbours, and that we might ere long have occasion to draw a line beyond which they would not be allowed to pass. That line should be the crest of the Anam hills and the present northern and western frontiers of Cambodia. Beyond that line are the empire of Siam and the independent Shan States, through which country lies our land route to China.

CHAPTER XII.

The home of the Shans—Various names for diverse races—Origin of tattooing—Description of the Youe—Tattooing tribes—The operation—Different styles—The History of Siam—A strange story—Scepticism of the King of France—Regal brooms at work in the monasteries—The maxims for monks—Difference between Buddhism and Christianity.

ALTHOUGH I use the word "Shan" to denote a race of people stretching from the valley of Assam, on the west, far into the interior of China, as well as from the borders of S'schuen, on the north, to the extreme south of Siam, it must be understood that the name is not used by themselves, but is merely that given to them by the Burmese. They generally call themselves Tai,[1] and add to the term the name of their clan. According to Ney Elias, who has studied the subject, the races in the first column of the following table call those noted at the top as indicated:—

[1] Or Thai. For information regarding the terms Thai-nyai (Great Thai) and Thai-nai (Little Thai), which latter term was "formerly applied to the Siamese in distinction from the Great Thai, their kinsmen of Laos," *vide* Yule's "Marco Polo," vol. ii. pp. 259, 267.

	Northern Shans	Burmese	Chinese	Manipurese	Khyens, Nagas, or Karens	Assamese	Kachyens	Siamese
N. Shans	Tai[1]	Man	Kyei		Kheng			
Burmese	Shan		Tarok, or Tayok	Kathei	Khyen, Kayen, or Karen	Athan, or Weithali	Han	Yodia Shan
Chinese	Pa-i[2]	Mien,[3] or Lau Mien				Weisali	Yeh-Jen[4]	Sien-Lo[5]
Manipurese	Kubbo,[6] or Pong	Awa	Khagi	Moitei[7]	Hau[8]	Tekau		
Assamese[9]	Sam	Man, or Montara	Khei	Moglu		Ahom	Singpo	Yutara
Kachyens	Sam	Mian	Mowa				Singpo, or Chinpaw	
Siamese		Mang	Khei	Kassei		Mung-lung		Tai

The Burmese call the Shans of Zimmé, Yun; of Kiang Tung, Gong;[10] of Kiang Hung, Lu; of Yunnan,

[1] Tai Niu, Tai Nyai, or Great Tai, otherwise Mau Tai, so called because their former capital was at Muang Mau. The classical, or Pali, name of Muang Mau was Kusambi.

[2] Or Peyih, Pa-yeh, or Pe-youe. (The Chinese word Pa is said to mean "cultivated highlands," and "i" barbarians.)

[3] Lau is written in Chinese with a character meaning "old."

[4] The same perhaps as I-Jen.

[5] The Laos, Lau, Lo-ho, or Lo, were in the south-east of Indo-China before the Sien, Tai-noi, or Little Tai, or Yun Shans, arrived there. A great many Shans must have left the south of China when the Chinese annexed it, B.C. 139–108. Regarding Sien-Lo, *vide* Yule's "Marco Polo," vol. ii. pp. 258–9.

[6] Called Phong and Tai Niu by the people of Kiang Tung.

[7] Perhaps Mau Tai, the name the Shans of the old Muang Mau kingdom were known by.

[8] This name is given by the Shans of Kiang Tung and Kiang Hung to the Chinese.

[9] Of the Shan race.

[10] The Gongs, Gungs, or Guens are said by the Burmese to have been cannibals living a little to the north-west of the Nattik pass (a descent from the Shan tableland towards Mandalay); they were driven thence by a Burmese king about A.D. 1017, and settled in

Shan Tarok, or Chinese Shans; and the country of Anam, or Cochin-China, Yun-gyee, or Great Yun. The Shans at Zimmé call the Burmese, Man; the Peguans, Meng; the Shans of Luang Prabang, Lau; of Kiang Tung, Khian; of Kiang Hung and Muang Yong, Li; of Muang Lem, Lem; the Chinese, Hau; Anamese, Min, or Kio.[1] The Shans at Kiang Tung[2] call themselves Khén; those of Kiang Hung, Lu; of Muang Lem, Lem; of Zimmé, Tai Nium; the Mau Shans, Phóng, or Tai Niu; the Moné Shans, Khum; the Siamese, Chou Tai, Tai Láo, and Tai Na; the people of China, Hau; and those of Anam, Kió. The Siamese call all the Shans living to the north and north-east of them, Laos, or Lau, merely dividing them into classes, the tattooed and non-tattooed, and designating them the "black-bellied" and the "white-bellied" Laos.

The origin of the tattooing is unknown, but there is no doubt that it is very ancient, for it was in existence before B.C. 130, as is shown by a petition from the prince of Hoai-nan[3] to the emperor of China of that day, in which he says that "the people

their present position, which is said to have then been inhabited by a similar race of Demons, which is merely a term which the Burmese used for the hill-races. They still call one of the Karen tribes Bhilu, or Demon.

[1] The Chinese name for them is Kiao-chi; the Min, or Min-youe, were the inhabitants of Fokien. The language spoken in Fokien is said, after the Sino-Anamite and the Cantonese, to resemble ancient Chinese more than any other dialect now spoken in China.

[2] At Kiang Hung the people of Kiang Tung are called Khen, and at Kiang Tung the people of Kiang Hung are called Lu.

[3] Quoted by Garnier.

A CAMBODIAN.

of Youe shave their hair and tattoo their body; they are light and changeable, weak and idle. The country they inhabit is full of impenetrable jungles full of serpents and tigers. The rains are continuous, and the heat of summer causes mortal illnesses." As the Chinese used the word "Youe" to designate all the tribes to the south of them, it is difficult to decide whether the Youe spoken of were Shans or not. The Anamites do not shave their heads, but the "Little Tai," or Siamese, do, all but a tuft at the top; and we know that they used to tattoo in the same way as the Northern Shans now do, although they have quite discontinued the custom for some time. The Burmese, the Shans, and certain Burmanized tribes are the only people in the south of Asia who are known to tattoo their body; whether any do so in the north I am not aware. The Khyen, or rather the portion of the race living on the western side of Burmah, used until lately to tattoo the faces of their young women with narrow dark-blue lines, pricked so closely together as to resemble a mask. The origin of the custom, which is dying out amongst those resident in our part of Burmah, is said, according to some of them, to have been to enable them to recognise their females when they had been carried off in a foray by some neighbouring tribe; others say it was to put a stop to the Burmese practice of carrying off their most lovely maidens.[1]

[1] "British Burmah Gazetteer." For further information regarding tattooing in Indo-China see Yule's "Marco Polo."

The operation is performed, except by the Khyens, only on the male sex, and never commenced until the lad has left the monastery. The whole person from the waist, in a line with the navel, down to the knee, and amongst the Shans of Muang Nan and Muang Pé from neck to foot, is covered with heraldic figures of animals, with tracery filling up the intervening spaces, so that the whole, at a little distance, resembles a pair of dark-blue breeches. The arms and back, amongst the Burmese, are sometimes more sparingly tattooed in red. The material used is lamp-black obtained from the smoke of sessamum oil, or vermilion, as the case may be, mixed, as occasion requires, with water. The pattern is generally, but not always, first traced on the skin with a fine hair pencil, and is then tattooed in by a series of closely adjoining punctures made by a long, pointed style, with a weight at the top, worked with the right hand, and guided by the left, which rests on the patient's body, with the fore-finger and thumb so joined as to form a sort of groove for the style to work in. The style is of brass, and consists of three or four portions; the bottom piece, which is solid, is pointed like an ordinary lead pencil, and divided by two slits at right-angles to each other, carried up for about three inches from the point; these are fine near the point, and about one thirty-second part of an inch broad higher up; these slits enable it to retain the colouring matter. The next joint, or two joints if there are four, is a hollow tube, and the last is either solid, or has a brass weight at the upper end, sometimes plain and sometimes fashioned like a bird or animal, in order to give weight to the tool. The operation, which in Burmah and the Shan country is considered indispensable as a sign of manliness, is painful, and is done in patches, and not all at once. On each occasion the child is put under the influence of opium, and death has frequently occurred through an over-dose of the drug being given.

The various clans have different styles of tattooing; that generally in vogue at Zimmé, although sometimes grotesque in its details, is not so fantastical nor well-imagined as the arabesques and wonderful scroll-work of the Burmese, and consists to a greater extent of bands. Some of the traditions as to the origin of tattooing, or what have been given to the public as such by certain humorous Europeans, are not worthy of belief; the origin of the custom is really unknown, but may have been either from the wish to make the tattooers more fearful to their enemies, or, what is still more likely, by tattooing charms on the body to make it invulnerable. To illustrate this last surmise, I will give an extract from a translation of the Pongsawadan, or History of Siam, which admirably displays the art the Siamese have of making "history a nurse's tale." In the year of the cock 1019 (A.D. 1658) the King of Siam, hearing wonderful tales about France from a French ship-captain, determined to send an embassy there, which only escaped being devoured by a whirlpool through their magician raising a wind which carried the vessel out of its gaping mouth. When the ambassadors told this tale to the French king, he believed it—or perhaps, being the monarch of a very polite nation, pretended to do so. I will now, having introduced the subject, allow the History to speak for itself.

"Some time after this the King sent for the ambassadors to come into the royal presence. He then ordered a company of five hundred French soldiers, all good marksmen, to be drawn up and placed in two ranks, directly facing each other—two hundred and fifty on each side. They fired simultaneously, and each man on either side lodged his ball in the barrel of the gun in the hands of the man opposite to him, without a single failure.

"The King then asked them if they had any as good soldiers, sharp-shooters, as these in Siam? The chief ambassador answered that the King of Siam did not esteem this kind of skill in the art as worth much in war. When the King of France heard this, he was displeased, and asked them what kind of skill in soldiers did the King of Siam value? The ambassador answered: 'The King of Siam admires soldiers who are well skilled in the magic arts, and such as, if good marksmen like your majesty's soldiers here would fire at them, the balls would not touch their bodies. His Majesty the King of Siam has some soldiers who can go unseen into the midst of the battle, and cut off the heads of the officers and men in the enemy's ranks, and return unharmed. He has others who can stand under the weapons of the enemy to be shot at, or pierced with swords and spears, and yet not receive the least wound or even injury. Soldiers skilled in this kind of art the King of Siam values very highly, and keeps them for use in the country.'

"The King of France did not believe this story, and remarked that the Siamese ambassadors were boasting beyond all reason. The King then commanded to ask them if they had any soldiers skilled in this kind of art along with them in the ship, and could they give him a specimen of their art?

"The ambassador answered, 'The soldiers we have along for use in the vessel are but common soldiers; but we can give your majesty a specimen of their skill.' The King asked, 'What can they do?' The ambassador said, 'I beg your majesty to arrange this company of five hundred soldiers—sharp-shooters—in a position far off and near as you please, to fire at my soldiers, and they will ward off the bullets, and not suffer a single one to touch them.'

"When the King of France heard this proposal, fearing lest his soldiers should kill the Siamese, and thereby destroy the treaty of friendship about to be formed between them, he was unwilling to make the trial. The ambassador then answered: 'Your majesty need not fear in the least. My soldiers really have an art by which they can ward off the bullets, and not suffer one of them to touch them. If it please your majesty, then to-morrow let them prepare a platform here, having an awning of white cloth, and surrounded with flags, and place upon the platform some refreshments and wine; then spread the word, and let all the people of the town come to witness my feat.'

"The King then prepared all these things as was requested. The following day the ambassador requested his magic teacher to select and prepare sixteen persons and clothe them entirely with the panoply of figures (tattooing) for making the person invulnerable,—the teacher and all together seventeen persons. When everything was ready, they came into the presence of the King, and took seats upon the platform. He then addressed the King, 'If it please your majesty, let these five hundred sharp-shooters shoot these seventeen persons seated upon the platform.' The King then commanded his soldiers to fire.

"The French soldiers then fired several rounds, some at a distance and some near, but the powder would not ignite, and their guns made no report. Those seventeen persons, uninjured, partook of the refreshments on the platform without the least fear or confusion. The French soldiers were wonderfully surprised and startled. The magic teacher then said: 'Don't be discouraged; fire again. This time we will allow the guns to go off.' The soldiers then fired another round. Their guns went off, but the bullets fell to the ground, some near where they stood, some a little distance farther off, and some fell near the platform, but not a single man was injured.

"When the King of France saw this, he believed all the Siamese ambassadors had said, and praised their arts very much, remarking he had never seen anything to equal it. He then presented the Siamese soldiers with money and clothes as a reward, and also feasted them bountifully. From this time forward the

A MONASTERY LIBRARY IN THE SHAN COUNTRY.

King believed everything the ambassador said. He did not doubt a single word."

Not only are the histories, but also the theological works of Siam and other Buddhistical kingdoms, filled with similar legends and absurdities. The late King of Siam, whilst he was associated with the priesthood, determined to purify the text of the Pali books. Many of the more childish observances of the modern ritual were pronounced to be without authority, and a vast mass of commentaries and fables were declared to be interpolations and corruptions of pure Buddhism. The present King is doing his utmost to purge the monasteries, which, from laxity in carrying out the rules, and the dislike of reporting acts which would, according to the law, lead to cruel punishments, had in many cases become mere nests of debauchery. Before noticing the present degraded state of Buddhism in Zimmé, I will give the maxims of the priestly orders in Siam, which, according to La Loubère, are as follows :—

" Kill no human being.
Steal not.
Avoid the sins of the flesh.
Boast not of your own sanctity.
Do not break up the ground.
Destroy no tree.
Kill no animal.
Drink no intoxicating beverage.
Eat no rice after mid-day.
Regard not song, dance, or music.
Use no perfumes about your persons.

Neither sit nor sleep in a place higher than that occupied by your superior.

Keep neither gold nor silver.

Speak of nothing but religious matters.

Do nothing but what is religious.

Give no flowers to women.[1]

Take no water from a spot where worms are engendered.

It is a sin not to provide water after nature's necessities.

Do not court secular persons for the sake of alms.

Borrow nothing from secular persons.

Lend nothing on interest, not even a cowrie.[2]

Keep neither lance, nor sword, nor warlike weapon.

Eat not to excess.

Sleep not much.

Sing no gay songs.

Play upon no instrument; avoid sports and games.

Judge not your neighbour; say not, this is a good, and that is a bad man.

Swing not your arms in walking.

Mount no tree.

Bake no bricks and burn no wood.

Wink not in speaking, and look not round in contempt.

Work not for money.

Give no strong medicine to pregnant women.

---

[1] Love is shown by offering flowers, and is repulsed by the refusal to accept them.

[2] A cowrie is a shell: 1,200 of them are worth $3\frac{3}{4}$*d.*

Seek not pleasure by looking upon women.

Make no incisions which bring blood.

Buy not, sell not.

When you eat, make no noise like dogs—chibi, chibi, chiabi, chiabi.

Sleep in no exposed place.

Administer no poisonous medicine.

It is a sin to walk in the streets in a non-contemplative mood.

It is a sin not to shave the head, the eyebrows, and to neglect the nails.

It is a sin to stretch out the feet when sitting.

Keep not the leavings of your meals.

Have not many garments.

It is a sin for a priest to love and caress young priests as if they were women.

It is a sin to appear as austere as a priest of the woods, to seem more strict than other priests, to act differently in public from in private.

To receive alms and to give them to another is a sin.

To speak to a woman in a secret place is a sin.

It is a sin to meddle with royal affairs, except where religion is concerned.

It is a sin to cultivate the ground—to breed ducks, fowls, cows, buffaloes, elephants, horses, pigs, or dogs, as secular people do.

It is a sin to preach in any but the Pali tongue.

It is a sin to think one way and speak another.

To sit on the same mat with a woman is a sin.

To cook rice is a sin.

To eat anything which has not been offered with joined hands is a sin.

To dream of a woman, and to be awakened by the dream, is a sin.

It is a sin to covet another man's goods.

To make water on fire, on the earth, or in water, is a sin.

To speak injuriously of the earth, the wind, of fire, or water, or anything else, is a sin.

It is a sin to mount an elephant or a palanquin.

It is a sin to be clothed in costly garments.

It is a sin to rub the body against any substance.

It is a sin to ornament the ears with flowers.

To wear shoes which hide the toes is a sin.

To plant flowers or trees is sinful.

It is sinful to receive anything from the hand of a woman.

It is a sin not to love everybody alike.

It is a sin to eat anything having life, such as seeds which may germinate.

To cut down or tear away anything which has life is a sin.

It is sinful to make an idol.

It is sinful for the priest not to fill up a ditch which he has dug.

It is a sin to fold the end of the garment, unless there is work to be done.

To eat out of gold or silver vessels is a sin.

It is a sin to sleep after meals, instead of performing religious rites.

TEMPLE OF MOUNT CROM NEAR ANCOR.

Having eaten what is given in alms, to say that it was good or not is a sin.

To exhibit self-glorification, by saying, I am a mandarin's son, or my mother is rich, is sin.

It is a sin to wear red, black, green, or white garments.

It is a sin, in laughing, to raise the voice.

It is a sin, in preaching, to alter the Pali text in order to gratify the hearers.

To employ charms, in order to become invulnerable, is a sin.

To boast of being more learned than another is a sin.

To desire gold or silver, saying, When I leave the convent I will marry and live expensively, is a sin.

It is a sin to mourn for dead relations.

To go out at evening in order to see any one but mother, or sisters, or brothers, and to amuse one's self by talking on the way, is a sin.

To give garments, or gold, or silver, to any but father and mother, brothers or sisters, is sin.

To leave the monastery in order to recover garments, gold, or silver, supposed to be stolen, is sin.

To sit on a carpet of wrought gold or silver which has not been given, but ordered to be made, is a sin.

To sit down without stretching the garment appropriated to sit upon, is a sin.

To walk in the street without having buttoned the proper button, and to enter a boat without unbuttoning the same button, are sins.

To cough or sneeze, in order to win the notice of a group of girls seated, is a sin.

Q

It is a sin not to have the under garment hemmed; and it is sinful to wear over the shoulders a garment in one piece only.

Not to put on the garments at break of day is sinful.

To walk in the streets as if some one were following is a sin.

After washing the feet, to make a noise with them on wood or stone, and then enter the house of a secular, is to commit a sin.

To be cognisant of the influence of numbers[1] is sinful.

It is a sin to make a noise with the feet, or to walk heavily on ascending a staircase.

It is a sin to raise the garment in making water.

It is a sin to pass judgment on other men, or to say this is well, this evil done.

To look fiercely at other people is a sin.

To clean the teeth with certain long pieces of wood, or while speaking to others, is a sin.

To eat and to talk at the same time is a sin.

To eat so that the rice drops while eating is a sin.

If, after eating and washing the mouth, the teeth are picked, and the lips whistled through in the presence of seculars, it is sinful.

To gird the garments below the navel is a sin.

To take the garments of the dead before they are percolated is a sin.

To menace a person with arrest, with the cangue,[2] with blows, or any other punishment, with complaints

[1] Lucky numbers. [2] Wooden collar.

against him to the King or any high personage, in order to excite alarm, is sinful.

To be moving anywhere without thinking of keeping the commandment[1] is sin.

It is a sin to wash the body in a current of water above the spot any older priest is washing in.

It is a sin to forge iron.

It is sinful, in thinking of religious matters, to dwell upon that which is not clearly understood, without consulting another priest who might give an explanation.

Not to be acquainted with the three seasons of the year, and the conferences which belong to each, is sinful.

A priest who knows that another priest owes money, and who enters the temple with the money-owing priest, commits a sin.

A priest in enmity with another priest, and who nevertheless accompanies him to religious conference, sins.

It is a sin to cause alarm to any one.

If a priest arrest any one, knowing he has no money, he sins, if the amount is less than a tical;[2] and if it be more than a tical, the priest must be driven from his religious profession.

A priest who gives medicine[3] to a man not sick commits a sin.

A priest who whistles for his amusement sins.

It is a sin to shout as thieves do.

---

[1] The Buddhist law.

[2] *2s. 6d.*

[3] Love potions, most likely.

The habit of envy is sinful.

To light a fire, or to cover a fire, is a sin.

To eat fruit out of season is sinful.

It is a sin to eat the flesh of man, elephant, horse, serpent, tiger, crocodile, dog, or cat.

To ask alms every day in the same place is a sin.

To make a bandage or cup of gold to receive alms therein is a sin.

A priest sleeping in the same bed as his disciples, or any other persons, commits a sin.

A priest who puts his hand into the cooking-pot sins.

A priest who crushes, fans, and cleans rice, or draws water to cook it, sins.

To serve sin is a sin.

A priest sins who, in eating, slobbers his mouth like a little child.

A priest asking alms, and taking more than he needs for a day's use, sins.

He commits a sin by yielding to nature's necessities in an open place.

If he take wood, or anything, to make fire in a place where an animal is accustomed to rest, he sins.

If he coughs in order to be noticed when he asks alms, he sins.

He sins if, walking in the streets, he covers his head with his robe, or wears a hat, as seculars sometimes do.

He sins if he removes his robes in order that his body may be seen.

If a priest go to sing or to recite near a dead person,

SCENE IN THE GROUNDS OF A MONASTERY.

he sins if he do not reflect upon death, and that everybody must die, and on the instability of mortal things, and the fragility of the life of man.

A priest sins if he eats without crossing his legs.

If he sleeps in a place where others have slept together, he sins.

A priest sins if, when speaking with seculars, he stretches out his legs.

A priest may not wash himself in the twilight or the dark, lest he should unadvisedly kill some insect or other living thing."

The term "monk" would have been a more fitting translation of the Siamese word *phra*[1] than "priest," as a monk, whether cenobite or solitary, abandons the world to save his own soul; and the priest, at the very least, takes some little concern in the spiritual welfare of others, which the above maxims show that the phras are neither required, nor allowed, to do. Buddhism is, in fact, a religion of unthankfulness and utter selfishness; of fear, and hope, without the divinest attribute of religion—love.

[1] In Burmese *pya*.

CHAPTER XIII.

Influence of education upon habits—Woman's superiority in Burmah and Siam—Training girls—A moral people—Bishop Bigandet's opinion of Burmese and Siamese women—Equality of sexes—Rules of the novitiant—Duties—Life in a monastery—Condition of priesthood—Zeal dying—Gross pictures of purgatory—The Zimmé military—Visit from a chao—The tsobua and his wife—A dominant queen—Morganatic marriages—A moral police—The chao hona—American exiles—A Cingalese "woondouk" in his cups—A married man—Number twenty-three.

ALTHOUGH the poongyees, as I have shown in the preceding chapter, are not ardent in attending after the spiritual welfare of their flocks, yet they have been from time immemorial the sole educators of the male portion of the people. This being the case, and as the boys at the early age of eight or nine are put under the charge of the poongyees, it is important, when judging of the habits and morals of the people, to consider what influence the example and training of their schoolmasters has had upon them. It is noticeable even in Burmah, where the monks are much more strict in their livelihood and in the observance of their rules than in Zimmé, that the women are far more industrious and virtuous than the men; and I think this chiefly arises from the difference of the schools in which they are educated.

The girls are kept at home under the immediate supervision of their mothers, who teach them to be industrious; and train them, from their infancy, in the acquirement of common sense, which has justly been called the most uncommon sense of all. Nearly before they have left the breast, they seem to become far-sighted little women of the world. Walk through any village or town, and you will see damsels squatted on the floor of the verandah with diminutive, or sometimes large, stalls in front of them, covered with vegetables, fruit, betel-nut, cigars, and other articles. However numerous they may be, the price of everything is known to them; and such is their idea of probity, that pilfering is quite unknown amongst them. They are entirely trusted by their parents from their earliest years; even when they blossom into young women, *chaperons* are never a necessity; yet immorality is far less customary amongst them, I am led to believe, than in any country in Europe.

Bishop Bigandet, the Roman Catholic Bishop in Burmah, who has lived amongst the natives for forty years, and is famed for his learning and just appreciation of the people, fully testifies to the high position that women hold. He says: "In Burmah and Siam the doctrines of Buddhism have produced a striking, and to the lover of true civilization a most interesting, result; viz. the almost complete equality of the condition of the women with that of the men. In these countries, women are not so universally confined in the interior of their houses, without the remotest chance of ever appearing in public. They are seen circulating freely in the streets; they preside at the *comptoir*, and hold an almost exclusive possession of the bazaars. Their social position is more elevated, in every respect, than that of the persons of their sex in the regions where Buddhism is not the predominating creed. They may be said to be men's companions, and not their slaves. They are active, industrious, and, by their labours and exertions, contribute their full share towards the maintenance of the family. The marital rights are fully acknowledged by a respectful behaviour towards their lords. In spite of all that has been said by superficial observers, I feel convinced that manners are less corrupted in those countries where women enjoy liberty than in those where they are buried alive by a despotic custom in the grave of an opprobrious slavery." I am of opinion that the Bishop has, perhaps, given Buddhism more credit in the matter than it really deserves, for the same equality of the sexes prevails amongst the Indo-Chinese races that have not been converted to Buddhism; besides which, the equality of the sexes prevailed long before Buddhism took any hold upon the country.

When the boys are about twelve, they are clothed in the yellow robe of novitiants, and are supposed to obey, not only the five commandments which are obligatory upon all Buddhists—viz. not to take life, not to steal, to avoid adultery and fornication, to tell the truth, to avoid intoxicating liquors—but

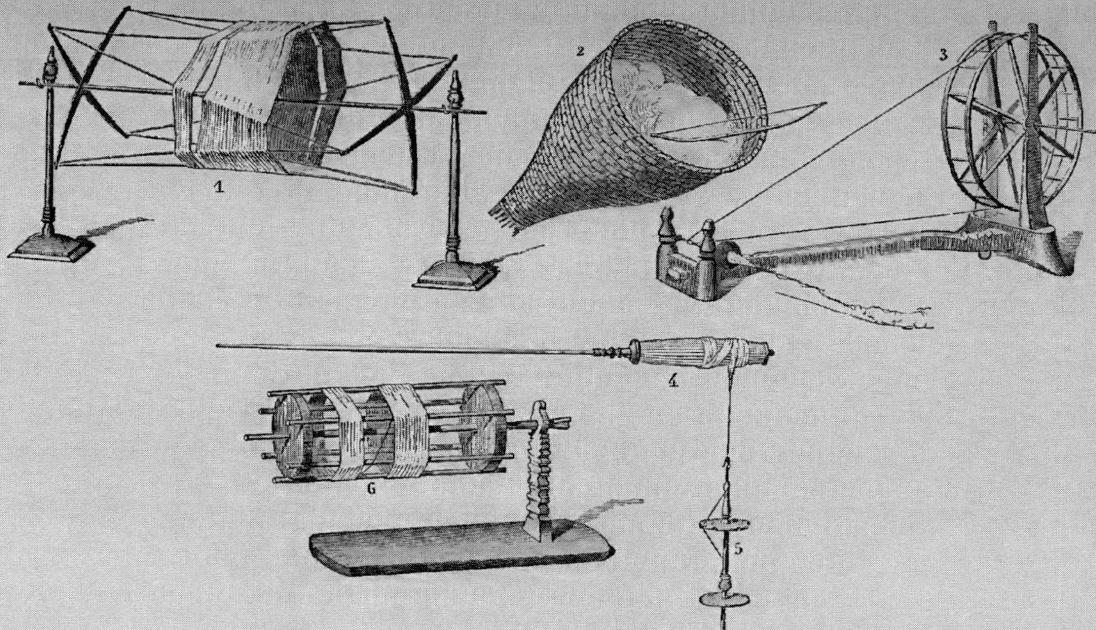

IMPLEMENTS USED BY SHAN WOMEN FOR COTTON AND SILK.

1. Divider for cotton. 2. Basket and bow for carding cotton. 3. Wheel to spin cotton. 4, 5, 6. Divider and spinner for silk.

the following five in addition: not to eat after midday, not to sing, dance, or play on any musical instrument, not to colour the face, not to sit or lie down on an elevated place not proper for them, and not to touch or handle gold or silver. Their duties are to minister to the wants of the poongyees of the monastery, to bring and place before them, at fixed times, the usual supply of water, their betel-boxes, and their daily food, and to attend them when they leave the kyoung on some pious errand. The remainder of their time, when not at their lessons, may be passed in contemplation, rest, or in any other seemly manner. The education in a kyoung, even if carried out in the full spirit of the precepts, is not invigorating either to mind or body, and many years passed in such seminaries must tend to develop a taste for apathy and indolence. All strict Buddhists hold that no male human being who has not been a probationer can count this existence as human in his numerous transmigrations, therefore all boys have to become novitiants, and the habits thus acquired account, I believe, for their being so much more lazy and apathetic than the women are. From my experience in Zimmé, and from what I learned from the missionaries, whatever may be the preaching of the monks, their practice is about as bad as it could be, and must tend to demoralize their pupils, and therefore in time the whole people of the country.

We found, on visiting the kyoungs, that, although

their code, for very good reasons, considers it a deadly sin to permit a woman to cross the threshold, women were not only frequenters of the kyoungs, but in cases were actually living there. The young monks, and even the novices, were ogling women and maidens, and joking freely, amidst an interchange of amorous glances which were obvious to every chance passer-by. Notwithstanding their laws forbidding them to speak to a woman except in public, to sit on the same mat with one, to endeavour to attract their attention, to receive anything from their hand, the monks do all these things, and many more, without the slightest shame or hesitation. Bishop Pallegoix, who for many years resided in Siam, expressed his disgust at the conduct of the depraved Buddhist monks, and declared that he had never seen in any other monastery he had visited what he saw at the Prabat monastery, where the kitchen was under the care of a score of young girls. With such an unpardonable state of immorality pervading the kyoungs, it is not wonderful to find all religious zeal dying out amongst the people, the temples and pagodas, or wats, decaying, and no new kyoungs being erected—indeed, I have reason to believe that none have been built since the Burmese left the country. Hardly any of them are properly maintained. Many of the brick pagodas are the work of "Jerry" builders; the bell-shaped building is run up with a good facing, whilst the inside is merely clay "and nothing more." As one example of this, I may state that the most famous one in Zimmé has succumbed; the outer face has slipped, and left the earthen inside visible, where it is not covered with jungle growth. In Zimmé the influence of the monks over the people is fast dying away into a mere traditional respect. The learning of most of the monks may be summed up in their knowledge of the three "R's." Their breviaries, though inscribed in the Laos tongue, are full of Pali interpolations, which they do not understand, though they repeat them with an amusingly devout air. Until there is a police in Zimmé for the correction of the monks similar to that in Bangkok, the poongyees will grow from bad to worse. In Bangkok, according to Sir John Bowring, the *phras*, or poongyees, are subjected to a police, which is under the command of one of the princes. These are authorized to bring them up for judgment. On the proof of their delinquencies they are unfrocked, flogged with rattans, or condemned to prison, or other penalties, according to the gravity of their offence. Earlier in the narrative I have mentioned that the priests are good handicraftsmen, but the specimens we saw in the kyoungs at Zimmé were very poor. The pictures on the walls and pillars are bad imitations of subjects borrowed from the Chinese. Their highest idea of art seems to lie in a thick covering of gold. Alongside such decoration it is no uncommon thing to find the walls and thatched roof in decay.

Sometimes coloured glass is used in the windows, but the effect is coarse and out of keeping with the sacred buildings, except when the sun is shining through the panes. The frescoes with which they disgrace the walls are the veriest daubs, gross in excess and grotesque at the same time, being delineations of the cardinal sins and their appropriate punishment in another world. I need hardly say that the sins of the flesh are selected before those that would be less suggestive to a sensuous mind.

However they may have been in an inward and spiritual sense, outwardly the military were much worse in appearance than the Church militant. Just opposite our *cottage orné* there stood a low, open bamboo shed, thatched in the usual style of the country, and about as miserable a den as could well be imagined under the name of a barrack. This was the guard-house, the house of our guard of honour. It contained two companies, or detachments, of the local Zimmé force, the total strength being seemingly about sixty men. They were, without exception, the drollest and most fantastic-looking warriors I ever set eyes on. A French regiment of light infantry had apparently supplied most of them with its cast-off clothing, which had since been worn into the resemblance of the garments of a scare-crow. The officers and sergeants, however, compensated for the poor appearance of the rank and file. Their uniforms were bedizened with tawdry gold lace, stitched on apparently at whatever places suggested themselves to the individual fancy of the wearer. Their swords were of European pattern, but so hung as if for the special purpose of tripping up their wearers. The most curious surprise was to hear the words of command given in Indian-English. "Who com dar?" had even taken possession of Zimmé. It was very amusing to watch them receiving the

CAVE TEMPLES NEAR LUANG PRABANG, ON THE MÉKONG.

chaos, or officials, who came to visit us, and it was difficult to restrain our laughter, which, had we given way to it, would have caused them grave offence. The formula never varied. It was a case of "guard, turn out," and out they turned higgledy-piggledy, one on the top of the other, this fellow in full war-paint, that one in a dish-clout, another one in half uniform and half native garb; such a comical guard as would make the fortune of a Christmas pantomime, could it only be reproduced faithfully on the stage. The chao arrived, each warrior saluted as pleased him best, and at the time which suited him, the only fixed rule—rather a curious one—being that no two men should do reverence at the same time or in the same manner. After the salutes had been performed, came the ordeal of shaking hands with ourselves, and we used to pity greatly the poor chao, who, after receiving the sixty separate salutes, had to bestow on each member of our mission a more or less pretentiously cordial grip. Watching him, we could fully understand how weary royal personages must be of public receptions. When on a formal visit, like that our visitor had just undergone, the chaos are carried about on a seat, resting on a wooden frame which is suspended from two poles, fixed crosswise and borne by coolies. The seat itself is a gorgeous affair, soft, and covered with rich velvet trappings, the amount of gold lace in the decoration denoting the rank and wealth of the occupant.

Naturally we had a good deal to do with the tsobua, or head chief, of Zimmé, as our mission was principally official. At our very first visit, we discovered that there was one still greater than the great man himself,—to wit, his wife, of whom more by-and-by. A very plain and unostentatious man is the potentate in question; and his sixty-two years, or so, gave him a certain gravity of demeanour becoming to his rank. On formal occasions he donned a white jacket and a silk sarong, or waist-cloth, worn Siamese fashion; these, together with embroidered slippers of handsome Zimmé work, completed his princely costume. When subsequently meeting him *en famille*, he discarded his jacket altogether, but not without an apology for the exceedingly airy nature of his garb. The people gave him the character his features convey, of being a simple and good old gentleman, weak of will, but a just ruler. Speedily we discovered that this weakness was not so much inherent as it was due to the dominating nature of his wife, who, nevertheless, usually employed her very real power for the benefit of their subjects.

She was evidently a perfect lady, quiet and self-possessed, received us with a gracious and dignified manner, and offered us the usual refreshment of tea, as though she had been accustomed to European society all her life. There was neither *gaucherie* on the one hand, nor effrontery or undue familiarity on the other, in the manner she adopted when conversing at any time with the various members of our party. In person she was delicate-looking, by no means devoid of good looks, and perhaps from thirty-six to forty years of age. Firm and intelligent, and possessed of excellent business capacity, yet she was quite illiterate,—neither she nor her husband could read or write. According to common report, on one point in particular she was firm, and, according to Zimmé ideas, severe. Before his marriage with her, the chief had indulged himself, after the manner of his kind, with several left-handed wives; but, no sooner was the royal knot tied, than, hey! presto! they all vanished like a rainbow, and she became Lady Paramount as well as Lady Regnant. I will not say that the green-eyed monster troubled her much—she was too powerful for that—but wisely she took precautions that her matrimonial peace should not be disturbed. When the little wives were bundled off, one and all, about their business, the chief was sent to a kyoung, or monastery, for a time, to cleanse him from former iniquities. The purification accomplished, he was forced, whether he would or not, into the blameless paths of domestic bliss, cleaving only unto her. The prospect did not please him, but he accepted the inevitable, and is probably the most praiseworthy husband in the whole country. Rumour has it, however—Rumour that would defame a saint—that his access of virtue is not from choice, but from that stern tyrant necessity. Lady Rumour certainly in this case had some slight grounds to go upon, as we could not help noticing that not one of the thirty female slaves in the household was young, or even passably good-looking. Not one of these unprepossessing ladies was permitted on any pretence to wait on their master alone, nor even to prepare his betel-nut in a leaf when the mistress was present; the choice *morceau* was invariably manipulated by her own delicate fingers, and by no other hands would she allow him to receive it. The people laugh immoderately when they talk over these precautions, and say that even the fifteen or twenty followers who accompany him in all his rounds are in his wife's pay, and are a sort of moral police.

The next in rank to the tsobua is the chao hona, a younger brother of the ruler, who is said to be of a very different disposition. He has a bad, cruel face, and his reputation is quite on a par with his appearance. He is fond of ostentation and the show of power, and often has hundreds of retainers attending on him. The few attendants and small state of the tsobua are no criterion as to that of the smallest chaos, who generally are masters of about a thousand slaves and serfs.

Shortly after our first interview with the missionaries, who seemed to think their generous hospitality more than repaid by having the opportunity of talking to Anglo-Saxon cousins after so many years of exile, we made the acquaintance of one of the most eccentric-looking individuals it has ever been my lot to encounter. Imagine a short, stout, wheezy old fellow, of about sixty, or perhaps older, with a nose so broken and flattened on one cheek, that any good looks he may once have possessed were completely destroyed. He was dressed in a Siamese jacket and sarong, and wore on his pate a cap of fur, shaped like a Scotch bonnet of the Balmoral pattern, ornamented with a

HILL WOMAN, SOUTHERN FRONTIER OF YUNNAN.

silver badge,—such a strange costume. He was a dignitary, and was possessed of the Burmese title of Woondouk. We were informed that he was a Cingalese who had come many years ago to Siam. Not knowing better, we had taken him for a half-breed Portuguese cook, of the type common in the Bombay Presidency of India; but this opinion, of course, went no farther than ourselves. He proved to be a most amusing old man, and expounded his views on Siam, the Shan States, and every place he had visited, as well as on affairs in general, with such frankness and vigour as to be eminently refreshing after the vapid languor we had been accustomed to expect in our intercourse with the officials. *In vino veritas*,—after imbibing I won't say how many glasses, his frankness reached a remarkable stage, and his vigour became rather too unpleasantly demonstrative. He had picked up a few words of English when attached on some occasion to a Siamese mission sent to England; but in what capacity he acted, even brandy could not get him beyond the *non mi recordo* stage. My own suspicion, and that of my companions, was that at that time he had not attained to higher rank than that of deputy or assistant in the culinary department.

One of his favourite remarks was that in Siam there were "too much plenty men; before they do nothing—all gentlemen, no coolies. In Bangkok they have now to make coolie a little." This we understood to mean that whereas, in his palmy days, the Siamese were lazier than they are even now, at present they find it necessary to do at least a little work. In another respect, besides his humour, he would have delighted the soul of "Artemus Ward," for he was in truth one of the "most married" men I ever met. Already he rejoiced in no less than twenty-two lawful wives; but so far from being satiated with the joys of matrimony, he coolly told us one day that he was going to be married to a twenty-third within a few days. It was sad to think of a charming girl—many of the Zimmé women are very charming—being linked for life to such an old reprobate. The news solved for us one mystery, which had puzzled us exceedingly: we now knew why so many of the women looked so hopelessly depressed and sorrowful,—a small wonder, if they have incurred, or even if they have a chance of incurring, the dreadful fate of playing number twenty-three to an effete old scamp like our notable woondouk.

CHAPTER XIV.

The Siamese commissioner—The power of Siam—Phra Yahna Rangsee—A well of information—The confidence trick—Description of chiefs and people—Light taxation—Elephants of chiefs—Value of slaves—System of slavery—*Corvée* and Military service—The King of Siam extirpating feudalism—Regeneration of Siam—A patriotic king and minister—Progress under the present King—An Augean stable—The long purse wins the day—Law and justice—Trials—Ordeal by water—Contented people.

THE Siamese Commissioner in Zimmé was a shrewd, astute man, in spite of his appearance. His face appeared to be shrivelled up, and his little blinking eyes were furtive, and invited no confidence. He assured every one that he cared nothing for the things of this world—a statement the reiteration of which is apt to rouse suspicion, and create the idea, "Methinks he doth protest too much," which we found true. He was the accredited Resident and representative of the King of Siam, and is undoubtedly powerful in Zimmé, although the officials in Bangkok were rather reticent on the matter. Even in McLeod's time, in 1836, the power of Siam was paramount; he found that the tsobua of Zimmé could do nothing without the King's permission, and at length was told by a man, whom he avoids mentioning, "Why do you waste so much breath on them here about the roads?

they have it not in their power to comply with your request. Go to Bangkok and obtain permission, and stick the order up here; then let them refuse if they dare."

The most intelligent man in Zimmé, and assuredly the best educated, was Phra Yahna Rangsee, a Peguan poongyee who had come from Maulmain. After being ten years a monk, he unfrocked himself, and proceeded to Bangkok, where he learned Siamese, and subsequently went up to Zimmé, where he acts as interpreter and chief writer to the Resident. We found that he could speak, read, and write Burmese, Siamese, and the dialect of Zimmé; was acquainted with Pali, but not to such an extent as with the other languages. He was certainly much better informed about whatever concerned the Shan country than any other official in the place, and was ready and manifestly willing to impart his information, which had been acquired with much acumen and evident interest in the subject. Most of his colleagues were dull and unthinking, and, perhaps owing to their ignorance, dogged and reticent; but this man, finding a good field for talent in Zimmé, had nourished his ambition, roused his faculties, accumulated whatever information might be useful, and was rapidly displaying a proof that knowledge, if properly digested and used, is, indeed, a real power. If I am not mistaken, this Peguan is certain to attain to eminence, and has a career of considerable importance before him. Siamese officials, as a rule, are the very opposite of Phra Yahna Rangsee; their one diplomatic receipt is,

GRAVES OF THE KHMER-DOM OR KUIS IN THE FOREST AT AMNAT.

"Delay, delay, delay again and again; and, if pressed, ask, as a last resource, for the advice of the person who is pressing you; then say that you must refer it to headquarters; and thus keep the ball rolling, until he, perhaps, gives it up, in despair of ever getting to the bottom of your diplomacy." This "confidence trick" of asking for the advice of the person who wishes action to be taken, until it has occurred too often, flatters the person who is urging them to act, staves him off for the time being, and gives them another chance, in the Micawber line, of "something turning up."

The chaos, or chiefs, are generally very fine-looking men, tall and fair, with good noses, and light eyes. The other men are tall, stout, hardy, and active. The women are also tall, and remarkably well-proportioned, very fair, and decidedly a handsome race. Their mouths are, however, disfigured with betel, and many are subject to goitre. The children are particularly fair, frequently having light eyes, and hair slightly tinged with red. It is not unlikely that the white women noticed by travellers, more than a thousand years ago, amongst the black people of Cambodia were Shan or Karen captives, both of these people being remarkably fair for Easterns. In Zimmé the Shans are not oppressed with heavy taxation, like their brothers in parts of Siam, no compensation being levied in lieu of *corvée* labour. The taxes, according to McLeod, were three and a half baskets of paddy for each buffalo and plough in use; one viss (3·65 lbs.) of cotton for each basket sown; two viss of tobacco for every thousand plants; two viss of safflower for the same number of plants; two hundred and eighty-eight nuts of betel for each plantation, no matter whether large or small; one viss of chillies per garden; twenty viss of salt per boat-load from Bangkok, and it mostly comes from the capital. Any person who sells an elephant after catching it gives thirty per cent. of what he has received to his immediate chief; but should he be very successful, and catch ten or more, his master, after taking his share, presents one to the tsobua, and one to the chao hona. The principal emoluments of the chaos, or chiefs, arise from the produce of their own fields, the trade they carry on, and the presents they receive. Dr. Richardson, when at Lagon, found that there were no taxes levied on specific articles; but every cultivator, without exception, paid into the Government treasury, at the close of the harvest, a quantity of grain equal to that he had sown. Besides the above, each household paid half a tical of coarse silver (1*s.* 3*d.*) on account of sacrifices to the nats, or protecting spirits of the country. These sacrifices are another name for public feasts, as the buffaloes, pigs, and poultry, together with the spirits, which are provided, are consumed by the people.

As in Upper Burmah, the people place themselves under the protection of some chief, and become his followers. They gladly work for him, and are often sent on trading excursions, receiving occasionally a portion of the profits. In the Siamese-Shan states the chiefs, besides slaves and serfs, are possessed of numerous elephants. The tsobua, at the time of our visit, owned over a hundred and fifty; the kyoukoopone, or sister-in-law of the tsobua, one hundred and thirty-five; the chao hona, a hundred; and every chao, from five to twenty.

Slaves are bought in Zimmé as elsewhere in Indo-China, the average price for a woman, provided she is under forty-five years of age, being about £6¼; while that of a man, the inferior animal, is about £4. The tsobua is said to possess fifteen hundred; the chao hona, one thousand; the kyoukoopone, eight hundred; and the other chaos from seventy to a hundred each, according to their wealth. The puniahs, or minor officials, have generally from fifteen to twenty apiece. You hear of people selling themselves for as small a debt as twenty rupees, or about thirty-six shillings. Any relentless creditor can enforce the sale of his debtors at their full market value. Even gambling debts are so discharged. In the state of Zimmé in case an owner is well off, or is generously disposed, he sometimes allows some of his slaves to settle in an outlying district to work for themselves; but they can always be claimed, unless they are of the classes which are allowed to purchase their freedom, and are able to settle their debt and claim their privilege of doing so. Captives taken in war, and their male offspring, as I have shown already, cannot purchase their freedom. From what we learnt there is little doubt that the sparsity of the hill-tribes in the hills neighbouring Zimmé has been chiefly caused by their having been, in the olden time, systematically

S

hunted like wild cattle, to supply the slave-market; but the King of Siam has set his face against the practice, and has entirely put a stop to it. Serfs, of course, have the same privilege as bondslaves of changing masters, but are bound to give notice of their intention; unless they can get a new lord more powerful than their old one, their instinct usually persuades them to remain. But of course the ability to leave whenever they choose prevents undue hardships being imposed upon them. The effect of this serfdom—or clanship, as perhaps it might be more properly called—and slavery is not pleasant to contemplate; it is a case of "the big fleas and the little fleas" from the top to the bottom. The peasant crouches before the village headman, or puniah, the latter before a petty official, the petty official before a chao; whilst the chao himself, swagger and flaunt as he may before his inferiors, is humble and subservient to the tsobua and head chiefs. Everybody is in fact a serf, if he is not a slave, to some one else. Under such a system forced labour is easily administered, and all public works are carried out by its means. All transports, including an adequate supply of men and elephants when officials are travelling, are forced. Food and forage has to be sent in abundantly and gratuitously. Military service is compulsory when required. In fact, no matter what is wanted for the public service, or for the private comfort of the officials, from an elephant down to a piece of firewood, from a thousand men down to a boy to drive a pony, or a child to keep the flies off, it has to be supplied at the behest of the nearest headman, or of a servant, if no puniah happens to be crouching at the officials' feet.

It is the same in Upper Burmah, and was the same in British Burmah before we enfranchised the people by taking their country under our government. The King of Siam is doing what he can to put a stop to this oppression, but feudalism is always more or less dangerous to deal with. The smaller chiefs are gradually being deprived of their power, and replaced by paid officials sent direct from the court of Siam; and all the provinces, with the exception of Zimmé and Luang Prabang, are now under the direct government of officers deputed by the King. Even in M. Mouhot's time the exactions of officers and chiefs on circuit had been restricted by order of the King; but until the salaries of the governors and other potentates are raised, this blot upon the administration of the country will not be erased. At present the remuneration of the officials is so small that not only is there flagrant bribery in courts of justice, but, according to the French, extensive peculation, particularly of money received for the remission of *corvée* labour (this latter does not apply to Zimmé), was practised as late as 1867, in districts at a distance from headquarters, and was said to be winked at, particularly in the provinces in the valley of the Mékong, by high officials whose duty it was to supervise the accounts.

The King of Siam has set his heart upon the regeneration and advancement of his kingdom; and, in judging what he has already done, it should be remembered that he has to struggle against the power of feudalism, and that his country is but now recovering from the disastrous effects of two thousand years of almost constant internecine warfare. His predecessor, who, according to Sir John Bowring and the evidence of subsequent events, had for his prime minister the noblest and most enlightened patriot the Oriental world has ever seen, abolished the monopolies which were impoverishing his people, greatly reduced the burden of their taxation, did all he could to improve the administration of law and justice, took a firm grip of feudalism, and undermined the power of the nobles by placing his own officials as governors of the provinces, and by removing all obstacles encouraged the healthy flow of commerce throughout his dominions. He had his children educated by Europeans, insured freedom of worship in his kingdom, and proved himself to be a most friendly neighbour to us throughout his reign.

The present King is determined to advance even more rapidly in the path of civilization and progress than his father did. During his travels he has visited British Burmah and India, and taken intelligent notice of all that was tending to the advancement and happiness of our people. On his return he has had his capital connected by telegraph with our provinces and the French possessions, carried out schemes of drainage in the delta of the Ménam, so that rich but inundated country might be brought under cultivation; improved his communications by

THE LATE KING AND QUEEN OF SIAM.

the construction of canals, whereby produce could be brought to the markets and sold at a price that would remunerate the cultivators; placed Europeans in charge of his customs, ports, mines, architecture, schools, navy, and telegraphs, and is even now developing a system of post by which all parts of the kingdom will be developed and benefited. It is a long cry from Bangkok to Zimmé; thus, notwithstanding the presence of a Siamese Resident, a good deal of dirt still remains in the Augean stables. Might is still Right in this part of the kingdom. Justice is a mere mockery in some of the inferior courts, and the heaviest purse gains the day. The puniahs, or judges, are often the *attachés* of the chiefs, and, not being salaried, the presents they receive and the fines they levy are their only emoluments. Visiting at Zimmé a so-called judge one day, and asking him for information, he laughed cynically, and said with evident frankness, "The judge, they say, should be, like a pair of scales, evenly balanced; it is wonderful how the scale goes down on that side into which some gold is dropped." Later and closer observation assured me of the absolute exactness of the intimation; bribery was the order of the day, and no concealment was affected in the matter.

When a man wishes to take proceedings against another, he reports his intention in writing to two judges, who fix the day for the trial. The plaint is made in writing, the defence only verbally. Both parties to the suit commence operations by making a "present" of a hundred betel-nuts, or so, to the court official who has summoned the witnesses to appear. Each of the latter is supposed to have £1½ for his trouble, but in reality most of it is retained by the court, and in all cases the loser is eventually mulcted of the whole cost.

Previous to the commencement of the suit, the plaintiff has to pay the amount he is suing for into court; and if the suit is found to be groundless, this should be handed to the defendant. I need not say that most of this is pocketed by the officials. If the defendant loses, he has to pay double the amount of the debt, one-half of which is the perquisite of the judges. If he makes no defence, the debt has to be paid, with the addition of ten per cent. as a court fee. If there are no other assets, he is sold, and his wife and children, or as many of them as will cover the debt and the perquisites. However the case goes, the court generally handles most of the plunder. Justice may be said to be a very paying commodity in this part of the country, a remark which I have often heard. Offences against morality are closely watched by the law, not for the sake of morality to be sure, but because all concerned have to pay heavily to the court for their peccadilloes. Such are, in any case, fettered and chained; and if there be no funds forthcoming to satisfy the officials, they have to become bond-slaves for the amount. Naturally, it is much to the advantage of the administrators of the law to gain a conviction; and as, when thefts are proved, three times the value of the article stolen is decreed to the owner, a good part of which cleaves to the

A COTTAGE IN THE SHAN COUNTRY.

hands of the judge, the accused are sometimes beaten until they confess, which, of course, often leads to the conviction of perfectly innocent people. At Zimmé important trials are held before a judge sent specially from Bangkok. In every case there is an appeal, first of all to the head judges at Zimmé, secondly from them to the tsobua, and from the tsobua to ordeal by water. This last appeal is not often resorted to; but we heard, during our stay, of one case in which a man failed in this ordeal, and he and his family had to become slaves. One of the most iniquitous rules of their law is that the fines for assaults, abuses, etc., vary according to the rank of the party complaining.

In spite of slavery, serfdom, and injustice, it cannot be said that the people of Zimmé are unhappy or of a discontented temperament. The slavery, as I have before mentioned, is of a mild character, and the forced labour is very unlike that in Spanish and Dutch colonies. There is no cruelty or brutal nigger-driving in the Laos *corvée* system. The whole country would flare up in rebellion if such were attempted, besides which the chaos are naturally clement in their dispositions, and public opinion has some power in Zimmé as elsewhere.

CHAPTER XV.

Tyranny in Burmah—Character of Shans—Weapons—Warfare—Rewards for killing tigers—Monkeys with tigers and crocodiles—Chasing deer—Killing a rhinoceros—Buffaloes our foes—Pocketing the French flag—The breeding-ground of our cattle—Cattle disease in Burmah—Difficulties of travel—Rivers unbridged, and without ferries—Pestilence and heat—Fate of Dr. Richardson's party—A quack and his medicines—Causes of disease—Various cures—Burial and burning—Theatres—Child actors and actresses—Plays—Marriages—Go-betweens—Girls in hiding—Enforced matrimony—Divorces—Monopoly of spirits—Gambling-houses—Opium—Children.

THE people of Zimmé are very well off in comparison with the peasantry of Upper Burmah, who dare not display the slightest show of ease or comfort, for fear of drawing upon themselves further exactions; they are truly sucked dry by the vampires of officials. The tyranny they suffer from is such as has driven one-third of the population to take refuge in our country. Emigration is made as difficult as possible for them, and no women or children are allowed to cross the border without permission; these have therefore to be smuggled along by-paths in the jungle; for if left behind, and the man were to settle in our provinces, his wife and family would be subjected to torture, and imprisoned as hostages for his return. Without such precautions, the King of Burmah

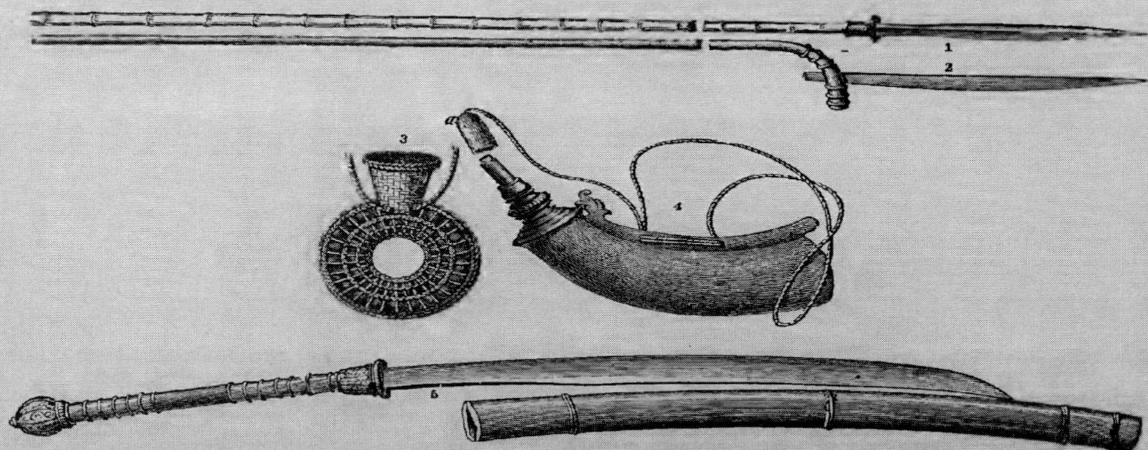

1, 2. Shan lances used in the chase. 3. Bamboo holder for bullets. 4. A powder-horn and measure. 5. A Shan dha, or sword, with scabbard.

would soon have only his own officials to rule over. The Yun, or Zimmé, Shans are by no means a quarrelsome race, but are subject to sudden outbursts of passion, if they think they are ill-used; and can give an excellent account of their enemies. They are more hardy than either the Siamese or Burmese, and are more manly in their bearing. In addition to a sturdy staff, not unlike the *lattee* of India, they habitually carry a *dha*, or short heavy sabre, and know how to use it, either in cutting their way through the jungle, or in self-defence. When in dangerous districts, or anywhere where danger from man or beast may be expected, they carry, in addition to these, a flint-lock musket or a spear.

They are considered to be adepts at lying in ambuscades and at night-attacks—are quick of sight and hearing, and creep through the forest in a surprisingly quiet way; their constant life in the woods gives them this advantage. McLeod says that all Shan attacks on their neighbours' villages have been made at night. They never wait to make a regular attack, or fight by day; if they fail in their attempt, they retreat, and watch for a more favourable opportunity. They are not so light-hearted as the Burmese, but neither are they so braggart as those imitators of the Gascons. Somehow or other, on seeing the two races together, one cannot help thinking that the quiet, self-possessed Shan has more real grit and manliness than the Burman.

Although the forests are said to be full of game, yet we saw little as we went along our beaten track; but tigers are so numerous in certain parts that huts have to be built in the trees as a protection from them. In Siam rewards are offered for killing them; a slave receives his liberty, a free man is exempted from military service, and a soldier is raised a grade in the service who kills one. McLeod, in his journal, frequently mentions their depredations; one party of Chinese he met had just lost two men and four ponies by their raids; and his party were constantly kept on the alert by their neighbourhood, and at one time they saw three of the beasts moving about. In north Siam the natives generally say that the chattering of monkeys indicates the likelihood of a tiger being in the vicinity; their fright is not at all unnatural, as tigers are as fond of them as the carpenter was of the oysters he so deeply sympathised with. The plan followed by these tigers is curious. When they see the monkeys sporting on the branches, they crawl through the grass to the tree, give it a sudden blow with the shoulder, as children do to get apples or nuts, and the poor creatures, which the blow shakes down, are devoured forthwith — so report says. Monkeys are not timid with all their enemies; for instance, M. Mouhot, when writing of the crocodiles in the Ménam, says: "It is amusing to see the manner in which these creatures catch the apes, which sometimes take a fancy to play with them. Close to the bank lies the crocodile, his body in the water, and only his capacious mouth above the surface, ready to seize anything that may come within reach. A troop of apes catch sight of him, seem to consult together, approach little by little, and commence their frolics, by turns actors and spectators. One of the most active, or most impudent, jumps from branch to branch till within a respectful distance of the crocodile, when, hanging by the claw, and with the dexterity peculiar to these animals, he advances and retires, now giving his enemy a blow with his paw, at another time only pretending to do so. The other apes, enjoying the fun, evidently wish to take part in it; but the other branches being too high, they form a sort of chain by laying hold of each other's paws, and thus swing backwards and forwards, while any one of them who comes within reach of the crocodile torments him to the best of his ability. Sometimes the terrible jaws suddenly close, but not upon the audacious ape, who just escapes; then there are cries of exultation from the tormentors, who gambol about joyfully. Occasionally, however, the claw is entrapped, and the victim dragged with the rapidity of lightning beneath the water, when the whole troop disperse, groaning and shrieking. The misadventure does not, however, prevent their recommencing the game a few days afterwards." Of course monkeys are only a *bonne bouche* to the tigers; their real food consists of deer, ponies, and wild cattle, all of which are very numerous in certain localities, particularly the deer called gyee, and the zat, or sambhur. Pheasants, partridges, jungle fowl, and pig were the principal game that we came across.

Deer are chased with spears and nets, the latter being spread across their paths, down which they are

T

driven by the beaters. Often in Burmah a hunt is carried on by torchlight, the inquisitive deer coming so close to the torches as to be easily cut down with their dhas by the hunters. At other times they are hunted down by dogs, which are seemingly a cross between a stag-hound and a pariah dog. These dogs are of great value, as much as £10 being sometimes given for them, and they are now very scarce. Elephants and rhinoceroses are numerous in the wilder parts of the country, and the natives are very bold in their attacks upon them. Mouhot, when passing along the hills that separate the Mékong from the Ménam, was invited to be present at a rhinoceros hunt, and thus describes it: "Our party consisted of eight, including myself. I and my servants were armed with guns, and at the end of mine was a sharp bayonet. The Laotians (Laos Shans) had bamboos with iron blades something between a bayonet and a poignard. The weapon of the chief was the horn of a sword-fish, long, sharp, strong, and supple, and not likely to break.

"Thus armed, we set off into the thickest part of the forest, with all the windings of which our leader was well acquainted, and could tell with tolerable certainty where we should find our expected prey. After penetrating nearly two miles into the forest, we suddenly heard the crackling of branches and rustling of the dry leaves. The chief went on in advance, signing to us to keep a little way behind, but to have our arms in readiness. Soon our leader uttered a shrill cry, as a token that the animal was near; he

SHAN METHOD OF HUNTING DEER.

then commenced striking against each other two bamboo canes, and the men set up wild yells to provoke the animal to quit his retreat.

"A few minutes only elapsed before he rushed towards us, furious at having been disturbed. He was a rhinoceros of the largest size, and opened a most enormous mouth. Without any sign of fear, but, on the contrary, of great exultation, as though sure of his prey, the intrepid hunter advanced, lance in hand, and then stood still, waiting for the creature's assault. I must say I trembled for him, and loaded my gun with two balls; but when the rhinoceros came within reach, and opened his immense jaws to seize his enemy, the hunter thrust the lance into him to a depth of some feet, and calmly retired to where we were posted.

"The animal uttered fearful cries, and rolled over on his back in dreadful convulsions, while all the men shouted with delight. In a few minutes more we drew nearer to him; he was vomiting pools of blood. I shook the chief's hand in testimony of my satisfaction at his courage and skill. He told me that to myself was reserved the honour of finishing the animal, which I did by piercing his throat with my bayonet, and he almost immediately yielded up his last sigh."

It may seem strange to those who have not been in Burmah or the Shan country that buffaloes are more hostile to Europeans than any other animal; such is, nevertheless, the case. They are fine, large animals, of an exceedingly suspicious disposition, gentle and obedient to those they know, but violent and dangerous to strangers. Europeans seem to be their pet aversion; and it is curious to see, as one sometimes does, a stalwart Englishman protected from a buffalo by a little Burman lad of ten or twelve, who quietly leads away the startled animal, which, but for his appearance on the scene, would have charged and possibly killed the unoffending but detestable white man. Such accidents have occurred in Burmah. Even the French, as they proceeded through the country, had to doff their flag to these ferocious natives, who will not respect a treaty, no matter how much "protection" it has in it. Coming across a herd of buffaloes, M. de Carné relates how, "at the sight of the French flag, carried by a native, they moved, and presently made ready to charge us, as we were hurrying to hide the colours from their sight; yet they are far less wild in Laos than in Cochin-China. In our colony, even close to Saigon, the sight of a Frenchman exasperates them, as if they resented the conquest more than the Anamites themselves." Their innate savageness is shown in those trained to fight, as at Mergui, Tavoy, and Amherst, which sometimes turn upon and fatally gore their attendant.

The extensive grassy plains and the wooded country in Northern Siam form a great breeding-ground for elephants, ponies, and cattle, which are carried into British and Upper Burmah, and there bartered for merchandise. In 1881 no less than 41,588 head of cattle and 1,322 ponies were imported into British Burmah alone, from the Shan country. Its value as a cattle-breeding country for the cultivators of British

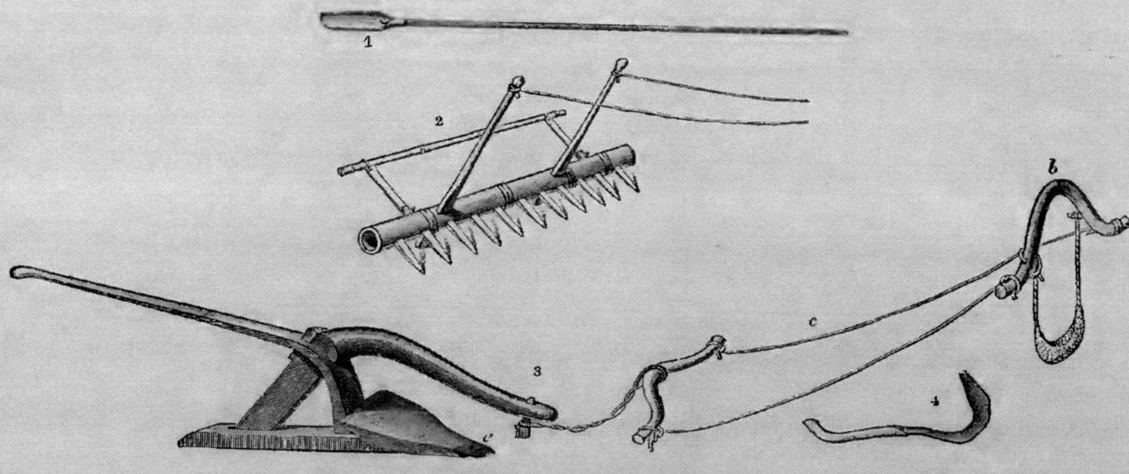

AGRICULTURAL IMPLEMENTS.

1. Hoe. 2. Rake. 3. Plough—(*e*) in iron; (*b*) yoke; (*c*) traces for a buffalo. 4. Scythe.

Burmah cannot be too strongly insisted upon. The main staple of Burmah, and the backbone of our trade with that country, is rice; and for its cultivation a very large number of cattle is an absolute essential. Owing to the epidemics which frequently occur in Burmah, the cultivation, which has so greatly increased of late years, would have remained stationary, or suffered serious decrease, had it not been for the source of supply found in the Siamese-Shan country. In 1866 upwards of a hundred thousand head of cattle—buffaloes and bullocks—died of the disease in Burmah. In 1877 one small district alone lost upwards of fifty-three thousand. In 1872 and 1874 an enormous number perished. In 1875 it interfered seriously with the cultivation of many districts; and in 1876 a serious outbreak again occurred—in Arracan alone fifty thousand buffaloes and ten thousand head of other cattle being swept away by it, whilst great numbers also died elsewhere throughout the country. In the deep jungles, elephants exist in a wild state, and are captured and sold to our timber merchants, who use them for the extraction of teak and other woods from the forests, and for the manipulation of the timber at the numerous saw-mills existing in the seaport towns.

The wild boar is more feared than any other animal by the hunters; for if a tiger, bear, or leopard is wounded, they may skulk away; but a boar, however little he may be injured, is certain to charge; and the amount of agility, presence of mind, and good luck it requires to succeed in getting out of his way only hunters are capable of imagining. The ground is generally beset with creepers or knotty roots, which on a sudden careless movement will nearly to a certainty trip you up, and then the boar has you at his mercy; and no one yet, even in fables, ever heard of the mercy of an infuriated and wounded wild boar. Their charge is made with blind fury, and with the rapidity of a tiger's spring.

Flint-lock muskets, particularly of the type seen in the Zimmé markets, are not only apt to burst, but are treacherous to use, for in a moment of peril they may fail to go off; a spear or dha has then to be brought into use, and the courage, nerve, and quiet coolness that is required in such an eventuality is seldom found in people who have not been bred up to face sudden dangers. Throughout the Siamese and Independent Shan States hunting has generally to be carried on in the dry season, the streams often being swollen and therefore difficult to cross in the rains. The fact of there being no bridges and few ferries in the country forces the people to face the difficulty of journeying across the hill-spurs or along the water-parting, for the streams near their entrances into the river are often too deep to be crossed without swimming or making rafts, and the latter would be a great hindrance to the carriage of merchandise.

This is the reason why the large caravans that come from China choose the route from Kiang Hung to Kiang Hai, which lies over difficult hills, in preference to that *viâ* Kiang Tsen, which follows the bank of the Mékong River, one or two of the streams entering

METHOD OF CROSSING RIVER IN FLOOD.

it being as broad as the Seine at Paris. All travelling, indeed, for any distance, except by boat or elephant, is put a stop to in the rains, and for some time in the dry weather the miasma is so deadly in the hills that travelling by land through the pestiferous districts should be restricted to from the middle of December to the beginning of May, and even then the heat has become so great that one feels as if facing a furnace. On our return journey from Zimmé we felt like hunted creatures, as though we would have given anything to escape into shelter to avoid the heat from the brazen sky and the bright red hills that were so hot as to force our followers to wear sandals to save their feet from blistering. McLeod mentions that the thermometer, in the country we were crossing, registered on the 18th of May 118° under some sheds, and 148° in the sun. Whether we had it hotter or no, I am uncertain, but a degree or two more than we had would have been absolutely unbearable.

A little later on the rains would have set in, and our party would have met the fate of Dr. Richardson's. He started from Labong, a town seventeen miles from Zimmé, on the 29th April; on the 9th May the rains began, and continued almost without intermission during the remainder of his journey. He arrived at Maulmain on the 21st May, suffering greatly from exposure; most of his followers ill, several of them, indeed, died shortly afterwards. The doctoring given to this gentleman's party on one occasion reminds one of our quackery in the Middle

Ages. The Shan doctor spread out all his medicines under a tree, and began prescribing for all the following. He had in his store of medicine the thigh-bone of a dog, the jaw of a monkey, the vertebræ of a fish, part of the grinder of an elephant, the fore-tooth of a rhinoceros, some bone of a turtle, and two or three pieces of broken china. The rest of his collection consisted of little bits of sticks, and roots of all colours, to the number of two hundred and eighty-one, the names and virtues of all which he professed to know, with the minute accuracy of the charlatan. Not the least curious part of the collection was his mortar, or substitute for one. It was a turned wooden bowl ten inches in diameter, with a handle to it, and inside, opposite the handle, a piece of coarse flinty sandstone, fixed with lac, about four inches square and sloping towards the bottom of the bowl; on this the various articles were ground down, in sometimes a quart of water, if the patient was very ill.

According to what was told us, the people seem to be free from hereditary diseases; small-pox sometimes rages amongst them, and they have no system of vaccination or even of inoculation. About one-third of the children are said to die before their fifth year; the greatest number of deaths amongst all classes and ages arises from bowel complaints and low-fever. The houses, though seemingly clean, are never scoured out; and as the floors generally consist of split bamboos, with sometimes matting spread about, the dirt gets into the interstices and remains there, often breeding disease amongst the people, until some day,

LAUNCHING A BOAT AT LUANG-PRABANG, ON THE MÉKONG.

by accident, their houses are found to be in flames, and they have to build new ones, just as in Burmah. In cases of disease, nats are generally propitiated, but at times shampooing and a cooling or a healing process is used; but anyhow, as a last resource, even with the most devout Buddhists, the nats are invoked in much the same manner as I have described when speaking of the Karen-nees.

When any one dies, the women of the house wail and beat their breasts, in token of their grief, in a similar way to that in vogue amongst the lower class in Ireland and Burmah; the coronach is joined by their friends, and often by every dog in the place. There are generally fewer funeral ceremonies than in Burmah; this much depends, however, upon the wealth of the family. Cremation, on a pyre of scented wood, is the rule, burying the exception; but in all cases of sudden death, contagious diseases, or bowel complaints, the body must be buried; this is the very reverse of what true medical science would teach.

Chaos and officials of rank are, strange to say, generally buried. Previous to the interment the body is embalmed and kept above ground for several months, during which period the friends and relations are entertained with Shan pwais (or plays), wrestling matches, dances, gambling parties, and other diversions more festive than funereal in their nature. The face of the dead chao is invariably covered with a mask of gold or silver; but we were unable to find out whether this was a religious, or merely a decora-

U

tive, custom. After a body is burnt, the ashes are gathered together and buried.

The pwais are often very well acted. In those that we visited, the characters were taken by female children from ten to twelve years of age; their training had been admirable, and they entered into their parts of princes and princesses, etc., as if born to them. The best company that we saw was at the house of the chief, who regaled us with an excellent dinner, cooked by a Chinese *chef;* the beverages, however, were execrable, and resembled those Greek wines Dr. Doran tells us about, that corroded the inside to the likeness of a sieve. On this occasion the stage was erected in the courtyard, and was made of an irregular up-and-down rockery work, with little houses on each side for entrances and exits, the whole reminding one of the pattern on a willow plate. It was more of a spectacle than a play, according to our European ideas; the children acted their parts in it to perfection, and the band was the best which we heard during our stay at Zimmé. The dresses were rich and very handsome; of course, not understanding the language, the plot was not very clear to us, but it consisted of the usual vicissitudes in the lives of princes and princesses, where forced separations and doleful occurrences ended at length in the mutual happiness and bliss, for ever after, of both parties. The assembly was arranged according to our High Church notions—the ladies on one side and the gentlemen on the other. Which had charge of the children, I forget; but as the Shans are proud and fond of the little ones, I presume they were equally divided.

Marriages are usually arranged by some old professional go-between, or matchmaker; but of course, in such a liberal-minded country, the young people have seen a good deal of each other beforehand, the usual amorous glances have passed, the excruciating moonlight serenades have been performed, and the little tale which, as some poet has truly remarked, "keeps the world from growing old," has been told and listened to. In the rare instances where a professional medium is not employed, the coy youth asks the blushing maiden for the flower in her hair. If she gives it, it is understood that he is accepted; and if the parents are willing, the nuptial ceremony follows in due course. All marriages, except on the occasions when officials marry below them, have to be accompanied with a fee to the poongyees, and the very smallest fee that is acceptable from the poorest man is three rupees, or five shillings; tolerably affluent people give £1; the sons of puniahs are mulcted in three times that amount; and the chaos are not let off under from seven hundred to a thousand rupees; but even they get off much easier than the tsobua, whose fee varies in accordance with the title which he receives on the occasion from the King of Siam, and is never less than ten thousand rupees.

Foreigners, besides the ordinary fee, have to pay seventy-two rupees into court for the privilege of being married to a damsel of such a high and distinguished race. It is to be hoped that the Cingalese woondouk was treated as a chao, and a foreigner as well, in which case this much-married man must have paid about three thousand pounds. A check upon such matrimony as he affected is decidedly desirable. A native of Ceylon to have only three less wives than the late King of Siam is preposterous. Although polygamy is allowed by the law, only the rich can afford to take advantage of it; and, for the sake of the women, it is to be hoped that the generality of the people will remain poor, until this abominable law is expunged from the code. Even now, if a girl chooses to resist firmly, even in the stage when fetters and imprisonment are resorted to, for the purpose of breaking her spirit, she can escape the fate of being mated to an old scoundrel that she never can care for; in case of so great a public scandal, the Siamese officials feel bound to intervene, and the fair one comes off triumphant.

To avoid becoming an inmate of a chao's harem, every pretty girl hides herself when one is paying a visit, as they prefer having a husband of their own to merely a very small share of one. The chief wife of a chao is generally taken from his own relatives, so as to keep the money in the family. The horrible union of brother with sister, which was not uncommon a few years ago, has now fallen entirely into disuse and, I think, only prevails in Indo-China in the Burmese royal family.

A Zimmé divorce is the most simple and unceremonious affair; as both husbands and wives have separate property, they simply divide partnership, the

SHAN METHOD OF EXTRACTING "TODDY," PALM-TREE WINE.

wife taking her goods and chattels with her. If only the husband wishes for the divorce, and his wife has done no wrong, he has to give her twenty-four rupees, and hand over half the property and the custody of the children. Should she have misbehaved, she can claim nothing whatever. In the same way, should the husband take to drinking, or otherwise misconducting himself, the woman has the right to turn him adrift, and to retain all the goods and money of the partnership. But the women are good little bodies, and will put up with a very great deal before they take such strong measures with a man they have once been fond and proud of.

Although the Shans are fond of strong drink, drunkenness seems rare amongst them, though, on the occasion of festivals, when they have not to pay for it, they are said to indulge very freely. The sale of spirits is a monopoly held by a Chinaman who is in secret partnership, it is said, with the chao hona. The price paid by the Chinaman for the license is twelve thousand rupees a year, and he is allowed to make, distil, and sell as much liquor as he likes, and in any locality he chooses. One rupee is charged for two bottles of oo-yay, a spirit made from the palm-tree; and half the amount for two bottles of sam-shu, or rice-spirit. English bottles of Old Tom, gin, brandy, whisky, etc., are likewise sold by him in the bazaar, the bottles being genuine, but the contents, I need hardly say, not unseldom of home make. The only two other monopolies that I heard of were gambling and opium, the first fetching twelve thousand rupees, and the second ten thousand. The monopoly for gambling applies to the keeping of betting and gambling houses for the public. The chaos and officials can play and bet as much as they like in their private houses, a practice largely followed. The poorer classes gamble to distraction, and it is common for a man to lose more than he and his possessions are worth, and to have to liquidate by the sale of the whole family. Even Monte Carlo cannot beat that. The "Hell" of the European gambler is "Heaven" in comparison with that of the hapless Yun Shan. The gambling is farmed by Chinamen. Opium is another curse of the country. Having paid for the monopoly, the Chinaman, like all purveyors to the public, does his utmost to create an appetite for his wares; he is said to entice young lads from their villages, deprave them with the drug, and send them back with such a supply as will lead a number of the villagers to become his regular customers. Once the taste is acquired by the Indo-Chinese, it is next to impossible to wean them from it; they will rob, and even murder, to acquire the wherewithal to satisfy their craving. The truth of this is well known to our police officers in Burmah, who would be much less troubled with dacoities if the consumption of opium was entirely put a stop to. Of course the prevention of its being publicly sold would lead to smuggling, whatever punishment might be inflicted, as the depraved appetite once formed will be satisfied at any cost.

Whatever their vices may be, the Shans are a

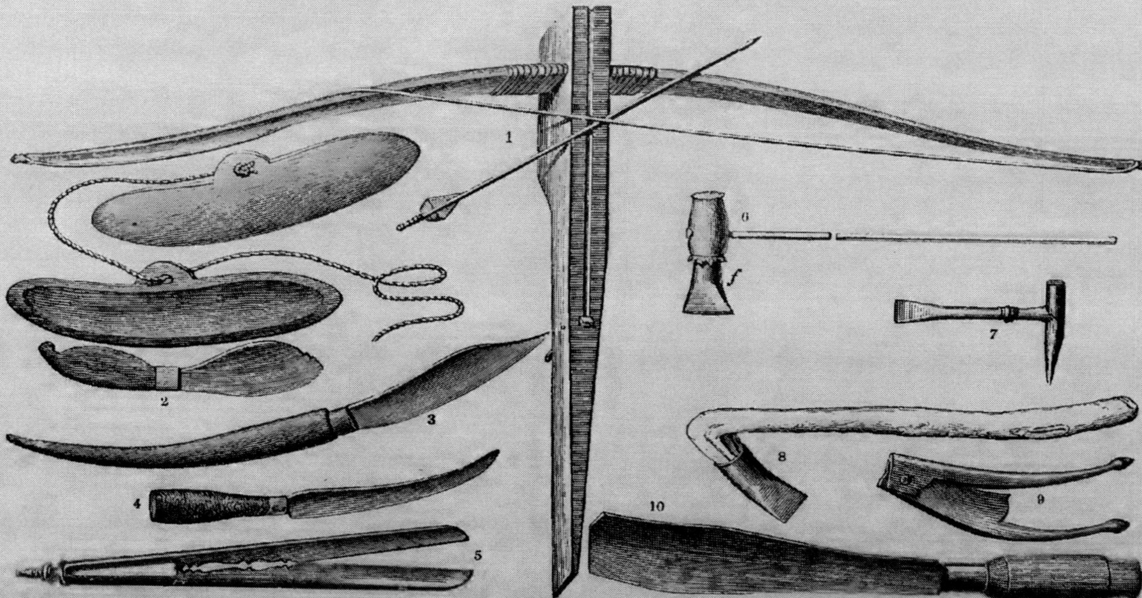

1. Bow and arrow in bamboo. 2. Razor, with case. 3. Pruning knife. 4. Dagger. 5. Scissors. 6. Axe for felling trees; the part *f* is moveable. 7. Screw-driver, etc., for guns. 8. Small axe. 9. Betel-nut choppers. 10. Heavy knife for cutting brushwood.

cleanly race, and water is in use morning, noon, and night. You see it led into their towns and villages by bamboo aqueducts, and one of their greatest pastimes is bathing. They are remarkably fond of the water; the river-banks, in the morning and evening, were crowded with bathers—men, women, and children—at every village we passed through. The children swim about and dive like water-fowl. They are most merry little folk, and one frequently feels inclined to caress the pretty little creatures—not to kiss them, however, for the disgusting habit of betel-chewing, which swells the lips and blackens the teeth of men and women, renders even the children more or less unsightly.

CHAPTER XVI.

McLeod's journey—The "Golden Road"—Advice of the Chinese—The former tsobuas of Kiang Tung and Kiang Hung anxious for trade—A great thoroughfare for Chinese—Bazaar at Kiang Tung—Siamese hostility to Burmah—Shan States independent—Trade route again opened—Zimmé towards Kiang Hung—Zimmé to Kiang Tsen—Carl Bock on Zimmé—Carl Bock on North Siam—Exploration required—Proposed railway—The field open to our enterprise.

THE great importance of reaching China through Zimmé and the Shan States has been acknowledged by the Government of India ever since McLeod's visit to Zimmé, Kiang Tung, and Kiang Hung in 1836–1837. That officer was urged by Chinese merchants, whom he constantly met and conversed with, to have the "Golden Road," their name for the trade route, so improved that they might bring their goods as far as Maulmain, in British Burmah. They complained that the road to Maulmain from the Méping valley was much worse than any part of the route they had to traverse between Yunnan and Zimmé, and, until it was improved, they could not bring their caravans through and return in the same season.

Owing to the streams and rivers being without

bridges, their journeys to and fro have to be completed in a little over four months. The absolute necessity of a railway from Maulmain to Zimmé, for the development of our trade, so as to enable the Chinese to reach British Burmah, and to keep communication open as far as Zimmé throughout the year, has been fully acknowledged by the press and by the mercantile community both at home and in Burmah. Far from difficulties being thrown in the way of improving the trade communications, the Chinese, the Shans, and the Siamese are all eager for us to take the matter in hand. The tsobua of Kiang Tung told McLeod that, if the English would only encourage their traders to come to his State, no duties, either export or import, should be levied upon them. He further promised to give them every encouragement and facility for trading. They might go where they pleased; and if they wanted cattle or anything, and did not wish to go out to the villages, he would order the owners to bring them in to Kiang Tung. The tsobua of Kiang Hung, McLeod says, "pressed me to send merchants up, but the mountainous country these would have to travel over is an obstacle; they could not return to Maulmain in the same season, even if they disposed of their goods at once, for their elephants would not be in a condition for the journey even to Zimmé (after having gone already from Maulmain to Kiang Hung), and they could not be disposed of here (at Kiang Hung)."

The Chinese trade with Kiang Tung is much dwelt upon by him, and the fact is brought out that Chinese labourers and artisans come to that place from China for the season's work. The importance of connecting it with British Burmah, which so much requires an increase to its labour market, is very great. He says: "Kiang Tung is a great thoroughfare for the Chinese, who pass through it and spread themselves over its territories, or proceed to Moné (a Shan State to the south-east of Mandalay) and other Shan States on the western bank of the Salween. They import the same articles as they do to Zimmé, with the addition of woollen cloths, carpets, thick cotton cloth, warm and fur jackets, and salt. For this last article the inhabitants are entirely dependent on them." Again, in another portion of his report, speaking of the wall of the town, he says, "parties of Chinamen are at work repairing these breaches, the inhabitants paying them for their labour. This industrious race furnishes the only artisans in the place. Many of them come in search of work, be it what it may, during the dry season, and after collecting a little money together, they return to their homes." At Kiang Tung there is a small bazaar held every day, and a great bazaar every five days. "On the present occasion (McLeod says) the people of the neighbouring villages assemble in town to dispose of their goods. The crowd was very great the whole day,—Chinese, Shans, Burmans, Ka-kuis and Ka-kuas, all mixed together. They erect temporary stalls, with a cloth covering to protect them from the sun." Owing to the Siamese hostility to Burmah, Siam having been attacked by it for centuries, traffic had

PANELLING IN A TEMPLE AT KIANG HUNG.

been nearly put a stop to between the Siamese and Burmese Shans, and had passed nearly entirely into the hands of the Chinese, who were interfered with by neither party, although they travelled, as is usually the case with them, without arms.

According to McLeod, the tsobua of Kiang Tung, with the King of Burmah's leave, at the time of his visit, 1837, "had sent an officer with letters and presents to the tsobuas of Zimmé, Labong, and Lagon, hoping that they were willing to forget their former differences and animosities, to become friends, and permit a free communication and trade between their subjects and through their country with the English at Maulmain. From forty to fifty merchants accompanied this officer, and brought a large sum of money to lay out in the Maulmain market.

"He was received with marked disrespect by the authorities, though many of the officers were inclined to accede to the tsobua's request; but the chao hona and chao raja wun principally opposed the concession. The chao hona would not permit the officer even to return, or the merchants to proceed to Maulmain, on the ground of their motives being suspected. The matter was quietly referred to Bangkok, and, under instructions from the court, a reply to the letter was sent, declining all intercourse with the Kiang Tung people, and stating that it was necessary that the King of Ava should address the King of Siam, whose subjects they (the Zimmé Shans) were, if the amicable disposition set forth in the letter really existed."

X

Thus ended the attempt, in 1837, to re-open the "Golden Road" of commerce between the rival States. Kiang Hai and Kiang Tsen were retaken from the Burmese by the Siamese in 1844, and have since remained under the King of Siam. Kiang Tung was attacked by the Siamese ten years later, but owing to the failure of their commissariat and to the commencement of the rains they were compelled to withdraw. Within the last few years the Burmese Shan States have succeeded in throwing off the yoke of Burmah, and, it is believed, will shortly put themselves under the protection of Siam. As the Burmese rule no longer exists in the Shan States, the King of Siam has withdrawn all opposition to the resumption of traffic. Under these circumstances the trade will rapidly revive, and the road to China will once more deserve its old title of the "Golden Road."

On his journey from Zimmé towards Kiang Tung, McLeod, for the first twenty-two miles, passed through a fertile and well-cultivated country irrigated by canals, and having numerous villages scattered over it; he mentions that the tea-plant grew wild in the hills. Tea and its cultivation is constantly mentioned by him all the way to Kiang Hung. In the next day's journey of twelve miles he came across teak and pine trees, and passing through a village met a Chinese caravan with no less than a hundred and thirty mules. The day following he wound about through the hills and crossed the water-parting between the affluents of the Méping and the Mékong, which Carl Bock lately found was five hundred feet above Zimmé, or twelve hundred feet above sea-level; an ascent of five hundred feet had therefore been made in about forty miles. There was thus no serious difficulty in this part of the route to prevent the construction of a railway.

He notices, on this part of his journey, having passed some fields, and within half a mile of a village, and mentions that "tea grows wild to the southward and westward of the hills passed to-day, before reaching the Mé Laú. These plantations are the property of certain chiefs, who collect the produce, and give 100 viss, or 365 lbs., for two plantations. It is gathered four times during the year, the best crop after the rains; all the care bestowed on the plant is to prune it occasionally." The next day he mentions, during his seven miles' march, traversing an extensive plain, which had been covered with grain, in the midst of which lay Muang Fue Hai, the capital of the district. Safflower, tobacco, and sugar-cane were cultivated in the gardens. The following day he proceeded through several villages and fields, and through thick jungle with fine thingan trees, which were used for making boats. There were about four thousand Lawas in the villages in the hills, who are miners, blacksmiths, and agriculturists. Most of the cotton taken away from the place was the produce of these people, who likewise cultivate indigo and sugar-cane. Each house paid a tax of 36½ lbs. of cotton, the same amount of chillies and tobacco, and half that amount of safflower. The distance traversed was fourteen miles.

His road thence led for fourteen miles through a valley, about eight miles broad, forming a splendid plain, in which numbers of cattle were grazing. The cultivation had been extensive, and wild sage was found growing in some deserted clearings, the inhabitants obtaining camphor from the sage. The next thirty-nine miles, through much the same class of cultivation and country, took him to the bank of the Mé Kok, down which affluent of the Mékong I propose to conduct the railway to Kiang Tsen, a town on the banks of the latter river, within easy access of Luang Prabang and Kiang Hung. Kiang Hai, the old town on the bank of the Mé Kok, according to Carl Bock, is eleven hundred and fifty feet above the sea-level, or fifty feet lower than the water-parting between the Méping and the Mékong, the distance from the water-parting being about sixty miles.

It will thus be seen that the railway from Zimmé to Kiang Tsen would lie chiefly through what was, even shortly after the Siamese and Burmese wars, a cultivated country, with such easy gradients that a railway could be carried across it without meeting with any but the most ordinary engineering difficulties. Kiang Tsen is admirably situated as a trade centre in an extensive plain surrounded by fine teak-forests. De Carné says: "At a little distance from Kiang Kong, the mountains retreat from the river, which winds along through a magnificent plain, in the centre of which is the town of Kiang Tsen. We were sailing for the first time in the waters of the kingdom of Zimmé. Teak is found for the first time in any abun-

A FALL ON THE MÉKONG, OR CAMBODIA, RIVER.

dance on the banks of the Mékong at Kiang Kong, but it is stunted there, and is badly cared for by the inhabitants. In the plain of Kiang Tsen, on the contrary, it formed magnificent forests on both sides of the Mékong." With reference to this place McLeod says: "Kiang Tsen is described as having been formerly a large and flourishing place; the lands about it are more fertile than elsewhere; the old town has a number of fine fruit-trees about it. There is near it a very large lake, which is never dry, and which supplies the people around with fish." This town is the present proposed terminus of the railway. Kiang Tsen is eight hundred and seventy feet above sea-level, or two hundred and eighty feet lower than Kiang Hai, which lies in the same plain, sixty miles up the Mé Kok.

Kiang Tsen lies some twenty or thirty miles within the Siamese boundary, and a hundred miles in a direct line from the boundary of Kiang Hung, the nearest province to it that has ever paid tribute to China. Ever since the Mahomedan rebellion in Yunnan, Kiang Hung has ceased to be tributary to China, and some years ago it threw off the yoke of Burmah, and has since been absolutely independent. The direct distance from Kiang Tsen to the nearest point of the Chinese frontier is one hundred and ninety-two miles.

With the assent of the tsobua of Kiang Tung, which there would be no difficulty in procuring, the railway might be produced as far as his northern boundary with Kiang Hung, or to within ninety miles of the Chinese frontier; but the State of Kiang Hung would not be entered until both the permission of China, to which it was once tributary, and of the tsobua of the State had been given. No possible political difficulties stand in the way of the construction of the railway as far as Kiang Tsen, the whole distance lying within British and Siamese territory.

In speaking of Zimmé, Carl Bock, who was there early this year, says: "I must observe here that only about a tenth part of the country is under cultivation, not counting the many mineral deposits, which are completely neglected. Gold in small quantities is found in the streamlets which intersect the district, and I have every reason to suppose that these streams pass through deposits of quartz. I had an opportunity of visiting excellent iron and lead mines in the neighbourhood of the town. To the north there are several petroleum wells.

"The country possesses immense resources, and I feel positive that, if a railway from Bangkok to Raheng were constructed, the road would soon be continued to Zimmé, a distance of only about one hundred and eighty miles, through Muang Tuun, Lagon, and Labong. Those who have not visited the country cannot, in fact, form an idea of its commercial importance, and of the great future which it may have. The principal revenue of the town is derived from the large forests of teak westwards of the town, which are worked by Burmans. Another source of revenue, though of less importance, is the export of lac, of which during the last year no less than 14,000

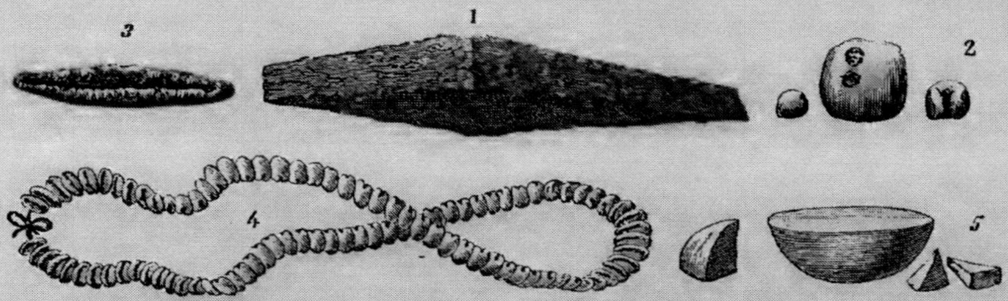

1. Iron money, made by the Kuys, or Khmer-dom, in use at Stung Treng on the Mékong River. 2. Siamese tical and its subdivisions. 3. Copper lats used at Bassac and Ubone. 4. String of cowries current at Luang Prabang. 5. Cast silver in use in the Independent Shan States.

piculs, or 1,862,000 lbs., were sent to Bangkok. The town contains within its walls about a hundred thousand inhabitants. Its favourable position between Siam and Burmah, thereby controlling the trade between these two countries, gives it a real commercial and political importance." In his journey up the Ménam from Bangkok, he found that Siamese money was not current at Raheng or in the country above it, but had been entirely replaced by Indian rupees; he was therefore obliged to change his Siamese money for rupees. This shows what a hold our trade has already upon the Shan country. He goes on to say: "The construction of a railway from Bangkok to Raheng would not meet with any great technical difficulties. The whole country is an immense plain, and far less obstacles would have to be overcome than for the railway through the American prairies; whilst, moreover, the traffic of the many villages of this region would greatly conduce to the success of the undertaking.

"The only natural highway at present existing—the river—is not sufficient for the growing wants of the local trade, it being only navigable to Paknam-Po, whilst the many sandbanks render navigation somewhat dangerous and uncertain.

"The journey from Bangkok to Raheng by boat takes, on an average, twelve days. The natives, as a rule, however, require much more time. The journey down takes them quite as many days, and often more; for, finding there is no current to contend against, they often cease all efforts, and simply drift along with the stream. By rail the distance of about three hundred miles, at twenty miles an hour, could be accomplished in fifteen hours.

"This country deserves in every respect to be opened up to European commerce and enterprise, and I feel certain that should a French company open negotiation for the construction of a railway, they could easily obtain the necessary concessions, and meet with the warm support of his majesty the King. I may here observe that his majesty is animated by a sincere desire to develop the welfare of his people, and would gladly avail himself of any means which modern civilization has put at his disposal."

Over six hundred elephants are employed in dragging the logs to the river, in the teak-forests near Raheng, by our Burmese subjects; besides teak, the district exports a great quantity of sappan wood, cut up in small blocks, and has an active trade in gum, corn, hides, and wax. The population of the town is given by Carl Bock as nine thousand, but he omits to say whether his estimate includes women and children. The next town he mentions is Muang Tuun, which, according to him, has about a thousand inhabitants, not counting women and children. Between Raheng and Kampheng Pet there are large teak-forests worked by Burmans from Rangoon and Maulmain; between these two places he was told there were sixty-eight villages, the distance being about a hundred geographical miles. He says that, although the Siamese are not a hard-working people, the difficulty in procuring labour is more apparent than real, as "Chinese and

Indian coolies may be obtained. The Chinese work hard for low wages." Muang Tuun is about sixty-four miles north-east of Raheng, and is the centre of a district producing an enormous quantity of tobacco; between the two places he came across a great number of small teak-trees.

The country about Lagon proved to be "an immense plateau, containing many villages of considerable size, the inhabitants of which were chiefly engaged in rearing cattle. Everywhere large farms were to be seen with thousands of cattle and buffaloes. They are employed as beasts of burden by those natives who cannot afford to keep elephants. They are also exported in large numbers to British Burmah." He proceeds to say: "This district produces large quantities of excellent cotton, which is sold principally to merchants of Yunnan; stick-lac and gum (damar, which is used as a varnish and is water-proof) are found in the neighbouring woods, and also exported." The main stream of the Ménam, the Ménam Yai, or Great Ménam, which joins the Méping at Paknam-Po, he says is "much larger and better navigable; running from the north-east, it traverses a rich and well-populated country."

From Zimmé to Bangkok the fall in the country is about seven hundred feet, the distance being about five hundred miles. The first sixty-nine miles were traversed by our party, the fall in the distance being about a hundred feet. The railway would follow the valley of the river the whole way to Bangkok; and the junction with the British Burmah system would either be *viâ* Muang Haut, or *viâ* Myawaddy and Raheng. The first route was crossed by us, and the other has been partly traversed by Mr. Hallett, who, when in engineering charge of the Tenasserim division, crossed the hills between Maulmain and the Siamese frontier. The pass crossed by him was a little less than two thousand feet above sea-level, and, according to him, a tunnel of no great length would reduce the height by several hundred feet. The only other pass which would have to be crossed on this route lies between Myawaddy and Raheng. It is much used by our traders, and, according to the data given us by McLeod, is about two thousand two hundred and eighty-seven feet in height; whether a lower pass could be found, or the height reduced by means of a tunnel, requires to be seen. With the help of the mercantile community, who have subscribed a fund for the purpose of an exploration, I hope to proceed to the Shan country with Mr. Hallett, who has most carefully gone into the whole subject of trade routes with me, and has rendered me great assistance, to bring back such information as will settle the course that the railway should take, and provide a rough survey and levels, together with an approximate estimate of the amount of money that will be required in carrying it out.

The route from Muang Haut, after leaving the banks of the Méping, is a gradual ascent for the first five miles, for the next six miles the path was a little steeper, and, to avoid the thick jungle, we kept a good part of the way in the bed of a stream. A steep ascent for about three miles is then met with, after which it becomes more gradual for nine and a half miles, when the crest of the Baw plateau is reached. The ascent from Muang Haut to the top of the plateau was about two thousand seven hundred feet in about twenty-four and a half miles. Any gradient that might be thought desirable for a railway could be constructed by properly aligning the railway. The descent from the Baw plateau to the Métiu stream, which joins the Hmine Long-gyee River, along which the railway would be carried to the Thoungyeen, which is an affluent of the Salween, is easy, and the distance five and a half miles. The distance from this point to the Salween is about fifty miles, and the principal descent would have to be made in this part of the route; but, as the crest of the Baw plateau at our point of crossing was only three thousand three hundred and thirty-seven feet above sea-level, it could be carried in the direction of the valley without any deviations on account of the descent. Probably a considerably lower crossing of the plateau could be found at the northern or southern edge. The difficulties in the way of crossing the hills lying between British Burmah and Siam have proved, therefore, to be nothing more than are met with and surmounted in ordinary engineering practice all over the world at the present day. If the gradient for crossing the Baw plateau be fixed at a hundred feet in the mile (about twice as easy as the one worked by locomotives on the South-eastern Railway leading to Folkestone Harbour), an engine could draw itself up and down the incline, and six times its own weight in addition.

The cost of a railway over this part of the route would not, in our opinion, be more than £15,000 a mile, and the remaining portion of the line could be constructed at about the same cost per mile as the Sittang and Irrawadi Valley Railways in British Burmah, or at £7,375 a mile. The total cost of the railway from the Rangoon and Maulmain (Martaban) line would be, if constructed to Kiang Tsen, which is on the banks of the Mékong River :—

336 miles at £7,375 per mile	=	£2,478,300
54 miles at £15,000 „	=	810,000
390 miles of railway at a cost of		£3,288,300

or if the railroad was only made to Zimmé :—

170 miles at £7,375 per mile	=	£1,298,300
54 miles at £15,000 „	=	810,000
230 miles of railway at a cost of		£2,108,300

Of course this estimate is merely approximate, as no detailed surveys or levels have been taken.

The prospects of a railway cannot be arrived at, nor even approximately calculated, without taking into consideration the effect that railways have had, under similar circumstances and in neighbouring countries. The Irrawadi Valley Railway, from Rangoon to Prome, was constructed through a country much inferior in fertility to the Shan States and Siam, covered for two-thirds of its course with scrub jungle.

Yet it is even now the best paying of the Indian Government Railways. It moreover had the disadvantage of having to compete with an admirable water-carriage, the magnificent steamers of the Irrawadi Flotilla Company running parallel to and within twenty or twenty-five miles of it for the greater part of its length.

The Irrawadi Valley Railway was constructed to connect the town of Rangoon, of 134,176 inhabitants, with the town of Prome, of 28,813 inhabitants; the Sittang Valley Railway to connect Rangoon with Toungoo, a town of only 17,199 inhabitants. The railway that I propose would connect Rangoon with Zimmé, a town of about 100,000 inhabitants, and, eventually, with Raheng, with 9,000 inhabitants (perhaps 45,000, if Carl Bock omitted the women and children), and with Bangkok, which is generally allowed to have between five and six hundred thousand. Not only would it do this, but it would be the link between British Burmah, with its three and three-quarter millions of inhabitants, and Siam and the Shan States, which, if the statistics are reliable, contain between thirty and forty millions.

The area of the Siamese dominions is about 260,000 square miles. The Burmese Shan States, which are now independent, contain about 80,000 square miles. The country is the most fertile in the East, and is universally acknowledged to be rich in minerals. The King of Siam is anxious to have it opened up; and it only rests with us to consider whether this magnificent field for our trade, throughout which our goods are at

Y

present found in small quantities, shall be opened up to our commerce, or whether we shall allow it to be annexed by the French, and permit our only feasible trade route to China to be blocked by their aggression. The King of Siam is one of the most enlightened of Eastern monarchs. He has by travel been enabled to see the results of the introduction of Western arts into lands similar to his own. The lessons which he then learnt he has never lost sight of. He recognises the fact that his people, though an intelligent and lettered race, are yet extremely backward in civilization. Siam is a country which only wants communications to become happy and wealthy. The capabilities are all there. With the introduction of railways, not only would the produce, mineral and agricultural, of the country be despatched to the marts of the West, but the welfare of the Siamese would be immensely increased. It is only by obtaining ready means of access to the remote parts of his dominions that the young King can hope effectually to suppress the bond-slavery which is the curse of Siam. With the sound of the railway whistle feudal oppression will disappear for ever.

The enriching of Siam by the introduction of railways means the opening up of an immense and yearly increasing market for our manufactures. Every fresh acre of paddy land, every new mine, made possible in Siam by the construction of the iron way, will imply fresh hands in Manchester mills and growing activity on Liverpool wharves. The cultivator who formerly never thought of growing more than was necessary for the support of himself and his family, will, when he finds money flowing into his coffers, not only be excited to fresh industry, but will discover new wants which formerly he had no thought of, new luxuries which hitherto he had no means of obtaining. The civilizing of the Siamese peasant and the Shan gardener and miner will return a splendid recompense to English commercial enterprise. The Straits Settlements have an export and import trade of upwards of £35,000,000. It may be confidently asserted that the connection of South China with Bangkok and British Burmah will imply a much greater increase to our commercial prosperity. The field is large, populous, and fertile, and the inhabitants are traders by nature.

SUPPLEMENTARY CHAPTERS.

SUPPLEMENTARY CHAPTERS.

HISTORICAL SKETCH OF THE SHANS.

BY

HOLT S. HALLETT, M.T.C.E., F.R.G.S.

PART I.

HISTORY OF UPPER SHAN.

Our neighbours the Shans—Extent of their location—Incorporated with the Chinese—La Couperie's remarks—The progress of the Aryans and Chinese—Death of feudalism—Annexation of Ss'chuan—Foundation of Yueh and Wu—Shan kingdoms B.C. 2208—Conquest by the Chinese—Migration to Burmah—Old towns—Birth of *the Mau empire*—Increase of Shan kingdoms—Effects of having no rule of primogeniture—Killing brothers—Rise of the Mau empire—Conquest of Shan States, Assam, Tali, and Arracan—Shattering Burmah—Conquest of Yun and the Malay Peninsula—Disruption of Burmah—Arrival of the Shan alphabet—A reign of a hundred years—Theinni as large as Paris—Conversion to Buddhism—A career of conquest—Killing monks—A Shan iconoclast—A Peguan emperor—Burning people by thousands—A depopulated country—The kingdom of Piao—Conquest of Yunnan—The *Karen* country—Advance of the Thibeto-Burmese—Kolarians and Dravidians—The *Mun aborigines* of Burmah—A mongrel brood—Resemblance of Talain to Kol—Indo-Chinese languages—Conversion of Malays and Thiamese to Mahomedanism—Lewas—Karen tribes—Connection of the Karens with China—Their early kingdom of Yun—Entrance of the Shans—Their vassalage—Yun and Yun-gyee—Kingdom of Lin-y, or Lam-ap—Karen kings—Zimmé a Karen State—Advance of the *Laos Shans*—Foundation of towns by the *Yun Shans*—Origin of the Siamese era—

Extent of Zimmé—A refractory infant—Contradictory chronicles—Conquest of Zimmé—Ousting of the Siamese—Shans in Yunzaleen—Changes of capital—Rebellion against Cambodia—Phra Ruang—Shan conquest of Cambodia—The ancient Khmer—A masterful language—Savage, a misapplied term—Civilized and courteous mountaineers—The Bannavs—Influence of China—An early phonetic language—Anam tributary to China—The end of the Thang—Disruption of China—Kublai Khan's conquests—*Lin-y*, a bar to the Shans—Movements of population—Absorption of Lin-y—A magic sword—Remains of great nations—Disastrous effects of independence—Wars and riches of Lin-y—*The Laos Shans* of Vien-Chang—Rise of their power—Zimmé annexed—Wars with Pegu and decrease of prosperity—Independence of Luang Prabang—Settlement in Bassac—Destruction of Laos cities—Attack of the Tonquinese—Conquest by Siam.

THE close of the Burmese war in 1826 left us in possession of the Burmese provinces of Arracan and Tenasserim, and we became the protectors of Assam, Cachar, Tiperah, and Manipur. Our eastern frontier in Indo-China had been carried in a continuous line as far south as the northern corner of the island of Ceylon, or nearly as far as the southern extremity of India. We could nowhere cross this line and proceed eastward without coming into contact with the Shans, and we were their actual protectors in Assam.

Not only do they stretch away far to the eastward, perhaps as far as the China Sea, but they actually form one of the chief ingredients that compose the so-called Chinese race. Mr. Colquhoun, in his journey through the south of China, came to the conclusion that most of the aborigines whom he met, although known to the Chinese by various nicknames, were Shans; and that their propinquity to the Chinese was slowly changing their habits, manners, and dress, and gradually incorporating them with that people.

From Kwangtung and Kwangsi the same race is found, called by the Anamites Muongs, spread throughout the hilly regions of Tonquin; and should the French, in pursuit of the Black Flags, enter the forests, they will find themselves, wherever they may go, amongst the Shans.

The origin of the Shans, like that of the Chinese, is lost in the mists of antiquity. Together with the Anamites, they have been in possession of the country to the south of the Chinese ever since the latter entered the north-western portion of the empire, and their forefathers most likely formed part of the same horde. The learned M. Terrien de La Couperie says, in his account of "The Oldest Book of the Chinese and its Authors":—"The influence of the advanced civilization and the mixture of the Ougro-Altaïc early Chinese immigrants with the native populations of China of several States (of which the primitive Tai, or Shan, was not the least important) were not confined to the area of their political power. This deep mixture, which has produced the Chinese physical type and peculiar speech, and accounts for several phonetic features common to the Chinese and many Indo-Chinese languages, as well as for the reciprocal loan of words, which amounts between the Chinese and Tai vocabularies to more than thirty per cent., had begun outside long before the extension of the Chinese political supremacy."

In the earlier hymns of the Rig Veda (about 3000

B.C.) we find the Aryans on the north-west frontiers of India;—the delta of Lower Bengal was reached by them about the fourth century before Christ. The earlier progress of the Chinese seems to have been more rapid; for although they had arrived at the north-west corner of China about the same time that the Aryans are heard of on the borders of India, they had already crossed the Yangtsi in the reign of Yaou (B.C. 2356). For many centuries they seem to have vacillated in their movements; in B.C. 1550 they are shown, in the Chinese calendar, as repulsing the inroads of the inhabitants of the country to the south of the Yangtsi, and therefore most likely had settlements on the north bank of that river; yet we are told by Professor Douglas that during the Chou dynasty (B.C. 1122–249) the empire merely covered the country lying between latitudes 33° and 38°, and longitudes 106° and 109°; therefore between the latter dates it comprised no portion of the basin of the Yangtsi-kiang. About B.C. 780, however, its power seems to have made itself again felt to the south of the river, and some of the princes ruling over the southern kingdoms may have acknowledged its authority.

The date B.C. 246 is a most notable one in Chinese history, for it marks the end of unruly feudalism, and the real birth of the solid Chinese empire. Up till then China had been divided into a varying number of principalities, governed by rulers called Chau, who at times acknowledged and at times denied their allegiance to the emperor. These princes not only made war on each other, but annexed on their own account neighbouring territory. For instance, part of Ss'chuan became feudatory to the principality of Ts'in, B.C. 316.

Kingdoms outside the empire seem to have been formed at various dates. Previous to the foundation of the Chou dynasty, Tai Peh and Chung Yung, elder brothers of the father of the founder, left the empire and formed the kingdoms of Yueh and Wu on the southern frontiers. According to the Anamite chronicles, many of the principalities south of the Yangtsi, which took their rise in the time of Yu, who commenced to reign B.C. 2208, were founded by a younger son of the emperor of China, and remained independent until they were conquered by the northern Chinese, B.C. 207 to A.D. 76.

Taking the above into consideration, and remembering that the chiefs of many of the Shan States bear the same titles as the old princes in China, and that others, the Muongs in the hills about Tonquin, are known by those which were used by princes to the south of the Yangtsi five thousand years ago, it is probable that at various times these States or their parents have been offsets from the empire of China.

The origin of the Shan kingdoms in the valley of the Irrawadi is evident from the Burmese chronicles, which tell us that some years previous to the building of old Pagan (B.C. 523), the Burmese had been driven southwards by an irruption of the Chinese from the upper valley of the Irrawadi. This shows that the Shans of Yunnan, who are called Shan-Tayoks, or Chinese Shans, by the Burmese, were already spreading down the valley of the Irrawadi. We have other evidence that this movement occurred about this date. The Shan chronicles, quoted by Ney Elias, mention that the town of Moné was founded B.C. 519; Theinni, B.C. 441; and Theebo, B.C. 423.

It seems likely that the Shans entered the basin of the Irrawadi by the valley of the Shweli, and, after founding the kingdom of Mung Mau, or Muang Mau, spread northwards, westwards, and southwards; and driving the Burmese southwards and westwards, occupied the locality west of the Salween, which they have retained ever since.

In A.D. 568 Muang Kaing, Muang Nyaung, and Muang Ri, Muang Ram, were the capitals of the Mau dominions. In A.D. 703 the capital was at Muang Kaung, or Mogaung, which was then known as Ma-Kau Muang Lung. The Shan kingdoms rapidly increased in numbers, partly from conquest and the habit of placing relatives of the ruling chief as princes of outlying provinces, and partly from the frequent splitting up of the kingdoms through rebellions and wars of succession.

Unfortunately for the kingdoms in Indo-China there is no rule of primogeniture; the ruler can choose his own successor from any member of his family; and if any other has a larger following amongst the people, or can get another strong power to aid him, he proceeds to dethrone his relative. The custom of assassinating all the royal family, with the exception of the children of the new king, on ascending the throne, was lately exemplified by King Theebau of Burmah.

The power of the Mau empire gradually extended.

At first it seems to have merely included the ten chieftainships, or muangs, of Kusambi—Mau, Ti, Wun, or Wan, La, Sanda, Sa (afterwards divided into Ho-sa and La-sa), Si-kuen, Meng Luang, or Momein, and a part of Yung-chang. In A.D. 703 the capital was at the residence of the prince of Mogaung, who had under him the portions of the basins of the Khendwen and Irrawadi, which included Khampti, Western Khampti on the Kyendwen, Kukung, Muang Kaing, Muang Nyaung, Mo Nyin, Taungthwot, Kalei, four Yaw, or Burmese, towns, and Mautshobo. In 1038 Bamo became a tsaubwaship, or principality, of the Mau empire; and in 1203 Momiet was added.

In A.D. 1220 the great Mau sovereign, Chau Kwampha, ascended the throne, and added the princedom of Theebo to his dominions. In 1223 Moné, and all the Kamboza, or Shan States on the tableland between the Irrawadi and the Salween, acknowledged his supremacy. In 1229 Assam was occupied by the Mau Shans, and a Mau prince was put on the throne; and about the same time, Nantien, Muang Maing, Kiang Hung, Kiang Tung, and Theinni, besides other smaller States, became principalities of the Mau empire.

Even Tali-fu had given in its allegiance before it was annexed as a tributary to the Mongols in 1234; and part of Arracan and Manipur are claimed as having been at this time included in the Mau dominions.

Between 1283–1292 the Mau shattered the Burman empire, and, perhaps with the aid of the Mongol-

Chinese, pursued Tarok-pyee-meng, the Burmese King, farther south than Prome. About 1293 they annexed Zimmé (most likely driving the Zimmé Shans to Cháliang, from whence the Siamese, to escape a pestilence, descended and founded Ayuthia in 1350); seized the Yun, or Karen, country; enabled Pegu to throw off the yoke of Burmah, under which it had groaned for two hundred and fifty years; received the Yunzaleen, which extended as far as the banks of the Beeling River, as a reward, together with the allegiance of the Peguans; conquered the Malay Peninsula as far south as Tavoy; and made their power felt in Java, Malacca, and Cambodia. In 1285 Muang Mau was founded, and made the capital of the empire; and a few years afterwards the whole of the Burmese empire was divided into States, and governed by princes of the Mau family. Until 1554, when it was annexed by Pegu, Upper Burmah and many other parts of the empire were governed by the Shans.

The Mau empire split up nearly as soon as it had reached the height of its power; by 1350 Siam had taken over the Mau conquests as far north as the boundary of Zimmé. Burmah from the first was divided into principalities; and the rest of the Mau empire resolved itself into independent principalities and kingdoms; Zimmé remained under a Mau prince, but whether dependent for any length of time on the Mau empire or not is not known. This prince is said to have brought the present Siamese alphabet into use.

The evidence of the various chronicles is conflicting in many cases, and difficult to compare. Arracan, according to the Mau, was conquered by them and made tributary; the Arracanese make no mention of such a conquest, but merely state that the Shans invaded them about 1174, but were defeated; and that between 1279 and 1385 the Shans, Burmans, and Talain more than once invaded the kingdom. The Arracan chronicles are not much to be relied on about this period, for they make their king reign a hundred and six years. This may be evidence of an interregnum, during which time it was governed by the Mau Shans.

Some of the old Shan towns were of great extent. Theinni, or Muang Siuen-wi, founded B.C. 441, was built in the shape of a square, each wall being fourteen thousand one hundred and twenty-two feet in length, fifteen feet thick, fifteen feet high, with foundations three feet deep; a moat surrounded the city, at a distance of twenty-one feet from the walls, fifty-two and a half feet wide, and thirty feet in depth. The town had eleven gates, each twelve feet wide.

Theinni proudly asserts that its people were converted to Buddhism B.C. 324, or about a hundred years before the Buddhist missionaries, Potera and Tauna, set foot in the south of Burmah, and Oupaha and Soupitha in Kiang Hung and Muang Yong, one hundred and eight years before they entered China, and seven hundred and forty-six years before they landed in Cambodia. The Burmese, on the other hand, state that all the Shan States were converted to Buddhism in 1556, when most of them became tributary to the emperor of Pegu. The truth seems to be that their Buddhism had lapsed from its ancient strictness, and he insisted upon its being reformed.

Sir Arthur Phayre, in his History of Pegu, shows that the reckless career of conquest of this emperor, which raised the kingdom to a height of dazzling but false prosperity, left it utterly exhausted, and the population so reduced by war, pestilence, and famine, that to this day it has not recovered. Having reformed the Shans, he became shocked at the thought of the Mahomedans, who resided in the country, killing goats and fowls; he accordingly had them collected in his capital, and caused the Tha-tha-na-paing to instruct them in the Buddhist religion, whereupon, with what amount of other persuasion the Talain chronicles fail to relate, numbers became Buddhists.

The deposed Shan emperor of Burmah certainly seems to have considered the safety of his dynasty more than religion; but the poongyees, or monks, in those days may have been as dangerous in conducting rebellions as those in Thibet have frequently proved. We are told in the Royal History that "he was of a cruel and savage disposition. He spared not men's lives. He respected not the three treasures (Buddha, the law, and the assembly). Pagodas, he used to say, are not the Bhoora (Paya), but merely fictitious vaults in which the Burmese deposit gold, silver, and jewels; so he dug into and rifled those shrines of their treasures. The poongyees too, he used to say, having no wives and children, under pretence of gathering disciples, collect guards around them ready to rise in rebellion. He therefore built a number of sheds on the plain of Toung-ba-loo, and pretending to do honour to the poongyees, invited all those round Ava, Tsagaing, and Panya to a feast. Then surrounding them with an army, he had them all slaughtered. He then seized all the books in their monasteries and had them burned. But some of the Shans had pity on the poongyees, and many thus escaped to Prome and Toungoo. More than three hundred and sixty were killed, but more than a thousand escaped."

The son of the zealous Pegu emperor seems not to have followed in the steps of his father, but in those of his Shan predecessor. The History relates how—"Pegu was now already exhausted; discontent was universal; and the emperor, suspicious of every one, became wantonly cruel. The Buddhist monks of Talain race excited his hatred. Numbers of them he forced to become laymen, and then either exiled or killed them. Thousands of the Mun people (Peguans) abandoned their country and fled, while those caught in their flight were put to death for the attempt. The country of the delta became depopulated, and an attempt was made to drive down the people from the Upper Irrawadi to fill the fertile land of Pegu. But famine raged, and there was no help."

The cruelties of this Peguan emperor seem to have surpassed the merciless acts of any African potentate. Faria y Souza reported that—"The King of Pegu in a rage for the death of his son turned his fury against the people, and some days burnt about ten thousand, throwing so many into the river as stopped the passage even of boats. He forbid them sowing,

Z

which caused such a famine that they not only ate one another, to which purpose there was a public butchery of man's flesh, but devoured part of their own bodies."

Boves, a Jesuit missionary, who was in Pegu in 1600, writes :—"It is a lamentable spectacle to see the banks of the river, set with infinite fruit-bearing trees, now overwhelmed with ruins of gilded temples and noble edifices; the ways and fields full of skulls and bones of wretched Peguans, killed or famished, and cast into the river in such numbers that the multitude of carcasses prohibited the way and passage of any ship, to omit the burnings and massacres of this the cruellest tyrant that ever breathed."

That many of the Shans were Buddhists long before 1556 is evident from the description of the kingdom of Piao given by Chinese writers of the tenth century. It appears from Ma Tuanlin, that there existed, after the Han dynasty, towards the tenth century of our era, an important kingdom called Piao, on the south-west confines of China; its capital contained more than a hundred temples. The population of the kingdom included two hundred and ninety-eight different tribes, who professed Buddhism; nine large towns were tributary to the King, whose dominions were nine hundred miles from east to west. The last statement must have incorporated the Kamboza, Mau, and Laos Shans, and then would be slightly in excess.

At the time of the conquest of Yunnan by the Chinese, B.C. 207 to A.D. 76, the Shans had extended far to the southward, and taken possession of the country which, before their arrival, was occupied by the Yun, or Karens, who, on their part, had driven the Lewa, or Lawa, the aboriginal inhabitants, to the southward and into the hills.

The hill-tribes in the north of Indo-China are much more mixed than they were before the arrival of the Thibeto-Burmese, about B.C. 923, or perhaps a little earlier. This mixture does not appear to extend as yet into the Shan States that are tributary to Siam. The northern frontier of that empire seems only to have been crossed by the Lewas, Karens, Shans, Chinese, and Anamites.

We know that, on the Aryans entering India, they encountered two different races, the Kolarian and the Dravidian. It is interesting to find that the aborigines whom the Burmese had to face on their arrival in Indo-China were the Mun, or Talain. The great adulteration that the Mun, a valley-dwelling people, must have undergone during the supremacy of the Shans and Burmese, as well as from the large immigration of Dravidians from the Madras coast which has been going on for probably more than three thousand years, has so altered their primitive type of countenance as to render them hardly distinguishable from the Burmese, and as their language has a deep affinity to that of the Kolarians of Central Hindustan, there is little reasonable doubt of their having had an early connection.

The Mun, or Talain, of Pegu, notwithstanding their intercourse with the Dravidians, Shans, Karens, and

Burmese, possessed a distinct language until they were forcibly compelled to disuse it during the time that passed between our first and second Burmese wars, 1826–1852. Many of these people, however, sought shelter in our province of Tenasserim, and thus retained their own language. According to Dr. Mason, the Talain is not cognate with the Chinese, or Thibetan, or any of the Tartar tongues of which specimens have been published. Its roots are not allied to Tai, or Shan, Burman, Karen, Toung-thoo, Kyeng, or Khyen, Kamee, Chinpaw, or Kakhyen, Nagar, or to Manipuri. Neither is it related to the Sanscrit or Hindu families of Northern Hindustan; nor to the cultivated dialects of Southern India and Ceylon, the Telugu, Carnataka, Tuluva, Tamil, Malayalam, Malabar, and Singalese. Here and there words are found of apparently common origin, but it is radically different.

The Talain and Shan languages and the Karen dialects have the same arrangement in sentences as the English, whilst the placing of words in all the Thibeto-Burmese languages is exactly the reverse. It will be interesting to test by the comparison of the structure of the languages, which is even more to be depended on than the vocabularies, whether there is an affinity between the languages of the Siamese, who are believed to be the aborigines of Southern Indo China, the Lewas, who are allowed to be the primitive people of Central Indo-China, and the Mun, or Talain, of Pegu.

The conversion of the Siamese to Mahomedanism,

which occurred perhaps as early as A.D. 1276, or at the same time as that of the Malays of Malacca, has perhaps kept them nearly as uncontaminated with other races as we may expect to find the Lewas and certain of the Karen tribes who live secluded in their hill-fastnesses.

The Yuns, or Karens, who occupied the country to the east of the Salween at the time of the arrival of the Yun Shans, are a most interesting people. They have no distinctive name for their race, and are merely a conglomeration of tribes all speaking dialects of the same language. The very name Karen, or Kayen, which is applied to them by the Burmese, is no longer used amongst them, if it was ever in vogue. It may have arisen from their inhabiting the kingdom of Tchen-Tching and parts of Tchen-la when the Shans conquered the latter in 707. Tchen is the exact equivalent in sound of the Burmese term Khyen, which is applied to the Karen tribes on the west of Upper Burmah and to the Pwo tribe of Karens lying to the north of our territory.

Dr. Mason says that the Karen traditions point unquestionably to an ancient connection with China; for the Karens believe in the ancient god of the Chinese Tie, or Tien, and offering to the manes of their ancestors is as common amongst them as it is amongst the Chinese. Their own traditions denote that they arrived from the west by the same route as that which was taken by the Chinese, whom they call their younger brothers.

On the advance of the Yun Shans, the Karen King,

whose subjects were very numerous, having accepted their allegiance, allowed them to settle in his country and build several large towns, amongst which were Kiang Hung, Kiang Tung, Kiang Tsen, Muang Lem, and a fortified town which was called Kiang Chang. As the Shans became more numerous, and therefore stronger, they became dissatisfied with their vassalage, and determined to throw off the Karen yoke. A son of the prince of Kiang Hung, who had been allowed to build and occupy the fortified town of Kiang Chang, invited Phya Ngam, the then ruling Karen King, to a banquet, and, having closed the gates of the town, slew him and all his attendants. This, according to the Muang Yong chronicle, occurred long before the time of Gaudama, B.C. 543.

Kiang Hung is still called Kiang Yun-gyee, or the large Yun town, by the Burmese, who likewise call the country to the east of the Salween, "Yun," and the Shans who inhabit it Yun Shans; even Cochin-China (the old Tchen-Tching), according to McLeod, is called Yun-gyee by the Burmese. It is therefore probable that the country of the Karens, who are at present found in the hills of Indo-China, must have been at one time very extensive.

About the time of the conquest of Tonquin, B.C. 110, by the Chinese, the kingdom of Yun-gyee was called by the Anamites Lam-ap, and by the Chinese Yueh-chang and Lin-y, and during the fourth century appears, to the south of the latter, the name of Tchen-Tching, corresponding with Cochin-China.

According to Garnier, Phan-ho-dat reigned in Lin-y

in A.D. 413, Phan-dzeuong-mai in 431, Phu-long in 436, and an army of the latter was commanded by Pham-con-sha-dat. P. Legrand de la Liraye remarks that these names are not Anamite or Chinese.

The date of the foundation of the kingdom is unknown, but it may have existed at a very early date, and most likely, if we may trust the resemblance between Karen titles and names, and those of the monarchs and generals of Lin-y, formed one of the great Yun or Karen kingdoms that existed at one time in Indo-China. The Karen States to the north of our border, at the time of Richardson's visit in 1837, were governed by three chiefs, Pha-pho, Pha-bhang, and Key-pho. The very name Dzeuong-mai (so pronounced by the Anamites) is without doubt the Tsching-mai (or Zimmé) of the Karens, which was probably a Karen principality, under Lin-y, in A.D. 431, as Labong, the first Shan town mentioned in the Ménam valley, was not founded until A.D. 574.

Whilst the Yun Shans were occupying the country to the south of Kiang Hung, the Laos, or non-tattooing branch of the Shans, were pushing down to the eastward through the country to the south-west of Tonquin. Their kingdoms were already in existence as far south as Vien-Chang, or Chandrapuri, at the time of the foundation of the Yun Shan towns of Labong, Lagon, Phitsalok, Kamphang, and Sang-kalok in the basin of the Ménam, A.D. 574 (or one thousand and ninety-three years after the foundation of the town of Moné). This is evident from the chronicles of Labong, which relate that the first King, reigning at that city, espoused the daughter of the King of Chandrapuri, the widow of a prince of Cambodia. It was in Sangkalok that the present civil era of the Siamese, which dates from A.D. 638, and seems to be founded upon that of the Chinese, is said to have originated.

The empire of Zimmé, before the Mau conquest of A.D. 1293, seems to have extended farther than it does at present; for we find, from the chronicles of Kiang Rai, or Kiang Hai, the ancient name of which was Tsan Katsa Lacón, that the King, who had been rather unruly as an infant, breaking every cradle that he was put in until an iron one was resorted to, received Kiang Tung as a dowry, and assigned the town of Zimmé, which was before known as Muang Lamien, for the maintenance of his son.

The different chronicles are rather conflicting, for the Labong one makes the King of Labong's son the founder of the new town of Zimmé in 1289, or about the time that the Mau Shans took possession of the country, and drove the Zimmé Shans, who were the forefathers of the Siamese, to Cháliang. It is most likely that the new town of Zimmé was founded by a Mau prince, on the same site as the old one, and that no mention is made of the change of dynasty in the Labong chronicle. At the same time, the Zimmé territories were extended by the Mau as far as the Beeling River, and the Yunzaleen was colonized by Shans.

The frequent changes in the capitals of the States to the east of the Salween add greatly to the confusion met with in the chronicles. The capital of the empire of Zimmé has been at various times at Kiang Hai, Kiang Tsen, Labong, Lagon, Zimmé, and at other places.

In 638 Phra Ruang, the King of Sangkalok, a principality of Zimmé, refused to pay tribute to Cambodia, which at that time was supreme in the south of Indo-China, and, rebelling against the ruler of Zimmé, became monarch of that realm. Phra Ruang's dynasty was but short-lived, for shortly after the succession of his son, the King of Kiang Tsen took the lead of the other States, deposed him, and founded the cities of Phitsilok and Lophaburi, or Lavo.

On the death of the King of Kiang Tsen, the King of Kiang Tung seems to have been acknowledged ruler of the Yun, or Zimmé, Shans; for in 707 the son of the King of that kingdom conquered the northern half of Cambodia, settled there with a horde of Shans, and drove the inhabitants to the south amongst the Siamese, who were then in possession of the country to the south of the Great Lake. The first wave of the Yun Shans thus descended to the neighbourhood of the Gulf of Siam. From this moment the people of Cambodia were known by their present name of Khmer.

There can be little doubt that the great resemblance between the physiognomy of the Cambodians and the Shans, and the numerous words that are mutually used by them, arose from this early admixture. The language of the conquered race seems to have had the mastery, for the resemblance of the language of the Cambodians to that of the Siamese, Stiengs, Ja-Rai, and other neighbouring tribes, is much greater than to that of the Shans.

The term savages, used by so many authors to denote all the hill-tribes in Indo-China, is very inaccurate and misleading, as many of these tribes are often much more civilized and humane than the tax-ridden inhabitants of the plain country, and are indeed merely the remains of once mighty empires. M. Mouhot, after remarking that the Cambodians are an agricultural people, among whom a certain taste for art still shows itself in the carved work of the boats belonging to the better classes, and that their chief characteristic is unbounded conceit, says: "It is not so among the savages of the east, called by the Cambodians their elder brothers. I passed four months among them, and, arriving direct from Cambodia, it seemed like entering a country comparatively civilized. Great gentleness, politeness, and even sociability, struck me in these poor children of nature."

In speaking of the Ba-nhars, one of these tribes, M. Comte, a missionary in Cochin-China, after remarking that their language has nothing in common with that of the Anamites, and is very simple in its construction, soft, flowing, and easy, goes on to say: "These people manufacture the saucepans in which they cook their rice and wild herbs, the hatchets, pick-axes, and pruning-bills, which comprise all their agricultural implements, the sabres which serve them as weapons, and the long-handled knives used for various kinds of work in which they excel. Their clay calumets, tastefully ornamented with leaves or other devices, are the production of the most skilful among the tribe. The women weave pieces of white or black cloth, which they use for coverings, and which, coarse as they are, form the principal article of commerce between the Ba-nhars and the Se-dangs. The villagers who live on the bank of the river Bla make light canoes, which are both solid and graceful, out of the trunks of trees. Such are the principal articles produced by the Ba-nhars, who are more backward than any of the other tribes, having little inventive genius." Surely "savage" is a harsh term to apply to a people who are not savage in their disposition, and who possess more skill as handicraftsmen than most of our villagers in Europe.

The influence of China over the eastern and southern kingdoms in Indo-China seems to have commenced at a very early period. M. Terrien de La Couperie says: "In B.C. 1109, the Anamites had a phonetic writing, and in several instances we have tidings bearing on the existence of such writings, composed of a certain number of Chinese simple characters used according to the phonetic principle disused amongst the Chinese, as we largely know. These simple characters, selected by progressive elimination of the less easy to draw and combine, formed a special script, of which we know several offshoots, and have been according to my views, and as far as affinities of shape and tradition are to be trusted, the *Grundschrift*, with which has been framed that splendid monument of Brahmanic phonetic lore—the South Indian alphabet, or Lat-Pali."

From B.C. 110 to A.D. 900, Anam, which then comprised none of the country to the south of Tonquin, remained tributary to China, and was at times ruled by a Chinese governor. At the close of the Thang dynasty the tributary kings took advantage of the disturbances to free themselves, and even Kwangsi became nearly independent. Kublai Khan, the Mongol emperor, re-subjugated these kingdoms, and Anam was again under the domination of China from 1282 to 1418, at which time, a usurper having seized the throne, the Chinese entered the country and governed it as a province until 1428, when, owing to the harassing attacks of the hill-tribes and other neighbours, they considered it so fruitless and unpleasant an acquisition, that they withdrew, and ever since have been contented with its remaining a vassal governed by native princes.

Lin-y, Lam-ap, or Tchen-Tching, the Karen kingdom, for some time barred the onward progress of the Shans and Anamites, but ultimately moved downwards upon the Siamese, Lewa, and Mun, as they themselves were forced to migrate by the onward rush of the upper population. During the fourth century it is likely that Karens were the rulers of Cambodia, and that it and Lin-y formed parts of the same empire. The incessant wars that Lin-y carried on with its neighbours were futile to prevent their gradual absorption of its territories; and the magic sword, possessed by its rulers in the fourth century, and still treasured amongst the Ja-Rai, now only sways over portions of a shattered nation, the remains of which are found with the Siamese and other aboriginal tribes in the hills of Indo-China.

When the Chinese helped Anam to conquer Lin-y, in A.D. 543, its riches were said to be immense. Amongst the treasure were found eighteen massive gold statues of the predecessors of the reigning monarch. Most of the troops engaged during the campaign died of disease. In A.D. 979 the Chinese governors having been replaced by native chiefs in Anam, who were constantly warring against each other, the King of Lin-y sent a large fleet to attack the capital, which was dispersed in a storm. In 981 Anam retaliated, and the King, abandoning his capital, left in the Anamite hands abundant riches, a hundred of his wives, and an Indian monk. In 1020 and 1042 war was again renewed.

In 1282 Kublai Khan's ambassadors to Lin-y, or Tchen-Tching, who had come to demand that the King should become a vassal of China, were imprisoned by the King, and the ensuing wars did not always prove successful for the Mongols, nor end in the subjugation of the country. It seems to have been a thorough hornet of a neighbour, for in 1408 we hear of ambassadors being sent from Cambodia to China, imploring help to put a stop to the incursions of the inhabitants of Tchen-Tching. The power of the kingdom must have been rapidly decreasing and its dominions diminishing about this time, for the Anamites had already become neighbours of the

Cambodians. Between 1373 and 1385 we hear of them, for the first time, aiding Cambodia in its endeavours to repulse Siam.

The Laos Shan principalities were also growing in power, and contracting Tchen-Tching on the west. The seventeenth monarch of the Laos kingdom of Vien-Chang, or Lan Sang, who had married a daughter of the King of Cambodia, came to the throne about 1350, and carried on many wars. By 1373 Laos had arrived at a great degree of splendour; a census taken at this time gave for this kingdom three hundred thousand heads of houses, not counting slaves and mountaineers. One of the grandchildren of the King who was then reigning married a daughter of the King of Siam, and another a daughter of the King of Zimmé.

Between 1501 and 1558 Vien-Chang joined in the civil wars of Anam, and became ruler of Zimmé. In 1558 the King of Pegu seized the latter country and ravaged Laos. In 1571 Laos attacked Cambodia, but was repulsed. In 1592 it was conquered by Burmah, and its inhabitants removed to Pegu, where the population had been destroyed during thirty years of warfare, but they soon revolted and escaped back to their country.

The last period of prosperity for Vien-Chang was during the time that lapsed between 1628 and 1652; from that time a number of civil wars destroyed its power, and Luang Prabang declared its independence, and became a separate kingdom. Cambodia being weakened, emigrants from Laos settled at Bassac in

1712, and that portion of the country became part of the kingdom. In 1777 it was made tributary to Siam, at which time Vien-Chang, Bassac, and Attopeu were left in ruins. The Tonquinese destroyed its capital in 1791, and it was finally conquered and became a province of Siam in 1827.

SUPPLEMENTARY CHAPTER (*continued*).

PART II.

HISTORY OF LOWER SHAN.

Cambodia—Prea Thong—Entrance of Brahmanism, architecture, and sculpture—Conversion to Buddhism—Divisions of empire—Homage to China—Prosperity—Arrival of Portuguese and English—The commencement of the French empire in Indo-China—Brahmanism and Buddhism—Description of people—Conquest of Cambodia by Shans—*Wars* of Siam, Zimmé, Cambodia, Burmah, and Pegu—Peace after 2,000 years of warfare—Growth of French power in Indo-China—French action in Anam—Investiture of Anamese King by China necessary—Concluding remarks.

THE once mighty empire of Cambodia, which at one time had commercial relations with the Roman empire, is first heard of in the Anamese chronicles, B.C. 1109, when an indigenous queen was ruling in Phonam, which is the name it was anciently known by to the Chinese. The next we hear of it is at the time of the advent of a Brahman, called Prea Thong, or Houen-houy, who is said to have come from Romanvisei, or Ki, and married the queen. This is reported to have happened in A.D. 68, which is the commencement of the old Cambodian era. He is believed to have introduced Brahmanism, architecture, sculpture, and astronomy into Cambodia; and there can be little doubt that between this time and 422, when

Buddhism was brought into the country, many of the ancient buildings which display the objects of Brahmanic worship were erected.

At the time of his arrival the empire was divided into seven principalities, which were governed by princes of the royal family. On the death of the Brahman's son, the people were so disgusted by the constant civil wars, which were consequent on the feudal division of the empire, that they are said to have elected the commander-in-chief of the army to the joint throne. This may imply that the empire was conquered and annexed by the Karens, for up to 422, when another native of India was raised to the throne, the emperors' names began with Phan, as was the case with the names of the rulers of Lin-y.

Phonam, Founan, or Cambodia, did homage at various times to China between B.C. 125 and A.D. 1435; and there are many accounts of embassies passing to and fro. From these it appears that early in this period Cambodia had reached a very great height of prosperity and gaudeous splendour. In the third century trade from its ports was carried on with countries as far west as the Roman empire, mention being made of merchants from that country being met with by the Chinese ambassadors. Palaces, towers, and theatres were erected for the reception and amusement of the guests.

The next Europeans who visited the Gulf of Siam seem to have been the Portuguese, who sent a messenger to Siam at the time they were besieging Malacca, in 1511. The first English establishment

A A

was founded at Poulo Condor in 1702, but in 1717 the Macassar portion of the garrison rose and massacred the Europeans, only two escaping. In 1777 Poulo Condor and the peninsula of Tourane were granted by Anam to the French, and this has formed the small edge of the wedge which may end in displacing the cruel Anamite dynasty from the shores of Indo-China.

The violent antagonism between Brahmanism and Buddhism, during the first centuries of our era, seems to have been at its height during the fifth century, and many Buddhist preachers are believed to have left India for Indo-China and the islands to the south of it. One of these, called Prea Ket Melia, or Kiao-tchen-jou, was raised to the throne of Founan about 422, and introduced the Buddhist religion and code of laws.

This Indian dynasty seems to have ended about 581, when the name of the empire was changed from Founan to Tchin-la. Previous to this time, travellers from China described the people of Cambodia as a black race, with long hair knotted on the top of the head; the rich wearing only a silk loin-cloth, and the poor one of cotton. The women had head-coverings, and decked themselves with beautifully carved silver jewellery set with precious stones.

The men excelled in making jewellery, gold and silver vases, furniture, and domestic utensils. Two crops were obtained from the land during the year. They were honest, and hated theft above all things.

There were no prisons, but the mode of trial was

worthy of the worst days of our Middle Ages. The accused was made to fast for three days, then hold a red-hot axe, or search in boiling water for iron rings. If their hands were not burned, they were declared to be innocent. Another way was to shut them up for three days with tigers, leopards, or with crocodiles, which were kept in the canals of the town, or to throw them into the river. If they survived, they were set free.

They had historians and learned men, and their literature differed little from that of the strangers from the north (India ?). The houses were constructed of wood, generally well raised from the ground, so as to have an extensive view; but some were low and small, and were thatched and not tiled. The boats were eighty and ninety feet long, seven broad, and shaped like a fish. Their delight was in cock and pig fighting, and their manners were the same as those of Lin-y.

When a relation died, they shaved their heads and beards. There were four modes of sepulture—throwing into the river, burning, burying, and exposing in desert places, where the corpses would be devoured by birds of prey. Offerings were made on a high mountain called Mi-tan, where the air was always hot, and the trees evergreen. The offerings consisted of five rolls of different coloured silks. The statues of their gods were made of copper, and some had two heads and four arms, others four heads and eight arms; in each hand was a bird, animal, child, the sun, moon, etc.

The walls of the capital were palisaded with trunks of trees. The King lived in a palace well elevated; he went out mounted on an elephant, white cloths being spread for it to kneel on, the people burning perfumes before him during his ride. The queen likewise appeared in public on an elephant. The people were not as warlike as the people of Lin-y, who were in constant collision with them.

The above description seems to refer to the inhabitants previous to the entrance of Buddhism in 422. A later description says that "the inhabitants are small and black, go barefoot, and perfume their bodies. They are active and robust, set great store on literature, have skilful astronomers, who foretell eclipses, and were in possession of many small horses. There are magnificent edifices, faced always to the east. The towns, thirty in number, have many thousand inhabitants. Their laws and manners are the same as those of Lin-y, with which country they are always at war. They go about armed, cut off the hands and feet of thieves to prevent them returning to their malpractices, bathe without distinction of sex or rank in the same tanks, one of which is dug by every two or three families, and clean their teeth with a twig. Some expose corpses to birds of prey, others burn them and preserve the ashes in gold or silver vases. They are skilful in rearing elephants, the five thousand which were kept for war being fed on meat."

Only the children of the legitimate queen could come to the throne, and each new King mutilated all his brothers by cutting off their fingers or noses, after which they had to live under a guardian in a separate place. Even as late as the end of the seventh century human sacrifices used to be offered up on Mount Bakheng, round which a guard of a thousand soldiers were kept. Each year, according to the Chinese historians, the King went to the temple in the night to offer up a sacrifice of this nature.

It shows how priestcraft can alter the pure religious and moral code of a religion, when not only were such sacrifices offered up by a monarch professing Buddhism, but when to this day (according to De Carné), at Phnom, a place on the Mékong, where Buddhists come to worship, the mutilation of pilgrims is encouraged by the monks, who perform the operation of cutting off pieces of fingers very cleverly, with the help of a chopper and a foot-rule, and measure the zeal of the pilgrim by the extent of the sacrifice.

For about a hundred years after the conquest of the northern half of Cambodia, or Tchin-la, by the Yun Shans in 707, the lower half was under the dominion of the Siamese, but at a period between 806 and 820 they became re-united. In 1296 the Mau Shans attacked Cambodia, and perhaps made it tributary. In 1352, two years after the founding of Ayuthia by the Siamese, or Yun Shans, Ancor, the capital, was besieged and taken by the Siamese King, who governed it, with the aid of his sons, until it became again independent in 1358. During this period Siam is said to have removed ninety thousand Cambodians as captives to Siam. In 1373 the Siamese again attacked Ancor, killed the King, and placed a Siamese prince, who was however soon assassinated, on the throne. The son of the King of Cambodia, who had taken refuge in Anam, returned, and with the aid of the Anamites regained the throne.

About this time, Siam, Zimmé, Cambodia, Burmah, and Pegu became so mixed up in constant warfare that by following the history of Siam we shall be able to display the progress of events that have rendered whole regions of a most fertile country nearly desolate, and to show how our humane influence, since we occupied the western coast of Indo-China, has brought the blessings of peace upon our own provinces and upon our neighbours, who were fast destroying each other in constant, senseless, and most ruthless warfare.

The Siamese empire may be said to have commenced at the founding of Ayuthia in 1350. In 1306 the King of Martaban and Pegu threw off his vassalage to the Mau empire, quarrelled with the Mau King of Zimmé, and added his country, together with Tavoy and Tenasserim, to his dominions. By 1330 the Siamese had taken the two latter provinces from the Peguans. The Zimmé Shans must have thrown off the yoke before 1350, for in that year mention is made of their having ravaged the Peguan dominions as far as the Beeling River. In 1382–84, five years after its last attack on Cambodia, Siam warred against Zimmé, and carried away many captives. During the absence of the Siamese army at Zimmé in 1384, Cambodia conquered several towns, and led six thousand Siamese into captivity.

On his return in 1385, the King of Siam took vengeance, drove the Cambodian monarch from his capital, took his son prisoner, and left only five thousand inhabitants in the once densely populated capital. A Siamese general remained with five thousand troops to keep the country in subjection. The Anamites again helped the King of Cambodia to recover his dominions, but in 1388 he was so harassed by Siam that he changed his residence from Ancor to Basan, and afterwards to Pnompenh, which is the present capital of Cambodia.

In 1430 Siam again pillaged Zimmé, and brought away twelve thousand of its inhabitants. In 1437 the King of Cambodia removed his capital back to Ancor, after which, for a hundred years, civil wars, encouraged by Siam, desolated the kingdom. Early in this period Ancor was finally abandoned, and the capital was fixed sometimes at Basan and sometimes at Pnompenh.

Hmine Long-gyee was seized by Pegu in 1480–1490.

In 1516 a clever and energetic monarch ascended the Cambodian throne, who re-conquered the whole kingdom, and in 1528 removed the capital to Lovec. The ruins of the magnificent temples that he built in this city are found to the north of Udong. In 1530 he seized a Siamese town, but was punished by the King of Siam, who entered his kingdom in 1532, and made him give up his sons as hostages. In 1540 the Siamese were worsted in a battle that took place in the suburbs of Ancor.

In 1544 Pegu conquered Burmah and Siam, and

remained supreme over Burmah until 1596. Next year Siam rebelled, and Burmah attacked Ayuthia, but was repulsed, owing to fifty Portuguese joining in and directing the defence. Two years later, in 1547, Pegu demanded two white elephants from Siam, and, on being refused, attacked it with nine hundred thousand men, seven thousand elephants, and fifteen thousand cavalry, but retired on receiving a recompense of four white elephants.

In 1555 Pegu took Ayuthia by treachery, and left only a thousand people in it, taking back innumerable captives and immense wealth. In 1557, 1560, 1562, and 1563, Cambodia attacked Siam, and nearly depopulated the country, but was defeated by the Siamese in the latter year, and the war came to an end.

In 1553 the first Catholic missionaries penetrated Cambodia, and regular missions were founded in Cochin-China in 1610, in Cambodia in 1615, in Tonquin in 1626, in Champa in 1630, and in Laos in 1632.

The first missionary to Tonquin was the Italian Jesuit, Julian Baldinotti, who arrived in 1626; he was followed in 1627 by Alexander de Rhodes, a Frenchman, and Antonio Marquez, a Portuguese; these were expelled in May, 1630, but numerous successors followed them. Persecutions ensued; Messari died in prison on the 15th of June, 1723. Buccharelli was beheaded, with nine Tonquinese, on the 11th of October, 1723. John Caspard Crats, born in Germany in 1698, Bartholomew Alvarez, born in Portugal in 1706, Emanuel de Alreu, born in Portugal in the same year, and Vincent de Cunha, born in Lisbon in 1708, were beheaded on the 12th of January, 1737.

After the persecution of 1737, there was a period of calm, and the King of Tonquin even sent to Macao for some mathematicians, and on the 6th of March, 1751, Father Simonelli and four other Jesuits arrived; but the King changed his mind, and did not require their services. The Jesuits were replaced by the envoys of the *Missions étrangères* in 1659. In 1679 Tonquin was divided into two religious provinces—Eastern and Western. The Spanish Dominicans took charge of Eastern Tonquin in 1693. It is now divided into four parts—Western, Eastern, Central, and Southern—the *Missions étrangères* having the Western and Southern, and the Spanish Dominicans the two other divisions. There are said to be four hundred thousand Christians now in Tonquin.

In 1563 an embassy was sent by Pegu to demand one of the four white elephants possessed by the King of Siam, and, on an evasive answer being given, the Pegu army attacked Zimmé, whose ruler refused to allow the army to enter its towns, and, after besieging and taking them, proceeded to Ayuthia, sacked it, placed one of the sons of the King on the throne, took many prisoners, and returned to Pegu, where a rebellion amongst the Shan and Talaing, Talain or Peguans, had broken out. This was quelled with great cruelty. The Peguan force was withdrawn from Zimmé in 1565.

In 1568 Siam, with the aid of Vien-Chang, or Laos,

rebelled, and conquered Zimmé. The Peguans returned, captured Ayuthia, by the help of treachery, and placed a Zimmé chief on the throne. Operations against Laos proved unsuccessful, and the troops were recalled in 1570. Other raids were made on Laos in 1571 and 1574.

In 1566 the King of Cambodia sent an auxiliary army of ten thousand men, a hundred elephants, and three hundred cavalry, to assist Siam in its struggle against Pegu and Zimmé; but animosity arose between the princes who commanded the armies, and in 1570 Cambodia attacked Siam and seized Korat and Prachim. It was equally fortunate against Laos, both by water and land, and destroyed the Laos war-boats near Stung Treng on the Mékong. During this time we are told that commerce declined; and Ancor, the old capital of Cambodia, according to Spaniards and Portuguese who visited it at this period, was completely abandoned.

In 1579 Zimmé tried in vain to shake off the yoke of Pegu.

In 1581 Siam, once more free, attacked Cambodia with an army of a hundred thousand men, but had to retire at the end of three months. The King of Siam returned in 1585, and, with the aid of treachery, captured Lovec, which was then the capital, and, in accordance with a revengeful vow, washed his feet in the blood of the Cambodian monarch.

In 1587, according to Ralf Fitch, who was then in Burmah, Pegu attacked Siam with three hundred thousand men and five thousand elephants, and invested Ayuthia, but was forced to retire. In the same year the King of Siam invaded Pegu, and took ten thousand captives. He then advanced upon Cambodia, which seems to have joined the Peguans in their war against Siam, and again bathed his feet in the same barbarous manner as he had done in 1585.

In 1594 Siam invaded Pegu and Martaban, and was joined by the whole of the Talain population, but being threatened by an advance of the King of Toungoo, a vassal of Pegu, retired, together with a large number of the population. This attack seems to have been the finishing stroke to the Peguan empire, which fell to pieces two years later. By 1600 Siam was in possession of Martaban, Tenasserim, and Tavoy.

In 1595 Cambodia drove the Siamese out of their kingdom; but, six years after, the Siamese returned, and placed a prince of Cambodia, who had been educated at the Siamese court, on the throne. The son of this prince shook off the Siamese yoke, and repelled two subsequent invasions. He died in 1627. From this date a series of civil wars and revolutions occurred in Cambodia, Siam and Anam taking opposite sides. One of the usurpers turned Mahomedan to please the Anamites and Malays, and moved his capital to Udong. The Siamese got the upper hand in 1690, and kept the provinces between Ancor and Korat as their recompense.

About 1610 the Burmese recovered Martaban, Tavoy, and, a few years later, Tenasserim and Zimmé. The Burman King shortly after this became emperor, and gave rise to the Burman empire, which continued until 1740. Zimmé rebelled in 1628, but was again subdued two years later. In 1658 the Chinese attacked Ava, the capital of Burmah, but were repulsed; the Siamese were no luckier in their raid on it three years later, but managed to conquer Zimmé.

In 1686 Constance Phaulcon, a Greek, who had risen high in the favour of the King of Siam, persuaded the King to apply to the King of France for a body-guard of a hundred men, to be commanded by their own officers. With these he garrisoned and strengthened the fortress of Ayuthia, and got the King to apply to the King of France for two hundred more troops, with which he intended to prevent the brothers of the king, who was dying of dropsy, from succeeding to the throne, and to raise, instead of them, a son-in-law, who would prove a mere puppet in his hands. The plot was discovered, Constance Phaulcon was executed, and what must have proved the annexation of Siam to the French dominions prevented.

In 1706 the Siamese succeeded in driving the Anamites out of Cambodia, and controlled the succession. The king who succeeded in 1748 was for four years at war with the Anamites, who had completely conquered the Siamese and annexed Champa. This war cost the Cambodians the provinces of Saigon and My-tho; and the next King, to gain his investiture from Anam, had to cede the coast provinces of Bassac and Tra Vinh. For doing this he was assassinated by his son-in-law. Another King was then raised to the throne by the Anamites, who received in return the province of Vinh-long and permission to build citadels at Sadeck and Chaudoc.

In 1740 the Siamese were the cause of the fall of the Burman empire, by enabling the Talains to drive the Burmese out of Pegu. The independence of Pegu did not last long, for in 1755 the great Burman conqueror Aloung-bhoora, or Alompra, came to the throne. In 1757 he annexed Pegu, Tavoy, and Mergui; in 1758, Manipur; in 1759, Tenasserim. In 1760 he laid siege to Ayuthia, the capital of Siam, but, falling ill, he retired, and died before he could reach Martaban.

In 1763 Zimmé recovered its independence, but was again conquered by Burmah two years afterwards, at which time the emperor of Burmah besieged Ayuthia for two years, took and set fire to it, nearly depopulated the country, and left a Peguan as governor. As soon as the main Burman army had departed, Phyá Tak, who was of Chinese parentage on his father's side, raised a guerilla force, and at length got so strong that he was able to drive the remaining Burmese from the country, put down the bandits who were disturbing the interior, and raise himself to the throne.

He had formerly been governor of one of the northern cities, and knew how to choose, and showed the good policy of remaining faithful to, his friends. By the aid of two brothers, sons of a nobleman of high rank, who were accomplished and brave generals, he succeeded in overcoming all other pretenders to the throne, and most luckily had time to recover the strength of the kingdom before another attack, as the

Burmese were engaged in resisting the Chinese, who attacked them in 1767 and 1769.

In 1771 the Burmese force which was sent against Siam happened to be chiefly composed of Peguans, who, on arriving at Martaban, massacred their Burmese fellow-soldiers, and carried on a revolt for three years, until they were attacked by a Burmese force and beaten at Martaban.

In 1769 Phyá Tak conquered Korat and Cambodia. In 1772 he again attacked the latter country with twenty thousand men, and took Hatien, and put a Cambodian prince of his own choice on the throne, who was dethroned by the Anamites the next year. Two years later, the Tayson rebellion having nearly ruined Anam, My-tho and Vinh-long were retaken by the Cambodians.

In 1774 Siam made Zimmé tributary. In the same year Burmah attacked Manipur and Cachar, which became tributary. In 1777, Laos, or Vien-Chang, was reduced to vassalage by Siam.

In 1780 the Anamites, who had re-established their authority at Saigon, made war on the Cambodian King, whose subjects were in rebellion, and replaced him by his son, who was only eight years old. The Siamese at once entered the kingdom, took possession of the young King, and returned to Bangkok, but replaced him on the throne in 1785. Soon after this the Anamite King had to take refuge from the Tayson in Bangkok, and it was only owing to French officers that Gia-long was enabled to recover his throne.

From 1740 to 1786 Canhung was King of Tonquin and the upper third of Cochin-China. At the latter date Huê Vuong was sovereign over the remaining two-thirds of Cochin-China. His brutality caused him to be so much disliked that the influential family of Tayson raised a rebellion and killed him. The kingdom was then divided between two of the brothers of the family. In 1786 the Tayson attacked Tonquin and annexed the upper third of Cochin-China.

In 1793 Gialong (who was then known as Nguyen-Anh), a nephew of Huê Vuong, with the help of French officers, recovered the lower third of Cochin-China, and by 1801 the whole kingdom was in his possession. In 1802 he attacked and defeated the King of Tonquin, which kingdom has since formed a province of Cochin-China, and gives the name Ngan-nam, or Annam, to the whole of the kingdom.

In 1790 the six provinces of Cochin-China, which are now under the French, were subject to Anam; and Cambodia, which was reduced to the provinces around the lake and to the part of the valley of the Mékong between the cataracts of Khong and Pnom-penh, was a mere tributary to Siam. It was only in 1795 that the Siamese allowed the King's family to rejoin him from Bangkok. In 1805 his son, a mere child, who had succeeded his father, was conducted to Bangkok to take the oath of fealty. In 1810 the Siamese acquired the provinces of Tonly-Repou and Mulu Prey, and shortly afterwards Battambong. In 1830 they annexed Pursat and Compong-soai.

On the death of the King of Cambodia in 1832, the Anamites raised his daughter to the throne, and placed an Anamite governor over it, who took the queen as his mistress. The Cambodian chiefs asked for the intervention of Siam, and the King of that country sent his famous general, who had annexed Vien-Chang in 1827, to their aid. Having driven out the usurper, he raised one of the Cambodian princes, who had been kept at Bangkok, to the throne in 1841. The sons of this monarch were educated at the Siamese capital, and the one who succeeded him fully acknowledged himself as viceroy under the dominion of the King of Siam.

In the meantime the wars between Burmah and Siam had been brought to a close by our taking possession of the sea-coast and the country lying between the Salween and the Thoungyeen, through which all the raids upon Siam and Burmah had been made, and there was only left the path across the now independent Shan States, which is of a most difficult and perilous nature. Many high ranges, some of which are between five and six thousand feet high, have to be crossed before Mandalay on the one hand, and the Mékong River on the other, is attained. The passes can be defended by a handful of men; and whichever party happened to be defeated in its attack would be nearly certain to be massacred by the hill-tribes who would join the victors. Besides which, it was understood that on no account would we have Siam attacked, as it was on friendly terms with us, and had become a field for our trade.

The wars between Burmah and Siam had always been caused by the Burmese, and by our action in 1826 and 1852 we had so reduced their power, that, however they might bluster and annoy us with their pretensions, they dare not attempt to do what they knew we would not allow.

Previous to the Franco-Spanish intervention of 1858, Peace seems to have thrown its cloak over the part of Indo-China to the west of Anam. It was at length at rest, after its two thousand years of nearly continuous warfare. Cambodia and Laos were perfectly contented with the Siamese dominion; and Anam was powerless against the strength of Siam, and was still hampered with rebellions which had been going on since its conquest of Tonquin in 1802.

In 1862 Anam ceded the Cochin-Chinese provinces of My-tho, Saigon, and Bienhoa to France, and Admiral de la Grandière, the French governor, seized three other provinces in 1867. In 1863 Admiral de la Grandière, according to M. de Carné, who was then on his staff, took advantage of the absence of the Siamese Resident from the court of Cambodia, and coaxed the King into signing a treaty. In M. de Carné's words—"The king, perhaps a little surprised, and hardly perhaps comprehending the meaning of the word 'protectorate,' which is as hard to define in Cambodian as in French, readily consented to set his seal to a treaty of nineteen articles, in which the protectorate of France over Cambodia, solemnly proclaimed, was surrounded by all the guarantees we wished to obtain." The King of Siam, on hearing of this, said that he had no objection to his becoming a vassal of France; but if he did, a new governor would be put in his place, and refused to crown him, which he had not yet done. The King of Cambodia at once signed a treaty with Siam, acknowledging that he was a subject of the King of Siam, and merely the governor of Cambodia. The French, however, persisted in their claim, which was not, however, allowed by Siam until 1868.

The present action of the French in Anam is precisely similar to that taken by them in Cambodia; but it is not probable that China will ever allow Tonquin to be made a base for the French to dismember the Chinese empire. Tonquin and Anam, as we have seen, have been under the domination of China, with but one interval (from A.D. 900 to about 1255, the time of the Mongol conquest), from B.C. 110 to the present time, and no amount of denial on the part of the French can efface this fact from its history. The King of Anam is not acknowledged by his own subjects as the rightful ruler until he has received his investiture from the emperor of China.

We have now followed the Shans as they gradually spread from the basin of the Yangtsi-kiang to the south of Indo-China; have seen how great empires have been broken up and their inhabitants been forced to take refuge in the hill-country; have watched the effect of the lust of conquest upon these countries, and seen the desolation it has brought about; have seen that a religion which makes it a sin to kill a fly is not strong enough to prevent the monarchs who hold it from massacring millions of their fellow-creatures, and attempting to force the whole world to grovel at their feet as their slaves. We have seen that the good old days for Eastern monarchs brought but cruelty, slavery, starvation, misery, and all the horrors of war upon a people who, even now, are the most hospitable, kindly, and charitable race of the East. Nowhere will you find greater geniality and a more courteous welcome than "Amongst the Shans."

I have pleasure in acknowledging the courtesy of H.H. Prince Prisdang, the Siamese Ambassador, in placing at my disposal papers and books which have aided me in writing this chapter. I am likewise indebted to Mr. Trelawney Saunders, of the India Office, and Mr. E. C. Rye, of the Royal Geographical Society, for the valuable advice they have given me as to the books and manuscripts it would be useful for me to consult.

HOLT S. HALLETT.

APPENDIX.

Opinions on Mr. COLQUHOUN'S Proposed Railway for the Connection of Siam, the Shan States, and S.W. China with British Burmah.

From The Times.

"It is in the East that we must look for the markets of the future. In Europe every nation is striving with all its might to become independent of our manufacturers, and when the Americans have in some measure finished their great work of possessing the land, their inventiveness and energy will leave us few openings. In the East are vast populations as yet very imperfectly thrown open to our commerce."

From The Chamber of Commerce Journal.

"'Across Chrysê' is just the book that is calculated to rivet the attention of all who recognise the advantage of opening up new markets for British goods."

From The Times.

"We think that his experiences and observations, which he has placed before the reader in such a clear and pleasant form, will not fail to bring home to the dullest and most apathetic mind the fact that the route advocated by him will, before very long, be one of the principal highways of commerce, and that these border lands of two great empires are destined to become, at no distant date, the scene of a most active and not less useful or remunerative trade. In 'Across Chrysê' the public will find solid stores of information about one of the most promising outlets for our future trade that we can see in any part of the world."

From THE GLASGOW HERALD.

"Members of Parliament and the commercial community generally have taken deep interest in the project; and Government not only granted Mr. Colquhoun full pay during the time of his exploration, but extra allowances during the six months employed in bringing his scheme prominently before the public in Great Britain. All this shows the universal interest that has been excited.

"Until Mr. Colquhoun's return from China, no practical scheme had been laid before the Government and the public, and therefore the development of the Shan country still remained a mere dream of the future. Mr. Colquhoun has been able to point out to the Government and the public, not only the enormous trade which may be created with the Shan and neighbouring countries, but has also been able to show clearly and uncontrovertibly the easiest direction from which the Shan country can be approached. In no single case that we have noticed has any member of the Government or of the commercial body gainsaid in any particular what Mr. Colquhoun has put before them, either as to the commercial value of the development of trade with the country, or the facility with which it may be attained. The scheme seems well worthy of all the support asked for it, and every effort should be made to secure the new market for this country."

Letter from PRINCE PRISDANG, *Siamese Ambassador, dated June 5th,* 1883.

"I have no hesitation in informing you that any well-digested scheme which has for its object the improvement of the commercial position of Siam, and the consolidation of the kingdom, will receive the attentive consideration of His Majesty and my Government; and that His Majesty will allow all facilities to be given for any purposes of exploration, or of gaining accurate knowledge, by properly qualified persons, of the nature of the country proposed to be traversed by the railway. . . . I shall be glad to take an early opportunity to inform my Government of your intention to visit Siam for the purpose of exploration with a view to the proposed railway, and I hope you may be successful in gaining whatever knowledge you may wish to get for this purpose."

From Royal Geographical Proceedings.

Lord Northbrook said: "He could assure the Society that Mr. Colquhoun's journey had attracted great attention from the Government of India, because he had recently received letters both from Sir Charles Aitcheson, Lieutenant-Governor of the Punjab, who was formerly Chief Commissioner in Burmah, and Major Evelyn Baring, Finance Minister of India, especially commending to his notice the journey of Mr. Colquhoun. From what he had heard to-night, certain parts of that journey were of great political importance to India, and more especially the discovery that the Shan States on the borders of Burmah and Siam were now independent both of China and Burmah."

Sir James Bain, as a director of the Chamber of Commerce of Glasgow, "felt sure that it was through the British provinces of India and Burmah that China would be approached in the most effective manner. Attempts had been made by the French to enter China by Tongking, but he was convinced that the true, and best, and most advantageous route would be through the British provinces."

Sir Thomas Wade said: "He wished to offer his congratulations to Mr. Colquhoun, not only for having completed a journey of singular interest from a geographical point of view, for he might be said to have discovered a new country, but also for the prospect he had given of commercial advantages by the route he indicated, whenever it became practicable in the manner which he hoped. Englishmen were to be congratulated on having found a new route, though they had not yet got the railways made, which they would be able to use without attracting the jealousy either of the French or the Chinese. He joined with Colonel Yule in the hope that Mr. Colquhoun would be enabled to continue his explorations without in any way suffering in respect to his official advancement."

From Chamber of Commerce Journal, *November 15th*, 1882.

"The article which we bring before the commercial public to-day deals more especially with the possibility of opening out one or more New Markets for British manufactures, of civilizing and educating new nationalities, of attaching them to us by peace and self-interest, and of teaching them how best to exchange their produce for our merchandise.

"Apart from the intrinsic value of Mr. Colquhoun's carefully collected facts, precedents are in favour of his proving his case. With energy and experience the British nation has built up, in India, one of the most successful instances of occupation-government which the history of the world records. Under our rule, the various peoples of our vast Indian Empire are bound together in friendly intercourse by the ties of civilization and commerce; whereas if they had continued to direct their own fortunes, there is little doubt that the dissensions, civil war and oppression, which are inseparable from the rule of native and rival princes, would have impoverished the country and rendered the existence of the aborigines one of misery and semi-slavery. Even more successful than in India have we been in Burmah. When we first took possession of British Burmah, whole provinces were so poor, and so sparsely inhabited, that we should have been glad to rid ourselves of what menaced, then, to become a costly and useless appendage. So unfailing, however, is native judgment, in its recognition of the peaceful protection of our paternal Government, that the population immediately commenced to increase by emigration from surrounding States, and has since progressed from year to year.

"We need not quote other examples in proof of this theory. We are a colonizing nation, and are open to learn and improve. That being so, success must, with a given amount of initiative, attend our labour. The past should encourage us to persevere in our forward course. New efforts are forced upon us, both by the growing necessity for new markets, and by the activity which French, Russians, Italians, are displaying.

"The two leading features of Mr. Colquhoun's paper can be briefly summarised without diminishing the interest which a perusal of the original cannot fail to raise. He is able to state, firstly, that the Shan country has recovered its independence, and no longer pays tribute either to Burmah or to China. When we bear in mind that the Shan people are a quiet, commercial race, and not an aggressive or warlike nation, that they grow the finest tea of all Asiatic countries, and that the mineral wealth of the country is great, we at once see in these facts alone that Mr. Colquhoun has made a discovery of considerable importance. When we are further told, as the second new feature, that the south-western portion of Yunnan is greatly more fertile and rich in produce and minerals than the north-eastern section of the province, then the importance of the peaceful and wealthy Shan country, as a means of access to Yunnan, becomes apparent. Mr. Colquhoun's suggestion is to carry a railway through this Shan country up to the south-west Yunnan frontier, and he argues that as both the surrounding country and the terminal province are highly productive, the proposed railway has every prospect of answering as well as those which have been so satisfactory in neighbouring Burmah. His argument certainly bears traces of serious logic.

"Our American cousins have developed the trade and growth of the United States by opening up roads and railways in advance of its population. Stanley commences his African campaign for the king of the Belgians by road-making and the establishment of stations. Let us show ourselves worthy of our reputation as a practical people by following these excellent examples. Communications are the basis by which trade is first generated, and subsequently increased. If we select for our operations States naturally rich, as the Shan country and Yunnan appear to be, we cannot do better than provide, in advance, for the commerce which our foresight and energy can create, and the due enjoyment of which is assured to us from our recognised power by land and sea."

Opinions of SIR ARTHUR PHAYRE, *formerly Chief Commissioner of British Burmah.*

Sir ARTHUR PHAYRE in 1862 wrote: "Direct British trade with the Shans and Western Chinese overland from Rangoon is of vast importance. To British Burmah it is all in all. Increase in trade and increase in population; and *this* increase from the finest population in Asia, the Chinese."

In 1865 Sir ARTHUR PHAYRE said: "To the north-east of British Burmah lies the country of the Shans, a people divided into small States, under independent chiefs. They are industrious and energetic, long for free trade, and possess a marvellous capacity for travelling as petty traders. Their country having no great navigable river, for the Salween *is* full of rocks and rapids throughout its course, all their trade is carried on by land. Having no carts, they carry their goods hundreds of miles *on the backs of bullocks, or on their own shoulders.* They come yearly in numbers to British Burmah. A road, railway or other, from Rangoon through their States to China, would extend commerce with this enterprising people, and bring the products of Yunnan direct to British Burmah and Rangoon."

In 1881 Sir ARTHUR PHAYRE said: "The great object of establishing and maintaining a *direct* trade with Yunnan has not been accomplished," and "the inland trade of British Burmah with Independent Burmah and the Shan States is only yet in its infancy, but it has made great strides within the last few years."

From CHAMBER OF COMMERCE JOURNAL, *June 5th*, 1883.

FRANCE AND ENGLAND IN INDO-CHINA.—This *Journal* was one of the first organs of the British press to direct public attention to the commercial value of Mr. A. R. Colquhoun's travels[1] in Indo-China. When we first discussed the possibility of opening up the Shan States and the Yunnan provinces to trade, by the creation of a railway, the question appeared to be simply an economical one for the consideration of Eastern and particularly of Indian and Burmese merchants. Since December last, however, the matter has entered on a new phase. The agitation which M. Dupuis has carried on for many years in France has at last borne fruit, and in conjunction with a somewhat feverish Colonial policy which has caused France to undertake simultaneous "operations" in Senegal, in Ashantee, on the Senegal, the Niger, and the Congo, in Madagascar, and in Tonquin, our interests in Indo-China would appear to be politically compromised.

Apart, however, from commercial relations, there is also a political aspect in the French expedition, of which this country must not lose sight. It is decidedly menacing to Siam. It is well known that France secretly desires to compensate herself in Indo-China for the place of which we deprived her in India.

England has every interest in protecting the integrity of the Siamese kingdom. The king of Siam understands our policy in India, Burmah, and the Malay Peninsula; he is entirely satisfied with the peaceful object of our rule, and, we believe, disposed to co-operate with us both politically and economically. In this respect both the king, the Siamese, and the Shans compare favourably with King Theebau of Native Burmah, who has, of late, given us so much

[1] See the *Chamber of Commerce Journal*, Nos. 9 and 10.

trouble by his renewal of his father's monopoly grants. Siam, Mr. Colquhoun shows, is more thickly populated and a more productive country than we have hitherto believed.[1] The Shan tribes, too, promise to be valuable allies from their highly developed capacities as travelling pedlars. Through them we could, apparently, easily develop the commercial future of Indo-China. We are glad to notice that Mr. Colquhoun includes Siam in his basis of operations. The branch line to his proposed railway, placing Bangkok, the capital of Siam, in direct communication with the Shan States, must prove highly remunerative. We only trust that means will be found to meet the French agitation in Cochin-China and Tonquin, by the creation of these Siamese railways

---

From THE SATURDAY REVIEW.

"What is wanted is a regular survey of the country by practical engineers, such as Mr. Colquhoun or Mr. Holt Hallett, who has assisted him in the construction of his maps and in the collection of details. The great difficulty of the route is undoubtedly between the Main Long-gyee and Muang Haut on the Méping River, where a range 3,000 feet high has to be got round. Whether this can be done by following the course of the branch streams of the two rivers is the question which Mr. Colquhoun has set himself to solve. The line of railway, if it is feasible, will be of great value, not because it will open up Yunnan. We have always been somewhat sceptical as to the enormous superiority in wealth and productiveness claimed for that land-locked province. But when the Chinese see railway traffic being carried on within a few miles of their own frontier, we may hope that the result will be the same which followed the arrival of steamships in their harbours. To be the introducer of the iron road into the Middle Kingdom is a position of which Mr. Colquhoun might well be proud, and provided this Burmese-Shan railway is constructed it is an almost certain result. The advanced young Chinese who, like Mr. Colquhoun's interpreter, quote Alfred de Musset and sit up half the night composing *vers coupés*, are not troubled with any superstitious fears on such a matter as a railway."

[1] According to the best authority, that of the Siamese ambassador, the population of Siam exceeds 25,000,000.

From THE FIELD.

"Mr. Colquhoun's main object in his adventurous journey was to practically test the commercial capabilities of South-western China; the neighbouring independent Shan States, and Northern Siam, as a main factor in the question of trade extension from British Burmah—a question which has occupied many thinking minds during the last quarter of a century. Various routes for tapping an undoubtedly once highly productive area have been proposed, and those interested in the subject will find an able account of them by no less an authority than Baron von Richthofen, in the "Ocean Highways" for January, 1874; and another by Mr. J. Coryton (perhaps more easily accessible) in the "proceedings" of our Royal Geographical Society for March 22nd, 1875 (vol. xix. p. 264). The whole question is also ably discussed by Mr. Colquhoun, in chapters xvi. and xvii. of his second volume.

"It was Captain Richard Sprye who, somewhere about 1858, first prominently urged the desirability and feasibility of a railway from Rangoon in British Burmah to Kiang Hung, a little south of Esmok, or Ssu-mao, on the southern boundary of Yunnan, the very point at which Mr. Colquhoun's explorations were brought to a compulsory and undesirable close. But the details of his route were, from an engineer's point of view, impracticable, as his line would have to cross four great rivers—the Sittang, Salween, Me Nam, and Me Kong or Great Cambodia River, besides an indefinite number of tributary streams—all separated by lofty and often precipitous ranges. These obstacles have been pointed out by Mr. Findlay in a report some years ago to the Glasgow Chamber of Commerce, who so far anticipates Mr. Colquhoun by observing that if a railway ever enters China from Burmah it will be by following, as far as possible, one of the valleys of the great rivers, across which it would be vain to think of driving. His proposed route is as follows:—Starting at a point some forty miles north of Pegu, on the existing rail, his line would strike east to Shuaygyeen (or Shwegyeen) on the Sittang, and follow the eastern bank of that river southwards to Sittang, continuing south east over the alluvial coast plain to near Dongwoon, and thence, after crossing the Salween at a point below the coastward extension of the chief ranges, would cross the upper Kokarit hills and descend to the valley of the Thoungyeen affluent of the Salween, following it to the junction of the Main Long-gyee, and ascending that river and its Me Lie affluent. From this point it would cross the water-parting (3,000 ft. high) and reach the Me Ping valley by the Me Papi, ascending it to Zimmé, and then go northeast to the water-parting between the Me Ping and the Me Lau tributary of the Me Kong, reaching the latter great river by the Me Khok affluent, and following its western bank northwards to Kiang Hung. The whole distance would be about six hundred and twenty-five miles, and a terminus could easily be made at Martaban opposite Maulmain, the junction to Dongwoon being effected over some sixty miles of plain. Mr. Colquhoun hints at official moral support and tangible aid from the leading Chambers of Commerce in the renewed reconnaissance which he intends soon to make from the British Burmah side.

"The success of the recently opened rail in British Burmah, the great expansion of its trade and population, and the vast promise of the rich country lying on its eastern and northern frontiers (which our French neighbours are striving their utmost to open up, *viâ* Tonquin), are strongly urged by the author, whose experience in South-western Yunnan enable him to promise the British consumer, in return for home manufactures, 'the finest tea drunk in China, cotton, silk, petroleum, and the most useful and precious metals, to an extent which will be enormous when European skill shall effect their development.'

"The discussion of the railway above noticed, and of the reasons in its favour, are properly introduced into Mr. Colquhoun's narrative as being his *primum mobile*, and the journey recorded in the present volumes contains the verification of his ideas as to the productiveness of South-western Yunnan, on which all that he writes is practically new matter."

From London and China Telegraph.

"There is a great deal of very valuable information in the article, especially where the disposition of the Shans and their loyalty to Siam are alluded to, and no one is better able to give an opinion on this subject than the author:—'The only means by which the King of Siam can hope to foil the French in their present policy and develop the material prosperity of his country is by opening it up by means of roads and railways. It is our duty, as well as our interest, to aid this friendly Power in the retention, consolidation, and development of his dominion. In no better and in no more effectual way can this be done than by connecting the interior of his kingdom with his own capital and with British Burmah by means of railways.' "

From St. James's Gazette.

". . . He has discovered that Central and South-western Yunnan are the most wealthy districts, and because these portions of the province are precisely those which are nearest to British Burmah. The additional discovery that the intervening Shan States, hitherto tributary to King Theebau, have now altogether thrown off the allegiance they formerly paid in a desultory way, is another of the most valuable results. It is still, however, a matter of doubt whether the country between Martaban (opposite Maulmain, the capital of our Tenasserim province) and Kiang Hung, on the Chinese frontier, is suitable for the railway which Mr. Colquhoun proposes. The few thousand pounds necessary for a preliminary survey from the Burmah side would be well spent, and there is every reason to believe that this sum will be subscribed by the Chambers of Commerce of the United Kingdom. Such a railway, if practicable, would undoubtedly be one of the most valuable in the world. It would not only open up the Shan States, in itself well worth the expense, but would develop the trade of the north of Siam and Yunnan, only languishing for want of customers. An immediate result would be the probable construction of connecting lines by the enlightened young king of Siam. It might even be hoped that it would lead to the introduction of the locomotive into China. That must come from within. Apart altogether from the trade which it is certain to gain for us, there is the certainty that it will lead to the emigration of great numbers of Chinese to British Burmah. Our great want there is increased population, and that not from India but from Indo-China. The Chinese and Shans are the finest agriculturists in the world; and it is only the heavy passage-money from Canton round by the Straits Settlement which has hitherto prevented the Chinamen from settling in our provinces in greater numbers. It will be seen, therefore, that the result of Mr. Colquhoun's explorations is not less important to the Indian statesman than to the English merchant."

From THE MANCHESTER GUARDIAN.

"A lively interest has already been shown in this city, and indeed throughout the entire cotton manufacturing district, in Mr. Colquhoun's plans for extending our commerce with Western China and its borderlands. In December last Mr. Colquhoun explained very fully his scheme at a special meeting of the Manchester Chamber of Commerce, and not only here, but also in London, Glasgow, and other commercial centres, it has produced an exceedingly favourable impression. Funds are being raised by the various Chambers of Commerce for the purpose of defraying the cost of surveying the route of Mr. Colquhoun's proposed railway from Rangoon to the south-western boundary of China, and there is good reason to believe that ere long the work will be begun. Mr. Colquhoun devotes two chapters of his book to a consideration of the various routes by which the trade of South-western China may be 'tapped,' and with his conclusion that the best and easiest is through the Shan States to the borders of South-western Yunnan, starting from Rangoon, our readers are already familiar. A full perusal of his book tends to confirm this view. The development of trade between Burmah and the Shan States is not an unimportant advantage of proceeding in this direction. Already the import trade from Zimmé and other points to British Burmah is considerable, and it seems certain that it would be enormously enlarged if the present slow and costly mode of carriage were superseded by such a railway as Mr. Colquhoun proposes. His modest proposal for a preliminary survey seems likely to be carried out; and if it should prove the first step in opening out a new trade route—as seems likely—the English commercial and manufacturing public will have good cause to rejoice that they have shown spirit enough to undertake and carry through without State aid an enterprise of such magnitude and importance. The problem of approaching South-western China from the west has long been under consideration. At last it seems to be in a fair way towards settlement."

From THE MANCHESTER COURIER.

". . . It is therefore the duty of England to awaken to her responsibilities in this matter. There is no need for armed intervention—in fact, anything of that kind would do infinitely more harm than good—but the schemes of the unscrupulous politicians who are waiting upon fortune in France at the present moment may be encountered from the other side only if the English Government has the smallest tact and knowledge of affairs. The king of Siam is a singularly enlightened monarch, and it is obviously our interest to strengthen our friendly relations with him. There is not on our side the faintest desire to annex any portion of his territory, or to treat him otherwise than with the most scrupulous fairness and honesty. Both he and ourselves will, however, be benefited if the ties between the two countries are drawn closer, and if communication be facilitated between British Burmah and the capital on one side and the Shan States on the other. Already there is one Burmese railway, and the plans for its extension to Bangkok and to Esmok in the independent Shan country have been drawn out. If they can be put in execution without delay, everything will be gained."

From THE GLASGOW HERALD, *May 16th.*

"We have dealt more fully with the adventurous portion of Mr. Colquhoun's book than with the chapters he devotes to the commercial aspect of his journey. One reason for this is that his observations on the latter subject were discussed pretty fully during his recent visit to this city. But their importance can scarcely be overestimated. He demonstrates beyond all doubt that a new outlet for British manufacture is to be found in the trade route he sketches between India and China. The railways he suggests for the purpose of effecting this object may be thought by some to indicate a project rather ambitious than practical; but those who possess most knowledge of the district and its resources will probably be of a different opinion. One thing Mr. Colquhoun makes clear, and that is, that if the wealth of Yunnan is to be tapped at all it must be by a line from British Burmah. The real agricultural wealth lies in the central, south-west, and western portions, and these can best be approached from our own frontier. Then there are the Shan countries to the south, as wealthy in minerals as Yunnan itself, and with no suzerain power to prevent their being worked. Already British goods are found in small quantities in the Shan States, having dribbled through the intervening territory and found markets at the trade centres. It is well known that the arguments he has already addressed on this subject to the leading Chambers of Commerce throughout the country have resulted in a practical resolve to develop the trade route he suggests, so that before long Mr. Colquhoun will, it may be hoped, be once more at work—this time with an ample staff—completing the necessary surveys."

From THE LIVERPOOL DAILY POST, *16th May.*

"'Across Chrysê' describes a route which is no doubt destined to become an important commercial highway, affording the means of direct inland trade intercourse between India and China. There seems to be no reason why the borderlands of the great empires of India and China should not be the scene of lucrative commerce, and with our possessions in British Burmah, and by the adoption of a conciliatory policy towards King Theebau, we have a better opportunity of doing this than the French can have from Tonquin or Anam. Mr. Colquhoun's opinion on this point is that the French annexation of Tonquin will mean an element of disquiet throughout Indo-China. The supremacy of French power there would, he thinks, not only deal a blow to all trade extension on our part with Indo-China and China from British Burmah, but would destroy the trade which we now possess, and lead in the end to serious complications between the two countries. And meantime it should not be forgotten in connection with our present interests that not only is Siam a friendly neighbour of ours, but that all European goods found in the Siamese provinces of the Cambodia and Ménam, as well as the independent Shan provinces, are of English manufacture, and distributed by English agency from British Burmah and the capital of Siam. . . . 'Across Chrysê' will, however, be most thoroughly appreciated by the mercantile classes as indicating so clearly the prospects of an important outlet for future trade."

From NATIONAL REVIEW *for June*, 1883.

"The value of the country as a field for commercial enterprise is fully evidenced by the character of the people, the richness of the soil, the mineral wealth, the vastness of the teak-forests, the fine quality of the tea, the large area available for cultivation, and the magnificent grazing-plains. The richness of the country is borne testimony to by the latest traveller in these parts, Herr Carl Bock, who recently made a journey up the Ménam from Bangkok to Zimmé, and thence to Kiang Tsen, on the banks of the Mékong. Mr. Bock remarks that the country between Bangkok and Paknam-Po is a low alluvial plain, thickly peopled and fertile, and that the country to the north-east, lying in the valley of the main branch of the Ménam, is rich and well populated. A railway from Bangkok, through Rahine (Raheng) to Zimmé, is strongly advocated by the traveller; according to him, absolutely no difficulties would be encountered as far as Rahine, and few above it, and the greater portion of the line would run through a plain thickly studded with villages. He lays great stress upon the commercial and political importance of both these towns, but more especially upon that of Zimmé, of which he says: 'This place controls the trade of the country with Siam, as well as British Burmah, and is politically and commercially of the greatest importance.' Again: 'The natural richness of the country is remarkable, and when the railway from Bangkok to Rahine, as indicated by me, is built, it will certainly be carried on to Zimmé in a short time . . . Whoever has not visited the town (of Zimmé) can with difficulty estimate the importance which the trade has already won, and how great its future prospects are. . . . Not only would a railway bring Zimmé and the neighbouring Shan States into direct communication with the sea, but it would draw to itself the greater part of the trade of the Shan States and Yunnan, which at present finds an outlet full of difficulty towards the east at Canton, or a still longer and more costly way to the Yangtse.' The Government of India and the commercial community of this country are now fully alive to the importance of the question; and with the cordial assistance of the king of Siam, a reconnaissance of North Siam and the Shan country will shortly be made, as the initial step of this policy."

INDEX.